THE EDUCATION OF GERALD FORD

The Education of Gerald Ford

Hendrik Booraem V

WILLIAM B. EERDMANS PUBLISHING COMPANY
GRAND RAPIDS, MICHIGAN / CAMBRIDGE, U.K.

Published 2016 by

Wm. B. Eerdmans Publishing Co.

2140 Oak Industrial Drive N.E., Grand Rapids, Michigan 49505 /

P.O. Box 163, Cambridge CB3 9PU U.K.

www.eerdmans.com

Printed in the United States of America

22w 21 20 19 18 17 16   7 6 5 4 3 2 1

Library of Congress Cataloging-in-Publication Data

Booraem, Hendrik, 1939- author.

The education of Gerald Ford / Hendrik Booraem V.

pages   cm

Includes bibliographical references and index.

ISBN 978-0-8028-6943-2 (pbk.: alk. paper)

1. Ford, Gerald R., 1913-2006 — Knowledge and learning.

2. Ford, Gerald R., 1913-2006 — Childhood and youth.

3. Presidents — United States — Biography.

4. Presidents — Education — United States.

5. Grand Rapids (Mich.) — Biography.

I. Title.

E866.B659   2016

973.925092 dc23

[B]

2015030834

The publisher and author gratefully acknowledge permission to reproduce illustrations from the following sources: pages 47, 48, 49, 50, 138, 139, 140: courtesy of Gerald R. Ford Library (GRFL); pages 47, 49, 50, 137: courtesy of Grand Rapids History & Special Collections, Archives, GRPL, Grand Rapids, Michigan (GRPL); page 137: map by Lynne Parker; page 140: from the 1935 *Michiganensian*, courtesy of Gerald R. Ford Library.

Contents

Contents

Foreword

On Thursday, October 17, 1974, Gerald Ford sat before the House Judiciary Subcommittee on Criminal Justice and laid his presidency on the line.

Five weeks earlier he had shocked the nation by issuing a pardon to Richard Nixon, absolving his predecessor of any crimes Nixon might have committed while president. Ford's popularity plummeted. Newspapers editorialized about how the new president had damaged his credibility. Indeed, hoping to move Americans beyond the drama of Watergate by pardoning Nixon, Ford seemed to have hitched his own administration to Nixon's wreckage.

Charges of a secret deal that exchanged the presidency for the pardon surfaced almost immediately. Democrats on Capitol Hill voiced such accusations while Republicans, stunned by Ford's act, stood by. The ominously titled House Judiciary Subcommittee on Criminal Justice sent Ford a Resolution of Inquiry, asking him to explain further his reasons for issuing the pardon. Ford's attorneys responded, saying the pardon's proclamation provided sufficient answers. More questions followed from the offended subcommittee's chairman.

By then, Ford had had enough. Turning to Jack Marsh, one of his lawyers, the president said, "Jack, the best thing for me to do is just go up to Capitol Hill, testify, and spell it out." To say the decision was bold understates it. No president had ever appeared publicly before Congress to explain himself. By taking this risk, Ford and his advisors knew any hope for a successful administration hung in the balance. Yet Ford was confident. Against the counsel of these advisors, Ford squared himself. "I've got nothing to hide," he told them. "I'm going up there."

Those who knew Gerald Ford as Jerry Junior, Junior, or Junie probably were less surprised than others by Ford's decision. "It's the Eagle Scout in him," his Scoutmaster, Chuck Kindel, might say. "That's the mettle he showed us on the gridiron," Coach Gettings of South High or Coach Kipke of Michigan could add. Any one of his three half brothers, Tom, Dick, or Jim, would tell America that Dad and Mother would have expected no less from him. "Tell the truth," his parents taught him, "and do nothing to embarrass the family."

Understandably, the antecedent of Ford's character, on display in the White House, is found in his youth. Whether facing down members of Congress who refused to fund humanitarian efforts in the closing days of Vietnam or placing his trust in homemakers rather than economists in crafting policies to fight economic uncertainties, Ford drew upon lessons learned in Grand Rapids, Michigan. Indeed, his famed bipartisan spirit was more a product of his mother's insistence that he look first for the good in people than it was a practical expediency for moving legislation on the Hill. When in the first month of his administration Ford invited the House Congressional Black Caucus to the White House (their first appearance since a contentious meeting with President Nixon in 1971), his opinions on race had already been shaped by his youthful experiences on Union Avenue, walking to and from school with Burt Garel, his African American neighbor, and playing football with Siki McGee and Willis Ward.

Americans crave the drama that punctuates the lives of their famous kin. Ford's youth is absent much of the drama that illuminates the lives of his presidential predecessors. At fourteen years old, Junior began waging war on the gridiron, tussling with other youths over a leather football. At a similar age, Andy Jackson was fighting in the American Revolution, a prisoner of the British army, and wearing a gash on his forehead for refusing to clean an officer's leather boots. At twenty-two, Ford left behind his playing days on the field of the University of Michigan to pursue coaching and a law degree. At twenty-three, in 1754, George Washington found himself entering a far different field in western Pennsylvania, starting a war that would reverberate around the globe, leading to the war that caught up young Jackson and revealed Washington to be arguably our greatest American. Early in his life, Junior Ford stuttered as he tried to speak. At about the same time in his life, Teddy Roosevelt gasped to breathe as his father raced him by horse-drawn carriage around the streets of New York, desperately trying to force air into the young boy's asthmatic lungs.

"Redeem the time," the apostle Paul told the church at Ephesus, an admonition no doubt taught to Ford at church, by his Scout leaders, or in the Horatio Alger novels he consumed. And Junior, whether sharing lunch with a father he was meeting for the first time, leading his South High football team in secret practices, or washing dishes to pay his university bills, seemingly made the most of every day. This growth — the making of the man — Rik Booraem explains in *The Education of Gerald Ford*, and in such a way as to illustrate that Jerry Ford was not born a "great man" (a shortcut we too often apply to our heroes), but he became one by forging his way through the valleys of character flaws, family drama, economic challenges, and more to reach the mountaintops. Like the paragons he read about in those Alger novels, Junior pulled himself up by his own bootstraps. But, again, as Booraem details, those straps already were being tugged by family, community, school, and friends.

Now, on that Thursday, only sixty-nine days into his presidency, Ford faced another valley, drama of the highest political sort. He sat alone, facing the assembled House Judiciary Subcommittee. For over an hour he fielded their questions. The purpose of the pardon, Ford explained, was to "change our national focus." Nixon already had been punished, having brought "shame and disgrace" to the office he held. Ford would not seek a trial for purposes of revenge. "Surely, we are not revengeful people," he argued, steering the committee members and, by extension, the American people away from baser motives. A New York congresswoman finally asked the pressing question about whether or not a deal had been struck for the pardon. "There was no deal, period, under no circumstances," the president stated.

In his youth, Ford exhibited the strength of character to confront a challenge by taking the initiative and moving on, a trait Booraem's study reveals time and again. It may be too much to say President Ford saved his administration on this fall day in 1974 — his party was only two weeks away from being spanked by the voters in the midterm election, and the specter of the pardon would haunt Ford's election bid two years later. But the man from Grand Rapids walked away from the committee room confident that he had told the truth and, having addressed the matter, was ready to move on from that valley to test his strength in others, against waiting opponents. The wellspring of that strength is found here, in the pages of Rik Booraem's text.

DONALD HOLLOWAY
Curator, the Gerald R. Ford
Presidential Museum
Grand Rapids, Michigan

Preface

This biography of Gerald Ford continues the narrative of my previous book, *Young Jerry Ford*, through the future president's graduation in 1935 from the University of Michigan. In addition, it revisits the high school years, covered in the previous book, this time with a full array of notes and discussion of sources. Finally, it examines in greater depth the society and culture of Michigan during Ford's youth, and endeavors to point out important themes in his early life.

By far the most important theme is the one stated in the title: education. Ford's character was the product of his education. Acquaintances, fellow students, and teachers of Ford at twenty-two agreed that he was a model young man, that is, he filled admirably all the roles that society considered important for a man his age: he was a superior athlete, an above-average student, a devoted son. These were roles he had learned, behaviors he had been taught since childhood by parents, teachers, and coaches. For obvious reasons, he was popular with adults: he not only accepted but also embraced what he was taught. He exemplified all the values they stood for.

One can only speculate why young Junior Ford, as he was called, was so extraordinarily teachable. Accounts of his early childhood provide glimpses of a reticent, hesitant small boy who struggled with stuttering and temper tantrums; then, in his early school years, the loving discipline of his parents, especially that of a mother who devoted hours to teaching him, gave him the skills he needed to succeed. Perhaps these years changed his attitude as well and created a thirst for structure in his life. From then on, at any rate, his standard approach to life was simple: learn the rules, master them completely, and play by them. Playing by the rules, a challenge to some young people, was a liberation for Ford: the feeling of confidence that it gave him allowed him to use all his talents, to be brave, committed, and devoted. The pattern repeated itself in school, in the Boy Scouts, in high school and college football, and in college society: devotion to the rules led to stellar performances. Of course, some performances lay beyond his abilities — Ford never could master foreign languages, no matter how much devoted effort he put in. But in most of the roles valued by his contemporaries and superiors, he shone.

A related question, which this biography also addresses, concerns not Ford but his society: Why did the particular kinds of behavior he practiced awaken such admiration in those around him in that particular setting, Michigan in the 1920s? What was the glory Michiganians associated with being a football player, even in a workaday position like center? What was the special appeal of the Boy Scouts? Why were the traditional forms of politeness so respected? What part did social class play in the life of a boy whose upbringing took place, more than that of any other president, in the midst of multiethnic, mobile urban America? And how was Ford's progress affected by the great mythic event that cut across his early life, the Great Depression?

To answer this second set of questions, one needs to examine deeply and in detail the milieus in which Ford grew up, urban western Michigan and Ann Arbor — and, more broadly, the urban Middle West of the 1920s and 1930s. In *The Education of Gerald Ford*, as in my previous presidential biographies, I have tried to do this by examining newspapers, statistics, local histories, and particularly the recollections of other men and women who were young at approximately the same place and time. Several vivid novels of Michigan in this era, and great sociological studies like Robert and Helen Lynd's Middletown books, helped give me a conceptual frame-work. Because Ford's life was relatively recent, it was possible to supple-ment these written sources with interviews. Some twenty people with firsthand knowledge of Ford and his activities shared what they knew and patiently clarified their memories for an inquisitive researcher. If the pic-ture of Michigan life in these pages falls short of accuracy, the blame rests not with the sources but with my lack of skill.

The biggest problem in describing the Michigan in which Gerald Ford came to maturity and acquired the bedrock of his character is that its soci-ety was superficially much like that of 2015, minus the effects of the com-puter revolution. Large hospitals; large urban high schools; automobile culture and college football; movies, dating, and dancing; the Boy Scouts and the Great Depression were central parts of Ford's experience eighty years ago, and a reader in our time is likely to assume that she understands these customs and institutions and how they appeared to a young person. Nothing could be more mistaken. Football was the same game, but its cultural meaning and extension were quite different. High schools had a similar structure, but very different personnel and expectations. We have a story of the Great Depression in our minds; but it looked quite different to middle-class Michiganders at the time, who did not know that story. For this reason I have devoted long paragraphs to these seemingly familiar institutions, to show in detail how they worked and how they differed from their present-day avatars.

The recency of Ford's life helps in creating an accurate background, but it also means that there are probably additional sources not yet available — family letters, memories of friends and neighbors — that, when they become public, will add new events to the story of his early years. In that sense, this book is a provisional biography, the best I can do with the information at hand. The general picture, however, has to be accurate; there is too much unanimity among the sources for it not to be.

More than one reader of this manuscript has commented, justly, that it contains too few examples of Gerald Ford speaking in his own voice — that often an event is presented and the reader is given no idea of Ford's attitude toward it. The reason for this has to do with the makeup of the sources, and with a deeper question that underlies the whole narrative. Ford was an active person, not a reflective person. He did not keep diaries or write long letters; the samples of his early writing we have are brief, factual, and conventional. The best quotes about his youth come mostly from retrospective interviews, where he talked freely and willingly about his early football games and about his family, and even those tend to be short.

Throughout his life Ford had little interest in crafting his communications; his statements were short and direct. More than once during his Washington years his critics interpreted this pattern as a sign of limited intelligence, and challenged his leadership ability on that basis. A close associate of Ford's commented, referring to these critics, that they were using the wrong yardstick for intelligence: where it counted for a leader, in personal relations and decision making, Ford had "a computer in his head." The implicit question is interesting: Communication skills are clearly desirable in a leader, but how essential are they? This study of Ford's performance in his high school and college years has ample data to help address that question.

Acknowledgments

Writing this book took far longer than expected, and the amount of help I have to acknowledge is correspondingly great. It has been an unfailing pleasure to work with scores of friendly, efficient people in gathering basic information and then filling in the gaps and packaging it for readers. My helpers in Grand Rapids were listed and thanked in the preface to my previous book, *Young Jerry Ford*, a popular treatment of Ford's boyhood, and I will just reprise the main ones: the Gerald R. Ford Presidential Museum, the Grand Rapids and East Grand Rapids Public Libraries, the Gerald R. Ford Foundation, Richard Ford, the president's brother, and a dozen or so members of the South High School class of 1931. It is a pleasure to mention them again.

Readers of *Young Jerry Ford* may recognize a debt of another sort. In chapters 2, 3, and 7 of this book I have reused individual sentences (in one case a whole paragraph) from the earlier book, concluding that I had already done my best on those particular topics and had nothing better to say.

I have two new debts to recognize from Grand Rapids: Canon Bob Schiesler of St. Mark's Episcopal Church allowed me access to the church records and enabled me to clarify the Fords' membership status. I used that data in *Young Jerry Ford* but failed to thank him for his help. Concurrent with the publication of that book, the Ford Museum mounted an exhibition, "Growing Up Grand," on the president's early years, and my conversations with the head curator, Don Holloway, on topics that concerned both of us were important in steering me to new sources and clarifying my thoughts as I wrote this work.

Acknowledgments

The Bentley Historical Library in Ann Arbor is the place to go for records of the University of Michigan and, to some extent, of the entire state. I spent weeks working in its rich collections, and in those of the Hatcher and Taubman Libraries on the main campus. The Ann Arbor District Library, efficient and helpful, is a mine of information on the town and environs. The Detroit Public Library contains the important Willis Ward Papers. And finally, the Library of Michigan in Lansing has important printed sources impossible to find elsewhere. Librarians and staff at all these institutions have my sincere gratitude.

Anyone with a computer and an interest in the University of Michigan rapidly learns that an avid, well-informed, continuous dialogue on Michigan sports history, especially football, exists online at sites like www.mvictors.com and www.mgoblue.com. Without knowing the names of more than a few individuals, I congratulate the participants on their work and dedication. Footnotes in chapters 9–12 make it obvious how much this book owes to their efforts.

Delta Kappa Epsilon, Ford's college fraternity, has its national office in Ann Arbor, luckily for me; Doug Lanpher, the president, helped this book along by searching out Deke material and putting me in touch with brothers who had firsthand knowledge of Ford and the chapter — Jim Grady of Bloomfield Hills and the late Lin Hanson of Chicago.

My greatest debt is, as it has been for many years, to my late husband Richard Bullock for his love and support.

Abbreviations

BHL	Bentley Historical Library, University of Michigan, Ann Arbor
DGF	Dorothy Gardner Ford
EBF	Elizabeth (Betty) Bloomer Ford
Ford-Cannon interviews	Gerald Ford interviews with James Cannon
GRF	Gerald R. Ford Jr.
GRFL	Gerald R. Ford Library, Ann Arbor
GRF Sr.	Gerald R. Ford Sr.
GRPL	Grand Rapids Public Library
Herald	*Grand Rapids Herald*
MD	*Michigan Daily*
Press	*Grand Rapids Press*
TTH	*A Time to Heal* (GRF's autobiography)

CHAPTER 1

The Stranger

An April morning on the South Side of Grand Rapids, Michigan, blue sky above, sun pouring down on a grid of grimy buildings — small businesses strung along Division Avenue, two- and three-story frame houses in close array, railroads and warehouses, coal smoke rising from chimneys and factory smokestacks. Not so much smoke as there had been last year; this was the spring of 1930, the aftermath of the great stock market crash — the beginning, although no one knew it at the time, of the Great Depression — and many factories had closed.[1] But much was unchanged from 1929: black sedans still jostled for space on Division and its cross streets with electric trolleys and horse-drawn ice wagons and milk wagons, at a speed limit of 15 miles per hour; now and then a small airplane appeared in the sky, flying the passenger service to Detroit.[2]

The South Side was working class, as was the West Side, across the Grand River where the big furniture factories were, where Polish and Lithuanian workers' families clustered around Catholic churches.[3] The South Side was more mixed: retail clerks and owners of small stores, railroad and trolley employees, craftsmen. Many families here were first- or

---

1. See the table in Ransom, *City Built on Wood*, p. 73.

2. Manfred, *The Primitive*, p. 103, evokes the excitement felt around 1930 by the sight of a solitary airplane overhead; *Herald*, July 25, 1926, mentions passenger service. Speed limit: *Herald*, October 21, 1930.

3. Elliott, *Grand Rapids*, p. 97; Carron, *Grand Rapids Furniture*, p. 46; Works Progress Administration, *Michigan*, p. 306. GRF described his South High School classmates in Ford-Cannon interviews, April 24, 1990, p. 3. Many railroad employees appear in the 1930 manuscript U.S. census of the 800 block of Lafayette Avenue on the South Side.

second-generation Dutch, a clannish, critical people who continually disputed with each other about religious differences.[4] There were two small
African American neighborhoods, and pockets of Lebanese, Greeks, and
Russians. Some houses had plumbing, quite a few did not; likewise with
electric power.[5]

(To the north, closer to downtown, was the other Grand Rapids, the
one that made visitors rhapsodize that nothing in town needed to be
changed to fulfill the concept of the City Beautiful. Broad, clean streets
sloped steeply upward from the downtown area to the "Hill District,"
where tall maples shaded the broad lawns in front of the imposing Victorian mansions of the furniture magnates, and their bankers and their
lawyers. The westward view from the hill was breathtaking — the high-
Victorian Romanesque city hall and courthouse, the new Michigan National Bank Building, the Beaux Arts library, the Italian Renaissance Fountain Street Church, and bustling Monroe Street, with the Grand River and
the furniture factories in the background. It all bespoke wealth, culture,
and civic pride.)[6]

In the middle of the South Side, at the corner of Hall Street and Jefferson Avenue, South High School towered over the surrounding buildings, a
proud assertion of the Progressive era's commitment to public education.
Originally designed as a combination high school and community center,
it was of red brick, three stories high, with a massive cornice, an imposing
main entrance, and two gymnasiums.[7] In contrast to early-twenty-first-
century American schools, in which a poor urban area almost automatically means a second-rate public education, South was one of the best high
schools in the city. Some people claimed it had the best faculty, although
that claim was also made by its two main rivals, Union High School on

4. Works Progress Administration, *Michigan*, p. 306; Schapsmeier and Schapsmeier,
Date with Destiny, p. 2; Ter Horst, *Gerald R. Ford*, pp. 32-22; Carron, *Grand Rapids Furniture*, p. 48.

5. DeJong, *With a Dutch Accent*, pp. 158-59, 184.

6. Logan, *Almost Lost*, is a beautifully illustrated, if slightly disorganized, introduction to the preservation and present state of what the book calls "Heritage Hill," the mod-
ern name by which the Hill District is known. See especially chapter 2, "Appearance and
Architecture," and the first pages of the following chapter, pp. 38-58. It also includes an
excellent photo of the old city hall, p. 8. Lydens, *The Story of Grand Rapids*, pp. 215, 217, and
Works Progress Administration, *Michigan*, p. 312, give basic data on downtown buildings.
On the general atmosphere, see the description by native son Arnold Gingrich in his novel
Cast Down the Laurel, p. 27.

7. Basic facts are from the South High School Scrapbook, GRPL.

the West Side and Central High School in the Hill District. Its principal, Arthur W. Krause, a small, trim, stern man, ran a tight ship; its faculty included remarkably gifted teachers in art and music, who sponsored programs like a string orchestra and three choruses, teachers who spent their summers in Europe, teachers who regularly produced state champion debating teams, teachers who chaperoned school groups to Washington and New York during vacations.[8] Reproductions of famous sculptures were displayed throughout the halls, and the library had a full selection of classics.[9]

And the students? In their medium-length dresses and long coats, their neat slacks-and-sweater outfits, they were a more formal and earnest crowd than one might have expected.[10] The real rebels, the boys who hated school, as well as numerous quieter kids from poor Dutch or African American families, had left after the eighth grade, as state law allowed; those who remained were generally serious about getting an education (though two sophomores would be arrested the next year for stealing cars).[11] Of course, there were outbreaks of high spirits, and in spring, particularly, students were apt to feel half-understood desires and longings stirring inside them. One very concrete desire was for warm weather to settle in so that they could get rid of the long underwear both boys and girls wore all winter, an embarrassment when it bunched up or peeped out from under one's clothing, but a necessity for students who walked to school, often a mile or more, through snow or bitter cold, carrying their books, lunch, and in some cases a musical instrument.[12] Only a very few students drove, although there were enough to produce complaints about their parking from the surrounding residents.[13] At the moment, most South High students, in time-honored fashion, were thinking about lunch.

Miss Marion Struik, who had left teaching at the beginning of 1930 to get married, still recalled her second-floor history classroom. It had

8. South High School *Star-tler,* June 12, 1931, GRF Scrapbook #1A, GRFL; *New Pioneer,* #39 (January 1989), #69 (April 1995); *Herald,* July 4, 1926; *Press,* October 15, 1934; *Grand Rapids Board of Education Official Proceedings, May 1, 1929, to May 1, 1930,* p. 38.

9. Interviews with Arnold Sisson, Don Daverman, William Schuiling.

10. Interviews with Don Daverman, Marshall Reister.

11. *Herald,* January 29, 1931; March 10, 1931.

12. Fifty-First Reunion, class of 1931, poem by Tena S. Streeter; *New Pioneer,* #43 (January 1990), p. 8, both author's collection; interviews with Arnold Sisson, Florence Moore, Don Daverman, Marshall Reister.

13. *Pioneer* literary magazine, October 11, 1930; *Herald,* September 24, 1930.

a view across Hall Street to one of the popular lunch hangouts — that is, for the minority of students who didn't eat in the cafeteria, go home for lunch, or bring their own. The place was called Bill's; it was a small wooden building with a large front window and a sign overhead advertising Hoekstra's Ice Cream. Most students would have described it as a hamburger joint, although the real specialty of the house, very popular with the adolescent patrons, was sticky, delicious cinnamon buns hot from the oven. It did serve a lot of hamburgers and cheese sandwiches, too. There was seating for twenty-five or thirty and a jukebox, but not enough room for dancing.[14] Bill Skougis liked to hire South football players, and through the window Miss Struik could see a familiar figure behind the counter flipping burgers: Jerry Ford, the star center of the team, the good-looking blond junior adored from afar by many of her girl students, in his white full-length apron. She taught him European history, and considered him an A student. Bill found him a good worker, quiet, friendly, and efficient.[15]

No one at South High had a bad word for Jerry Ford.[16] His popularity stemmed not from student leadership — he was involved in very few activities other than sports — but from his looks, his football prowess, and his low-key, pleasant personality. He hung around mainly with other athletes and was, like many of them, rather on the taciturn, expressionless side (although he could occasionally get fired up in class about politics or current events).[17] Miss Struik thought he was "pensive" at times.[18] But he was always friendly, unfailingly polite, never angry or moody or out of sorts. He made good grades; some classmates called him "intelligent," but "hardworking" might have been more like it. Imaginative he was not. His classmate Tena Sikkema was. A small sharp-featured Dutch girl whose family had recently emigrated from Europe to Grand Rapids, gifted in writing and full of rebellious ideas, she sometimes found herself debating with him in history. She liked him, but found his ideas totally "business-oriented," totally "provincial."[19]

14. Interviews with Gert De Vries, William Schuiling.

15. *Petoskey News-Review*, August 16, 1974, clipping in GRFL vertical file, "Childhood and Youth"; "Marion Blandford: Partner in Community Patronage," *Press*, December 28, 1983.

16. Interview: William Schuiling.

17. Ter Horst, *Gerald R. Ford*, p. 37; Cannon, *Time and Chance*, p. 12.

18. *Petoskey News-Review*, August 16, 1974, clipping in GRFL vertical file, "Childhood and Youth."

19. Interview with Tena Sikkema Streeter, December 18, 1997, author's collection.

This particular spring day, Jerry was busy serving burgers and washing dishes early in the lunch hour; then business slackened, and he went to his usual post by the cash register. As he did so, he became aware of a stranger who had been standing up front, by the candy counter, for several minutes — a fair-haired burly man, round-faced and self-confident, nothing like Bill's usual customers. His blue eyes looked steadily at Jerry. He came over to the register.[20]

"Are you Leslie King?" he asked.

"No," replied Jerry, puzzled.

"Are you Jerry Ford?"

"Yes."

"You're Leslie King. I'm your father. I'm in town with my wife, and I'd like to take you to lunch."

No, that can't be right, Jerry thought; he knew who his parents were, Mr. and Mrs. Gerald R. Ford, 649 Union Avenue, Southeast. His father was at work now, in the office of the struggling little paint factory he owned on the West Side. Who was this man? Then he began remembering: his mother had told him a few years before that she had been married long ago to a man named Leslie King, and —

Jerry looked him in the eye. "I'm working," he said.

"Ask your boss if you can get off."

Bill Skougis said it was all right. Jerry took off his apron and went outside with the stranger. A brand-new Lincoln sat by the curb, with a woman in it whom King introduced as his wife.

"Where shall we go for lunch?" King asked him. Jerry suggested the Cherie Inn, a pleasant restaurant not too far away, toward the fashionable East Side. South High boys sometimes took their dates there for

20. The episode narrated in the following paragraphs, GRF's meeting with his biological father Leslie L. King, was certainly one of the most dramatic in his early life. As such, it appears in every account of his youth, always based on his recollection, since he was the only witness. I have used GRF, *TTH*, pp. 47-48; Ter Horst, *Gerald R. Ford*, pp. 38-40; Vestal, *Jerry Ford, Up Close*, pp. 43-44; Schapsmeier and Schapsmeier, *Date with Destiny*, pp. 7-8; Cannon, *Time and Chance*, pp. 13-14; Hersey, *The President*, p. 88; Leroy, *Gerald Ford — Untold Story*, pp. 34-37, quoting an interview of GRF with Dick Cavett in 1974, and the Ford-Cannon interviews, April 4, 1990, pp. 6-7.

GRF was not entirely consistent about the year this incident took place, stating sometimes 1929 and sometimes 1930. The latter date, used in *TTH*, makes more sense, for it coincides with Charles King's death and the cessation of the child support he had been sending. The newly flush Leslie King used part of his inheritance, or the promise of it, to buy a new car from the factory in Detroit.

dinner.[21] As they drove, King explained that he had just bought the car in Detroit and was driving it home to the state of Wyoming, where he owned vast acres of land. He went on to describe to Jerry how he had found him: he had called every high school in the city, looking for a Leslie King or Junior Ford (Jerry had been called "Junior" until recently; he had come to dislike the name, although his mother still used it). Finally, at South, he had found what he was looking for. The people in the office knew Jerry, and directed him over to Bill's.

Lunch was perfunctory. Jerry was uncomfortable. King kept asking him questions about the football team and the football season. Jerry answered: yes, he had been all-city center as a sophomore; he hadn't done so well this season because of a knee injury, but that could be fixed; next fall he would be team captain. As he talked, he scrutinized King's face for signs of a physical resemblance between the two of them. There were some, he had to admit. But he and King didn't talk at all about King's marriage to his mother or his responsibility (if any) toward the son she still called "Leslie." The conversation, Jerry remembered later, was "superficial."

As they spoke, questions boiled up in Jerry's mind, questions he was too well brought up to utter; "I bit my tongue to stop myself from being impolite," he remembered years later. Why had King suddenly intruded into his life from out of nowhere? Did he want to boast of his son, the football hero? Did he just want to show off his affluence? In reality, did his son mean anything at all to him?

When the meal was over, King drove Jerry back to South High and let him out. He gave him twenty-five dollars. "Now, you buy yourself something you want that you couldn't afford otherwise," he said grandly, and he and his wife were gone.

Jerry was preoccupied the rest of the day, his actions mechanical — afternoon classes, track practice with "Pop" Churm, the long walk home, two and a half miles up Madison, across Franklin, up Union (if he didn't catch a ride with his friend Bob Eckhardt, who owned a car). As he thought back, the meeting with King seemed to take on a slightly furtive, underhanded quality. The contrast between King's wealth and his family's moderate, almost austere lifestyle bothered him, too.[22] What would his parents think about it?

He need not have worried. After supper, when the younger kids —

---

21. Ford, *TTH*, p. 48; *Herald*, December 5, 1930; Marshall Reister interview.

22. Hersey, *The President*, 113. Distance from school: Ford-Cannon interviews, April 25, 1990, GRFL, p. 1.

Tom, twelve, Dick, five, and Jim, two — had been put to bed, he sat at the table with his parents — tall, silver-haired, serious Jerry Ford Sr. and his stout, warmhearted mother Dorothy Ford — and haltingly told them what had happened. If they were angry or surprised, they didn't show it; their first thought was to deal with their son's evident distress. Both reassured him: he could count on them for love and support.

His mother filled in some of the blanks for him. She had met King, who was from a rich family in Omaha, when she was at college in Illinois, rooming with his sister. They had fallen in love and gotten married; but he had turned out after their wedding to be violent, suspicious, and physically abusive. She had left him once and come back. After their son Leslie Jr. was born and he threatened her again, she left him for good and got a divorce. King was to pay three thousand dollars alimony and (coincidentally) twenty-five dollars a month for child support.

Leslie King had evaded paying the alimony and child support. In some ways, it had been easier for Dorothy King to forget the unpleasantness than to contest the point; besides, two years after leaving her husband she met Gerald Ford, a young salesman, in Grand Rapids, and in 1917 they were married. They had brought Leslie Jr. up simply as "Junior"; most people assumed he was Jerry Jr., named for his stepfather. The boy's grandfather Charles King had picked up the court-ordered child support, to make up for the payment his son refused to send.

In a way, Leslie King's sudden appearance at this time was understandable. Charles King had died in March, and the support checks had stopped coming. His death might explain the trip to Detroit by his newly flush son to buy a new car; maybe it also connected with King's stop in Grand Rapids to size up his firstborn offspring. But what would happen next? Jerry was shaken by the willingness of this brash, big-talking man to suddenly breeze into his life apparently without any real concern for him. Dorothy Ford reminded her son of a Bible verse that had always been a source of comfort to her, and was to become one of his own favorites, Proverbs 3:5-6: "Trust in the Lord with all your heart, and lean not unto your own understanding; in all your ways acknowledge him, and he will direct your paths."

Jerry went up to bed trying to trust in the Lord with all his heart and erase the image of Leslie King from his mind, or at least find something in the man to respect. He couldn't do it. His real father was a stranger to him and always would be. The football star cried himself to sleep.[23]

23. Ford, *TTH*, p. 48.

CHAPTER 2

City on the Grand

Dorothy Gardner King had not expected to live in Grand Rapids. To her, it was just a city where her father, Levi Gardner, a developer who worked out of Chicago, selling real estate in Grand Rapids and Toledo, had an office. But when her marriage broke down in 1913, after barely a year, and her parents helped rescue her and her baby from a violent husband, she had little choice but to move in with them.[1]

Dorothy had had what seemed a storybook wedding back in 1912, in her hometown Episcopal church, to the tall, blond, big-talking brother of a college friend. He was the only son of a rich merchant and wool broker who lived in Omaha and did business in several western states. But her dreams of a happy married life fell to pieces on the honeymoon, when her husband Leslie King turned out to have an uncontrollable temper and became physically abusive, threatening her with words, fists, and weapons. She ran back to her parents in Harvard, Illinois, and then discovered she was pregnant. Dorothy tried to patch up the marriage, but in vain. By the time their son, Leslie Jr., arrived in July 1913 at the ornate home on Woolworth Avenue where her father-in-law lived, King was threatening her, her mother, and the attending nurse with violence. In fear of her own life and that of her baby, Dorothy slipped out of Omaha in a hired cab and joined her parents, who were expecting her, across the river in Iowa.[2]

---

1. Levi Gardner's business activities are described in his obituaries in the *Harvard (Ill.) Herald*, May 11, 1916, and the *Press*, May 10, 1916. *Polk's City Directory* shows that he had maintained an office in Grand Rapids since 1903, and the Toledo city directory for 1911 and 1912 shows one in that city as well.

2. This whole sequence of events is from Cannon, *Time and Chance*, pp. 1-5, based

Fortunately, this did not mean returning to Harvard, where divorce was something that did not happen to respectable people. She had a married sister in the Chicago suburbs, and her parents had moved to Grand Rapids, to a large, comfortable home on the far South Side. For a short time she worked in Chicago as a saleswoman, but when her father was diagnosed with Bright's disease (chronic kidney failure), her best course of action became clear. She would move to Grand Rapids, help with the care of her father, and present herself as a young widow, with her infant son, Leslie King Jr.[3]

She and her mother began to put down roots, using the connections that a respectable business-class family found natural — churches and clubs. The Gardners were Episcopalians, and they began attending the impressive St. Mark's Church, with two slender French Gothic spires, often called the "Pro-Cathedral" of western Michigan, in the heart of downtown. Mrs. Gardner and her daughter joined the local chapter of the Daughters of the American Revolution; they came from an old New England family, the Ayers, and were very proud of their lineage.[4]

---

on testimony in the records of the divorce case. It is noteworthy that King's violence was mainly toward women; when Levi Gardner spoke with him personally, he was rational and conciliatory. His own father, Charles King, who later said these events were much against his wishes, was away when the events occurred.

3. The account of Cannon, *Time and Chance*, p. 6, apparently derived from family recollections, is that the Gardners moved to Grand Rapids in 1913 to get away from the small-town Harvard gossip that followed DGF's divorce. But *Polk's City Directory* for 1913 shows Levi Gardner already residing at 1960 Terrace Avenue in the spring of that year, before DGF had left her husband.

Cannon, p. 8, gives the location of the Grand Rapids house as 457 Lafayette; this, however, is contrary to *Polk's City Directory* for 1913-1916, which shows the Gardners living at 1960 Terrace (now Prospect) Avenue, near Garfield Park. He describes it as a "fine" house. The house at 457 Lafayette was the home of GRF Sr. and his mother from 1913 to at least 1916.

The Chicago city directory for 1916 lists Mrs. Dorothy King, saleswoman, at 506 West Sixty-first Street, and the coverage of her father's funeral in the *Harvard Herald* gave her residence as Chicago; but she is also in Polk's 1916 directory of Grand Rapids, listed as "(wid. Leslie)."

4. Veronica McLachlan reminiscences, GRPL, p. 3; Lydens, *The Story of Grand Rapids*, p. 452; Sophie de Marsac Chapter, DAR, record book, GRPL. Cannon, *Time and Chance*, pp. 8-9, and other biographers (Ter Horst, *Gerald R. Ford*, p. 33; Vestal, *Jerry Ford, Up Close*, p. 49) have mistakenly stated that the Gardner women, and later the Fords, attended Grace Episcopal Church at this time. Grace, in fact, was later the Fords' church, but it was many years later. The family, along with others, left St. Mark's and joined Grace in the late 1930s after a bitter rift in the congregation involving the minister of music (Scott Scholten,

9

Levi Gardner's condition worsened rapidly, despite medical consultations and trips to Florida and various spas. In May 1916 he died, leaving his widow, daughter, and grandson on their own in a strange city where they were just beginning to make connections.[5] Fortunately, however, that same year, at a church social, Dorothy met a young salesman for a local paint and wallpaper company, Gerald (Jerry) Ford. He and his widowed mother lived on Lafayette Avenue, south of the business district.[6] Respectable people, they were a bit below the Gardners in social standing — Ford had dropped out of high school in the eighth grade after his father's death, and his relatives in the city were mostly small business proprietors.[7] But he was personally attractive: tall, friendly, steady, and even-tempered. The last counted for a good deal; Dorothy's experience had taught her to value steadiness over wealth.

Nevertheless, she was cautious about committing herself. The two were not married until February 1, 1917.[8] Dorothy, her mother, and Leslie Jr., whom the family were calling simply "Junior," went to live at Jerry Ford's new rented home, 716 Madison Avenue, in a somewhat less classy area than they were used to. Jerry's mother and sister lived in the other half of the two-family house. It was the beginning of a long and very happy marriage.[9]

"Ford Is 'Average Episcopalian,'" *Press*, December 15, 1973; anonymous informant in Grand Rapids). Perhaps because of these circumstances, people at St. Mark's often downplay any connection with the Fords. See chapter 3, p. 27 and note.

5. *Harvard Herald*, May 11, 1916.

6. Cannon, *Time and Chance*, pp. 8-9; Schapsmeier and Schapsmeier, *Date with Destiny*, p. 5. The sources agree that they met at a church social, but it was probably not at Grace Church; see preceding note.

7. Hersey, *The President*, p. 90. GRF Sr. had three sisters, Jane, Ruah, and Marjory. Marjory, unmarried at this time, had a dance studio downtown. Jane, much older than the other siblings, had a son, Harold Swain, almost the same age as GRF Sr., who managed a coal company in Grand Rapids. Ruah and her husband lived elsewhere. The Fords and the Swains were fairly close, and had regular family gatherings. (Ford-Cannon interviews, April 24, 1990, p. 8; April 25, 1990, p. 3; Richard Ford interview, May 31, 2012.)

8. Cannon, *Time and Chance*, p. 9, states that the marriage took place in 1916, but the official certificate in the city records, vol. 18, p. 179, gives a date of February 1, 1917. Cannon also says the wedding took place at Grace Episcopal Church. It did not, according to the record. The couple were married by a Congregational minister, the Reverend C. O. Grieshaber, apparently at Ford's home on Madison Avenue. Because of DGF's divorce, no Episcopal minister could marry them.

9. Marriage certificate; *Polk's City Directory*, 1917; Cannon, *Time and Chance*, p. 9.

It was also a turning point for Junior King's future. He would grow up in Grand Rapids, where he would be known as Junior Ford.

To grow up in a large modern city is clearly different from growing up in Shakespeare's London or Franklin's Philadelphia. The size of the city generates large, more or less self-contained neighborhoods and subcultures whose inhabitants have little occasion to interact directly with other residents. For adults involved in the business of government and public services, the city is obviously a unit; but for children and adolescents whose mobility and responsibility are limited, the influence of neighborhood and subculture is primary, that of the city as a whole only indirect.

Grand Rapids in the twenties, when Junior Ford was a boy, was definitely large enough to qualify as a complex modern city. Its population of 137,000 people in 1920, forty-seventh largest in the country, grew to 168,000 in 1930, forty-eighth largest, about the same size as Hartford or Des Moines. Industry rather than commerce or government was its organizing principle; eight major firms and a host of minor ones manufactured furniture and associated products like lumber, paint, and varnish. There were also large companies that made carpet sweepers, church pews, refrigerators, asphalt shingles, and flypaper.[10]

Its structure was that of any large American city at that time. It comprised a collection of residential neighborhoods, segregated by income and to some extent by ethnicity, all linked by public transportation to the central business district, the "downtown," in Grand Rapids, at the falls of the Grand River. Public transportation, in this case, meant the brightly painted electric streetcars of the Grand Rapids Railway Company, whose network of tracks extended down all the major thoroughfares in every direction from downtown. Thousands of workers and shoppers rode to and from downtown every day for ten cents a trip. "You could go anywhere you needed by taking a street car," a doctor's wife remembered. Passengers could even send letters as they rode — each coach carried a mailbox.[11]

The business district was the city's center of commerce and government, but beyond that, it was symbolically important. Downtown stood for the promise of city life, that the concentration of wealth and brains could produce high-quality amenities that more than compensated for the

10. Works Progress Administration, *Michigan*, 311; *Polk's City Directory*, 1927, p. 12.

11. Butler, *Live, Live, Live*, p. 73; Virginia Peck reminiscences, GRPL Women's History Collection. For the structure of American cities in this era, see McKenzie, "The Neighborhood," pp. 146-52.

discomforts of living in a large city. The comments, both contemporary and retrospective, of Grand Rapids residents suggest that it delivered on that promise. To them, the business district was an interesting, impressive place. Downtown meant Herpolsheimer's, the city's leading department store, where a woman played the harp in the quiet, elegant dining room, or a dim, stylish men's clothing store, "dark and subdued inside, with neat-carpeted silent floors, and hidden lights shining downward along the walls, and counters full of fresh new clothes: stacks of brown and black and blue and gray and burgundy wine." Downtown meant grand, striking public buildings like the imposing gray stone City Hall with its huge bell, or the brand-new Fountain Street Baptist Church, "impressive and effective," or the white marble Beaux-Arts library. It meant the grand Pantlind Hotel, focus of the semiannual Furniture Show but also "just about the most elite place in the city" for its dazzling dining room. "What beauty! What wonderful food! What service!" rhapsodized one local man.[12]

The rich inhabitants of the city — a 1926 estimate was that it contained thirty-six millionaires — had finer private luxuries in their homes, but downtown offered quality fare inexpensively to everyone. Lower Monroe Street had its theaters — the Powers, the Majestic, the Strand, the Empress — offering touring Broadway plays, local productions, vaudeville, burlesque, and motion pictures. The Isis, in 1926, was being remodeled "into a high class, handsome cinema temple." There was a Grand Rapids Symphony, and concerts in St. Cecilia Hall. And some of the city's greatest pleasures were free: making one's way down the "canyon" of Monroe Street's four- and five-story commercial buildings, amid crowds of secretaries, shoppers, policemen, and businessmen, and savoring the illusion of being in a really big city, a Chicago or a New York; or standing on Monroe Street late at night, looking up at the newly built, twelve-story Michigan National Bank Building, where a light flickered on an upper floor as a charwoman passed through, and feeling a sense of big-city grandeur and isolation.[13]

Downtown, as a source of shared quality experience for city residents, was possible only because of the cheap, reliable trolley network that connected it to the outlying residential neighborhoods. But during the 1920s

12. Cady interview; Manfred, *The Primitive*, p. 184; Works Progress Administration, *Michigan*, pp. 312-13; Turner, *The Good Old Daze*, p. 24.

13. *Michigan Tradesman*, February 10, 1926; Silbar, "Stars in His Eyes," pp. 6-7; Stanton Todd, "Let Me Live," Stanton Todd Papers, BHL, p. 20; Works Progress Administration, *Michigan*, pp. 311-12; Manfred, *The Primitive*, p. 127; *Herald*, July 11, 1926; March 27, 1931.

that connection was weakening, and the whole system of transportation in Grand Rapids was changing. The change was highly visible and very exciting; no one knew where it would lead. The force for change was the automobile.

Figures tell part of the story. In 1920 there were 17,618 "pleasure cars" registered in Kent County; in 1925 there were 47,415 "passenger cars," and in 1930, 60,271. But just as important was a sweeping change in the way people looked at automobiles. In 1920 they still retained much of their early image as a pleasure vehicle for rich and upper-middle-class folk, and a useful adjunct for farmers and small-town families who could afford them; they were seen mainly in a rural or suburban context, to be used in the pleasant weather of spring, summer, and fall. But in the course of the 1920s they muscled into the city center; people used the new closed cars year-round to go shopping and attend urban amusements. They competed with trolleys and pedestrians for space on downtown streets, posing new problems for Grand Rapids city police, from traffic control to time limits for parked cars. The city appointed an "accident recorder" to study the situation, and police learned to chalk the tires of parked cars to make sure limits were observed. In the midtwenties, pressed by increasing congestion, the city government began installing traffic lights at major intersections and taking the first steps toward regulating traffic throughout the city, like designating through streets. (Drivers resented the lights, one auto dealer said, but some liked using them to demonstrate their cars' rapid getaway.) Speed per se was not yet much of a problem; the twenty-mile-an-hour limit was frequently broken, but not by much. The real problem was that all concerned — motorists, trolley drivers, pedestrians, and the city government — were constantly having to adapt to new rules, or to make them up as they went along.[14]

Despite the massive changes that were obviously under way, the Grand

---

14. Figures for Kent County are from Michigan Department of State, *Registration of Motor Vehicles, Titles, Operators, Chauffeurs, Etc.*, for the years given. A story in the *Herald*, July 11, 1926, gives figures for Grand Rapids: 53,154 drivers, or about a third of the population, in that year. Carl Sanders, in the *Press*, estimated over 40,000 cars in the city on January 1, 1928. For comments on the changes in automobile use and city traffic, see Lynd and Lynd, *Middletown*, p. 253; Reid, *Finally It's Friday*, p. 45; Belasco, *Americans on the Road*, pp. 115-16; and especially Barrett, *The Automobile and Urban Transit*, pp. 132-33, 137-40, 156-57. On chalking tires, see *Herald*, March 3 and April 19, 1930; on traffic lights, *Herald*, July 4, 1926. Lewis, *Babbitt*, p. 75, has a brief family discussion, set in the early 1920s, about the comparative merits of open and closed cars.

Rapids Railway Company remained upbeat through most of the decade. In June 1926, with much fanfare, it put into service a new fleet of electric coaches with conveniences like automatic exit treadles; in July it published a statement by civic leaders urging residents "to ride the coaches more to and from work and to use their autos more for pleasure purposes." In 1927 it informed passengers that a survey in South Bend had shown that 58.3 percent of downtown shoppers had come by streetcar, as against only 19.4 percent by auto (and 13.3 percent on foot). Grand Rapids was probably not too different; people used the streetcars a lot. Junior Ford took his first date to a downtown movie on a trolley — and after the show, committed an early faux pas by putting her on the trolley to her house and then getting on the one that went to his own.[15]

As Junior Ford grew up during the twenties, he had varied reasons, besides the movies, to go downtown. His aunt Marjory's dance studio, where he learned to dance, was there. So was the YMCA, where he swam and played basketball. The Boy Scouts regional office was downtown; he would become a dedicated Boy Scout. Sometimes he took the trolley, and sometimes he walked. It was not a long walk; Grand Rapids was still fairly compact. Downtown was one pole of his juvenile world — by far the less important. The more important was his own neighborhood, Union Avenue, Sherman and Franklin and Pleasant Streets, on the border between the East and the South Sides — the mythic world, as John Thompson put it in an eloquent piece on growing up in Grand Rapids, where he picked up once and for all his basic life concepts: what Work was, what Play was, the roles of an adult Man and Woman, the meaning of Business, the implications of Religion.[16]

Because this is Ford's story, this survey of Grand Rapids views the city as he knew it in those years of growing up: downtown plus the East Side, with a secondary look at the South Side. The Catholic West Side was not in his world as he grew up; it was another planet, a space he crossed occasionally on his way to caddy for his father at the new Masonic Country Club. In his high school years it would become symbolized by his football team's main rival, Union High School. The industrial guts of the city, the

15. *Trolley Topics*, July 1926, April 1927. GRF told the first date story on himself; see *New Pioneer*, May 1988, referring to the ABC News program *Conversations with the Presidents*, April 16, 1988.

16. Thompson, "Yesterdays in Grand Rapids," pp. 299, 303, 305. In Manfred, *The Primitive*, p. 221, a college sophomore walks with his date from Calvin College to Fountain Street Church. The Boy Scouts are treated in more detail in chapter 4.

river valley with its furniture factories, was not really in his experience either. His family drove through it on the way to the Lake Michigan beaches, perhaps with the same sort of vague distaste described by a rich East Sider in his novel about Grand Rapids: "The route Jim picked to take to the beach jagged through the back streets of the business and wholesale district, past the gas plant and its area of squalid houses. Then it made a right-angle turn around the corner of the box company plant and entered the straight, mile-long stretch of [Grandville] Avenue, bordered by a row of furniture factories. . . . A network of tracks lay behind the factories where engines belched smoke and added to the grime."[17]

The valley was also the main approach to the city by rail, whether you used the Pennsylvania, the New York Central, or the Pere Marquette. At the end of his adolescent years, when he was taking the train regularly to Ann Arbor and other places in the outside world, young Ford would see, as he entered and left the city, the typical rundown chaotic industrial vistas: the "jumbled buildings . . . large factories, smoking chimneys, flimsy houses, a few trees" that David DeJong remembered from his arrival in 1918, or the view Thompson recalled from the thirties: "Plaster Creek and . . . the sidings of the gaunt old furniture plants . . . blown smoke and those junk-fenced back yards with dead hollyhocks and sunflowers that line all American railway tracks, and two- and three-story wooden tenements with washings on the back railings where the outside steps go up."[18]

The East Side was where Grand Rapids' business class lived — the salesmen, clerks, professionals, and corporation executives who, as Robert and Helen Lynd put it in 1925, "address their activities predominantly to people in the selling or promotion of things, services, and ideas."[19] Two landmarks, one at each end, defined the East Side in the 1920s. At the west end was the Hill District, a fifteen- or twenty-block area of stately mansions and tree-lined streets on a high hill overlooking downtown. From the 1890s on, this had been the place for Grand Rapids' corporate executives and successful professionals to live. The area was "regal," as one resident put it, with "huge old trees" and houses that had servants' quarters, third-floor ballrooms, swimming pools, libraries, circulating hot water, and all the appurtenances of upper-class comfort. Younger people might

17. Bissell, *A Sow's Ear*, p. 21.
18. DeJong, *With a Dutch Accent*, p. 156; Thompson, "Yesterdays in Grand Rapids," p. 292.
19. Lynd and Lynd, *Middletown*, p. 22.

criticize some of the older Queen Anne–style residences as "bulgy packing crates," but there were other styles; the area boasted two Frank Lloyd Wright houses and was still building up at the beginning of the 1920s. And not all the residents were rich; William Bloomer, for instance, a conveyor belt salesman whose daughter Junior Ford would one day marry, lived with his family on Fountain Street among the mansions.[20]

At the east end of the East Side, on what had been the outskirts of the city, was Reeds Lake, a mile and a half long, a popular place for swimming and boating in the summer, or skating in the winter. Before the turn of the century, the Grand Rapids Railway Company had extended its trolley line out Lake Drive and Wealthy Street and built an amusement park by the lake, complete with roller coaster, fun house, and rides. Ramona Park, by the 1920s, was an established landmark. From late May to early September, thousands of people rode the streetcars out to watch balloon ascensions and parachute jumps, ride the "Jack Rabbit," eat hot dogs and burgers, enjoy vaudeville or legitimate drama at the Majestic Theater, treat their children to pony rides or airplane swings, and spend a little money at the shooting gallery. There was a bathing beach, and a small double-decked steamer carried sightseers around the lake. A small, mixed community grew up, of concession owners and workers, and affluent families who owned houses on the water. In 1927 they incorporated as the tiny "city" of East Grand Rapids — Grand Rapids' first suburb.[21]

By the 1920s the far East Side was recognized as "the choice residential section of Grand Rapids," as a 1926 real estate advertisement expressed it. Lake Drive was its axis, bordered with large, often imposing houses and churches, punctuated occasionally with neighborhood commercial areas like the one at the intersection of Lake and Wealthy, with its small stores —

20. The phrase "Hill District" is used in, for example, Stanton Todd's reminiscences ("Let Me Live," pp. 1-2) — although the fashionable neighborhood he contrasts with the Hill District in that passage would today be seen as a southward extension of it — and in a real estate advertisement in the *Herald*, July 8, 1926, which describes a house for sale with "large dining room in mahogany and old ivory with crystal chandeliers and sidelights," "butler's pantry and airy kitchen"; "billiard room with fireplace in basement," "vacuum cleaning system and house phones," among other amenities. Other information comes from Betty Ford, *The Times of My Life*, pp. 8, 12; Turner, *The Good Old Daze*, p. 35; Thompson, "Yesterdays in Grand Rapids," p. 307; and the Mrs. Stuart Knappen reminiscences, Kent County Council Oral History Collection, GRPL.

21. Elliott, *Grand Rapids*, pp. 96-97, 108; Denham, *Growing Up in Grand Rapids*, p. 91; Silbar, "Stars in His Eyes," p. 7; *Trolley Topics*, May-June 1929. East Grand Rapids incorporated as a fourth-class city in 1927 (*Grand Rapids Mirror*, Fall 1933, p. 17).

cafe, shoe store, drugstore — and the neighborhood theater affectionately known as the Hinky Dink.[22]

During the 1920s Grand Rapids' geography began changing. Again, the automobile was a major disruptive force. Business-class families with money were in the market for larger houses with modern electrical wiring, and having a car made it possible to live at a distance from the streetcar line. In the middle of the decade real estate men developed a ten-block area well south of Lake Drive as an upper-middle-class residential area with stately two-story homes under the name of Ottawa Hills — "the synonym of Grand Rapids Beautiful," one ad called it. The curving streets were designated by Indian names. Buyers snapped up the lots. "Six years ago," declared a Real Estate Board ad in 1931, "Pontiac Road, Cadillac Drive, and Iroquois Drive were not even good dirt roads. There were scarcely any improvements and little or no building. Drive out there today . . . you can scarcely believe your eyes." Pretentious two-story period houses, Spanish, Tudor, and colonial, lined the streets. The area was described in the 1930s as "fashionable"; the students at its new high school struck many people as pampered upper-class youth.[23]

Toward the end of the decade, the rich families of the Hill District began joining the migration. Dorothy Leonard Judd, of the Leonard refrigerator-manufacturing family, married in 1925 and moved into a luxurious house in the southern part of the Hill District, with a library, dining room for eight, living-room fireplace, and the like. But by 1930, she recalled, she and her husband concluded that "it was time for us to follow the 'Madison Avenue Crowd' to East Grand Rapids," and they moved into a larger house on San Lu Rae Drive. Virginia Peck, who grew up in a Quality Hill mansion with a third-floor ballroom and chauffeur's quarters over the garage, began married life in 1930 in a new house, one of only three, on San Lucia Drive in East Grand Rapids. Bob Denham, son of a prosperous doctor, found himself transferred to East Grand Rapids High School in 1927 when his family built on a vacant lot on Plymouth Drive; within the next two years the street filled up with substantial new houses. A young surgeon and his wife in 1931 built "a delightful Dutch Colonial two-story house," with a breakfast nook, four bedrooms, a music room, and a full

22. *Herald*, July 18, 1926; Manfred, *The Primitive*, pp. 97, 136. A rich boy and his friends from the Hill District referred to this theater as the "nickel dump." Todd, "Let Me Live," p. 17.

23. *Herald*, September 12, 1926; March 22, 1931; Works Progress Administration, *Michigan*, p. 306. For more on Ottawa Hills High School, see chapter 6.

basement on East Paris Road. By the end of the 1920s, some of the imposing houses of the Hill District were vacant or being converted into cheap
furnished apartments.[24]

Along the fringes of the East Side, less affluent families of the business class — salesmen, secretaries, small proprietors — lived in decent
but modest one- and two-story homes of wood and stucco on tree-lined
streets. The houses were typically painted gray or brown, colors supposed
not to show the winter soot. Some were owned, and some were rented.
There were ethnic areas. On Henry Street, south of Lake Drive, was the
better of the city's two African American neighborhoods. Dutch immigrant families lived on some squalid dead-end streets on the East Side, frequently without indoor plumbing or electricity. The immigrant children
sometimes did odd jobs for the "rich Americans" (actually middle-income
families) who lived only a block or two away. Children grew up accepting
the juxtaposition — west of Fuller Avenue, one Anglo-American boy later
recollected, were houses "one size smaller" where "the Dutchmen live[d]
and past that the niggers." This was the part of the East Side where Junior
Ford's family lived, the part where it began to shade into the South Side.[25]

The South Side was primarily working class. Houses were closer together and populations were denser. Since a large number of families
rented, there was a great deal of mobility from year to year. All the railroads that served Grand Rapids had their yards and main lines on the South
Side, and provided employment for many of its residents. Other families
had breadwinners working downtown or in the furniture factories. Ethni-
cally the area was a hodgepodge. Its main artery, narrow, crowded South
Division Street, began "on the fringes of the downtown district, in the
midst of a conglomeration of boarding and rooming houses, Irish Catho-
lics and Syrians, temples of strange cults and spiritualistic parlours," and
ran straight south through neighborhoods of Greeks and East European

24. Judd, "A Lifetime in Grand Rapids," bound typescript in Dorothy Judd Papers,
GRPL, pp. 34, 44; Virginia Peck reminiscences, Grand Rapids Women's History Collection,
GRPL; Denham, *Growing Up in Grand Rapids*, p. 72; Butler, *Live, Live, Live*, p. 89. Emigration from the Hill District was slower than from less affluent areas, because many of the
owners were rich widows who preferred not to sell their houses, although they knew
their children would never live there. A mansion partitioned into furnished apartments
is depicted in Wickenden, *The Wayfarers*, p. 19.

25. DeJong, *With a Dutch Accent*, pp. 158-59, 182; Wickenden, *The Wayfarers*, p. 7;
Thompson, "Yesterdays in Grand Rapids," pp. 295-96; Todd, "Let Me Live," p. 17. On the
African American population, see Logan, *Almost Lost*, pp. 66-67.

Jews. The intersection of Division and Franklin, "a lower income zone or bracket whichever you wish to call it," according to a friend of Junior Ford's who lived there, was the center of Grand Rapids' Little Italy.[26]

Anglo-Americans made up a bare majority of the South Side population, but the largest immigrant group, and a very visible one, was the first- and second-generation Dutch, who occupied large neighborhoods on both sides of South Division. They fitted into the Grand Rapids economy in varying ways: some worked in the furniture factories, some were in the building trades, and the younger generation were frequently store clerks or secretaries. The city's business class approved of them as "clean folk . . . thrifty, hardworking, sober, non-rebellious." They were also clannish, traditional-minded, fervently devoted to their many varieties of Calvinism, and prone to endless earnest debates over proper morality — "believing strictly," as one of them wrote, "in the status quo, the Republican Party, and in ourselves as the special children of God." Many of the younger Dutch were bright and ambitious. Their Christian Reformed Church had established its own denominational college, Calvin College, and had "fifty-odd churches of the true faith" in Grand Rapids, their "new Jerusalem."[27]

Dutch piety, combined with the New England heritage of the business-class elite, gave Grand Rapids' religious and moral atmosphere a quality one might call "conspicuous Christianity" — conspicuous, at any rate, to the rest of Michigan and to Grand Rapids dwellers who happened not to share it. One of them, Dorothy Judd, called the city "remarkably conservative" in religious matters; Ford's own word was "strait-laced." "Little Jerusalem!" an Ann Arbor doctor exploded in the 1930s. "Everywhere you look in Grand Rapids, you see a church. They fill them up Sunday morning, Sunday evening, prayer meeting in the middle of the week. You're always praying for something over there in Grand Rapids." Sunday in Grand Rapids, to be sure, was a remarkably quiet day. The *Press*, one of the two major daily newspapers, did not publish at all, and many of the Dutch refused to attend movies or organized sports on that day. But Christian morality

26. DeJong, *With a Dutch Accent*, p. 213; Works Progress Administration, *Michigan*, p. 306; *Herald*, August 4, 1926; Art Brown interview, Grand Rapids Oral History Collection, GRFL.

27. The Dutch percentage of the city population at this time is variously given as 25 or 30 percent; on the South Side, it would have been considerably higher. Works Progress Administration, *Michigan*, p. 306; DeJong, *With a Dutch Accent*, pp. 197-202; Ter Horst, *Gerald R. Ford*, pp. 31-32.

was a seven-day-a-week affair. The *Herald* carried a Bible verse every day on its editorial page and was squeamish in its coverage of morals offenses; immorality was not to be mentioned, let alone encouraged.[28]

Grand Rapids, the second-largest city in Michigan, differed radically from the metropolis, Detroit, on the other side of the state. Detroit was a hotbed of ethnicity and crime, full of rich men and political malcontents; Grand Rapids was staid, pious, and orderly. On New Year's Eve in 1926 the Grand Rapids Railway Company held the "owl" streetcar — the last streetcar of the night — until 12:15 A.M. so that late celebrants had time to get home; a Detroiter observed sardonically that in the Motor City the parties were just starting at 12:15, and the last streetcar would probably not run before 4:00 A.M. Prohibition in Detroit generated rum-running and organized gangs; in Grand Rapids, it was a success, with the upper classes setting the example — at one high-society wedding, the guests toasted the bride and groom with water.[29]

One consequence of this pervasive morality was an equally pervasive community commitment to civic and charitable activism. Since the 1890s, the leaders of mainstream Protestantism in America, alarmed by what they saw as a social crisis in the nation, had been calling on their followers for self-sacrifice and social service. Grand Rapids Protestants had heeded their call. Charitable organizations flourished, from the Welfare Union to the Santa Claus Girls. Youth organizations like the YMCA and Boy Scouts multiplied. There were all sorts of organizations for civic betterment, supported by the leading people in town. As John Thompson put it, "Rich people in Grand Rapids, unless they have some really enormous pile of inherited loot, . . . tend to go in for some sort of civic enterprise." The less rich followed their lead. Social service was a prestigious activity; Grand Rapids, in the words of a local reporter, was "a town that rewarded virtue."[30]

This civic conscience bred a glow of self-satisfaction that could easily turn into smug complacency, as it did in the literature put out for the

28. Judd, "A Lifetime in Grand Rapids," p. 41; Ford, *TTH*, p. 46; Willard Ver Meulen oral history, Grand Rapids Oral History Collection, GRFL; Ter Horst, *Gerald R. Ford*, pp. 32-33; DeJong, *With a Dutch Accent*, p. 196.

29. O. J. Mulford to Benjamin S. Hanchett, January 3, 1927, Benjamin S. Hanchett Papers, BHL; Engelmann, *Intemperance*, pp. 61-65; Kay Whinery and Mrs. Noyes Avery interviews, Kent County Council Oral History Collection, GRPL.

30. Charles, *Service Clubs in American Society*, p. 24; Elliott, *Grand Rapids*, pp. 98, 100; Thompson, "Yesterdays in Grand Rapids," p. 301; Sherrill, "What Grand Rapids Did for Jerry Ford," p. 80.

Grand Rapids Centennial in 1926, an event celebrated with pageants, speeches, and a grand parade in which Junior Ford joined hundreds of other uniformed Boy Scouts marching down Monroe Avenue: "Grand Rapids is one of the best-governed cities in the Union. . . . The citizenship is contented, as is eloquently proved by the percentage of residents who own their homes. There is a minimum of poor and indigent persons requiring public aid, but a generous public, exceptionally well organized, provides for the support of those in need. . . . The city has no resemblance to the so-called 'slum districts' of some larger cities. It has no poor sections, no neglected districts."[31]

The writers of these statements had to know that they were exaggerating. The bloom that had surrounded Midwestern cities in the early twentieth century, making them exciting places to live, full of experiments in government and social service, began fading after World War I, as populations and economies stabilized. In Grand Rapids particularly, the furniture industry, the city's mainstay, was in trouble in 1926, facing an increasingly saturated market and stiff competition from North Carolina manufacturers; many signs pointed to its stagnation or even decline, with an eventual impact on the city as a whole. And as for "slum districts," every Grand Rapids male high school age or older knew of Commerce Avenue, the downtown thoroughfare between the business district and Union Station, with its cobbled street, cheap hotels, whorehouses, and mixed-race gambling parlors. Mel Trotter's City Rescue Mission had cleaned up a block of adjacent Market Street, but across the river, at Front and Bridge Streets, there were the beginnings of a skid row that a few years later would be among the worst in the nation.[32]

Grand Rapids was no paradise; but it did have an unusual level of civic consciousness, a conviction that the wealthy should set a high moral standard, and a confidence that united effort could solve most social problems. Jerry and Dorothy Ford were right in the middle of this civic activity.

31. The centennial celebration is described in the *Herald*, September 28-29, 1926. The quotation is in Elliott, *Grand Rapids*, p. 102.

32. Ransom, *City Built on Wood*, pp. 68, 73; Elliott, *Grand Rapids*, p. 106; interviews with Henry Moore and Charles R. Sligh Jr., GRPL oral history collections; Ter Horst, *Gerald R. Ford*, p. 33; Manfred, *The Primitive*, p. 242; Wickenden, *The Wayfarers*, p. 140; Vander Meulen, *Skid Row Life Line*, passim.

CHAPTER 3

Living on Union Avenue

Jerry Ford Sr. was not just honest, decent, and hardworking. He had goals. He wanted to be prosperous, to be his own boss. He wanted his family to live well. By the early twenties, he thought he was well on the way to success. Junior was in school. He and Dorothy now had a second son, Tom, born in 1918 the day after Junior's birthday. He had a good job as sales manager of the paint division of Heystek and Canfield, and money in the bank. The world war was over and business was booming. In 1922 the Fords decided to buy a lot and build a two-story house, the first they had owned, at 630 Rosewood Avenue, on a block that had just been laid out in East Grand Rapids.[1]

---

1. On GRF Sr.'s ambition, see Stanton Todd's comment, "To Benjamin Clough a synopsis of my experience in Republican politics, 1942 to 1947," Stanton Todd Papers, BHL. His prosperity in the early twenties is confirmed by his building the Rosewood Avenue house. GRF says (*TTH*, p. 43) that it was in 1919, but the city directory listings for the two following years, 1920 and 1921, show the Fords still living at 716 Madison Avenue. Only in 1922 do they appear at the Rosewood Avenue address. GRF also says that his father was working for Grand Rapids Wood Finishing at the time, with an additional interest in his nephew Harold Swain's coal company, but the city directory gives his job as sales manager for Heystek and Canfield, which the census confirms. GRF to Ray Phillips, January 28, 1975, White House Central Files: Presidential Personal, PP13, GRFL, mentions the position as head of the Paint Department but dates it inaccurately to 1924; the city directory shows him as department manager only in 1922. Ter Horst, *Gerald R. Ford*, p. 28, states that the Fords owned an open touring car and took Florida vacations during this period, but his statement is not supported by other sources and may stem from a misinterpretation of family photos that show GRF in Florida with his Gardner grandparents.

The 600 block of Rosewood was so new in 1922 that it does not even appear in the

His timing was unfortunate. In 1921 the head of Heystek and Canfield died; his son, thirty-year-old Henry J. Heystek Jr., took over and began a management shake-up that, within five years, wrecked the business. Ford, caught in the storm, lost his job in 1922 or 1923; unable to meet the payments, he also lost his house. The setback did not harm his high standing in the business community. "Well, I'll just have to work harder," he told Dorothy when they realized they were going to have to move back to a rented house. He took a job as salesman at a smaller company, Grand Rapids Wood Finishing, and moved his family back to his old neighborhood, the south fringe of the Hill District, at 649 Union Avenue.[2]

It was a marginal area in more ways than one. The luxury homes of the Hill District were only a couple of blocks away in one direction; in another direction, one block distant, were the small, slatternly African American homes of Henry Avenue. The chunky white houses lining the 600 and 700 blocks, where brick-paved Union descended a fairly steep hill to cross Franklin Street, conveyed an image of uniformity and stability; but in fact, the fifty families who resided in them formed a mixed, highly mobile group. They included all occupational classes, from unskilled laborers to officers of small companies. At one end of the scale, three had live-in servants. At the other, one family was African American. The great majority were headed by men (or occasionally women) either from the low edge of the business class, like salesmen, department store clerks, and stenographers, or from the top of the working class, like foremen and machinists. In any given year, just under half the families were likely to be of Dutch origin, good steady neighbors, disciplined and hardworking. Three-quarters of them owned their homes.[3]

1920 U.S. Census manuscript, in which the street numbers stop in the 300s. A picture of the house appears in the article "A Patriotic Edge," *Press*, July 1, 2001.

2. These events are mentioned in Ford, *TTH*, p. 45, and Cannon, *Time and Chance*, p. 10. GRF's account suggests that the family lived on Rosewood Avenue for two years; the city directory shows them at that address for only one year, in 1922-1923. An article in the *Press*, August 15, 1974, based on an examination of GRF's records in the Grand Rapids schools, makes the claim that he skipped a grade. The claim seems unlikely; most likely the reporter failed to find school records for one grade, because the Fords lived in the East Grand Rapids school district for one year. The article stated that the grade skipped was the fourth, which would have been in the year 1922-1923. Probably, then, the Fords moved to Union Avenue in the late spring of 1923.

The changes at Heystek and Canfield are recorded in *Michigan Tradesman*, April 13, 1921. After 1925 the firm disappears from city directory listings.

3. These generalizations apply to the 600 and 700 blocks of Union Avenue; since the

Despite that fact, families on the block were anything but permanent. When the Fords arrived in 1923, thirty-two of their neighbors had been living on the block for a year or more; when they moved away in 1930, only sixteen of those families still lived there. Of the eighteen families who moved onto the block the same year as the Fords, all but two had left by 1930. Over one-third of both groups had moved out of town; a large fraction of the rest migrated to more affluent neighborhoods farther out on the East Side. This part of Union Avenue, in other words, was for most of its dwellers a way station on the road to prosperous family life elsewhere in Grand Rapids.[4]

To a child, with no idea of the transience of adult life, everything seemed permanent. Seven years, the length of the Fords' stay on Union Avenue, was an era to the oldest Ford boy. The house and the block were fixed vividly in his mind as the scene of his childhood and adolescence. And in fact, there were enough families who stayed to create a semblance of continuity; moreover, those who moved away were usually replaced by families of the same sort, so that the character of the block changed hardly at all from 1923 to 1930, the years the Fords spent there. This chapter is about the Fords as a family in those years, their neighborhood, their life-

---

Fords' house was close to the junction of both blocks, I thought it best to include both. The total number of families, as shown in the city directory, was usually around fifty. I have traced the movements of each family shown as living on the blocks between 1920 and 1931.

The breakdown in occupational groups, which remained quite constant from 1920 to 1931, is as follows: Group 1 (professionals and company executives), 4.7 percent; Group 2 (managers and proprietors), 7.6 percent; Group 3 (salesmen and clerks), 55.5 percent; Group 4 (skilled workers), 24.2 percent; Group 5 (unskilled workers), 8.0 percent. Figures for home ownership are from the 1920 manuscript U.S. Census. Figures for ethnic origin are my tabulation, from the city directory, and are likely to be conservative — I counted only surnames that were unquestionably Dutch. In the 1920 census thirteen families (27 percent) were Dutch-born and eight others (16 percent) were second-generation Dutch. African American–owned homes in the area, according to the 1930 census, consistently had about half the value of those of their white-owned neighbors.

4. Data on change of residence come from the city directories. A family's failure to reappear in the following year's directory, on Union Avenue or at another address, could be due to emigration from the city or to the death of the head; I have assumed for purposes of this tabulation that emigration accounts for the great majority. Families that moved to other addresses in Grand Rapids or East Grand Rapids were classified by the area to which they moved. Of the 124 families who disappear from the two blocks of Union Avenue, 42 (34 percent) apparently left Grand Rapids; 37 (30 percent) moved farther out on the East Side; 22 (18 percent) moved elsewhere on the near East Side; and the remaining 23 relocated to other parts of the city.

style, their interests and aspirations in the changing world that was Grand Rapids in the 1920s.[5]

It was a neighborhood with a lot of children. As in most American towns of that era, they made the street their playground. On snowy days in the winter, when driving was dangerous, the city barricaded the hill and they could coast down on their Flexible Flyers or, for the poorer families, homemade bobsleds. All year long, they had the run of the neighbors' backyards; Sylvia English, a stenographer, remembered seeing Junior Ford swinging on Georgia Hopper's clothesline pole. They made friends on adjacent streets; two of Junior's best friends, Art and Ben Engel, lived on the other side of the Fords' backyard fence, in a house facing Paris Avenue.[6]

The roomy houses occupied small lots; their front and back yards tended to be compact. The Fords' front yard and those of several neighbors were a couple of feet above sidewalk level. Their house, like most of their neighbors' houses, dated from the early twentieth century and had a two-story stable from the horse-and-buggy era, now converted into a garage for the family car, at the end of the driveway. Junior and the Engel twins turned the disused second floor into a clubhouse and hideaway where they could indulge in daring activities like penny-ante poker, reasoning that his parents wouldn't want to climb the ladder. They were right about Mrs. Ford, who had weight problems and was not in the best of health, but wrong about Junior's father. "He caught us red-handed several times," Ford recalled, "and reprimanded us severely."[7]

Jerry Ford was a stern-looking man and a strict disciplinarian. "Stern-looking but not stern-acting," was the verdict of one family friend, and it was certainly true that he had the bonhomie necessary to succeed in sales, with the salesman's stock of jokes (a friend of his son recalled once seeing a set of fake dog droppings). Nevertheless, those who knew him well sensed that he was basically far less gregarious than his wife, and his view of life

5. Ter Horst, *Gerald R. Ford*, p. 29. Wylie, *Village in the Vaucluse*, pp. 351-52, points out that a small "core population" of families can give an illusion of permanence and stability to a community. His point is reinforced in Chudacoff, *Mobile Americans*, p. 75, for early-twentieth-century Omaha, where neighborhoods preserved their ethnic character even when almost all their families moved away, because other families of the same ethnicity moved in.

6. Sheridan, "Portrait of the Next President," p. 20; Sherrill, "What Grand Rapids Did for Jerry Ford"; Ter Horst, *Gerald R. Ford*, p. 29. Denham, *Growing Up in Grand Rapids*, p. 44, mentions Flexible Flyers.

7. Ford, *TTH*, p. 46.

was fundamentally serious. He worked hard at his job (with the requisite stomach ulcers of a hard-driving man), but found time to follow politics and civic affairs closely in the newspapers. What books he read were either nonfiction, especially on public affairs, or inspirational essays like Emerson's — and he gave his sons Horatio Alger books to read. Not only did he discipline his sons' conduct, but he also used conversations with them to reinforce moral lessons, admonishing them against stereotyping people poorer than themselves, or criticizing another person without considering his good points. A big, dark-haired man, 6 feet 1 inch and weighing two hundred pounds in maturity, he radiated moral authority. He "had the straightest shoulders I have ever seen," his eldest son recalled.[8]

From the time he achieved financial security, Ford was active in civic and charitable organizations; he was, in the parlance of the time, a "joiner." He took responsibility, frequently serving on the arrangement committees that did the real organizational work. Some of his clubs were practical adjuncts for a business-class man in sales: early on, for instance, he was president of the Travelers' Protective Association, an organization for traveling salesmen like himself. Others were mainly dining clubs, the kind of men's clubs satirized in *Babbitt*, valuable primarily for their friendly contacts with other businessmen. In the mid-1920s, when he was in his thirties, he served as president of the local Exchange Club. He was a devoted Elk, and became Grand Exalted Ruler of the Grand Rapids lodge in 1931.[9]

8. Philip Buchen interview, p. 6, and Mr. and Mrs. Paul Goebel interview, p. 3, both in Grand Rapids Oral History Collection, GRFL; Vestal, *Jerry Ford, Up Close*, p. 53; *The Almanac*, December 13, 1967, in Thomas Ford Scrapbook, GRFL; transcript of AOL interview with GRF, February 13, 1995, vertical file, GRFL; Richard A. Ford interview, "Family" vertical file, pp. 11-12, GRFL; Hersey, *The President*, pp. 90-91; Ford, *TTH*, p. 44. A small, undated selection of books from GRF Sr.'s collection, in the Thomas G. Ford Papers, GRFL, is my basis for this description of his reading; it may or may not apply to the 1920s.

9. GRF Sr.'s résumé of volunteer activities was so long that most acquaintances, in summarizing it, tended to mix affiliations from different periods and occasionally to credit him with activities he was not involved in. In later years, as an affluent manufacturer, he worked with organizations that had not been a part of his early married life. In these paragraphs I have tried to identify his commitments from the 1920s. The Travelers' Protective Association is mentioned in the caption of an undated photo in GRF Scrapbook #1a, p. 17; it belongs to his years as a salesman. Exchange Club: *Herald*, September 18, 1926. Elks: Benevolent Protective Order of Elks, *Golden Jubilee*, p. 14. Stanley Davis, a local politician, in an interview in the Grand Rapids Oral History Collection, GRPL, asserted (tape A, side 2, p. 5) that GRF Sr. was connected with the Rotary and the Lions as well, but I have found no confirmation of that connection for the 1920s or 1930s, and no mention of it in any other source.

But more important to him were the clubs with a philanthropic purpose. His earliest and deepest affiliation, which followed in his own father's footsteps, was with the Masons; from 1912 on he was a dedicated member of Malta Lodge. When the combined Masonic lodges of the city decided to set up a modern country club on a hill northwest of town, Ford, though unable to contribute much money, supported it faithfully. In 1924 he joined the Scottish Rite lodge and became more deeply involved in the ceremonials and pageants it produced at the new five-story Masonic Temple on Fulton Street. Dorothy Ford, like many women of her acquaintance, became a "Masonic widow" one or two nights a week as her husband worked on lodge activities.[10]

Church membership, too, had a strong component of social service. Jerry Ford had grown up attending a branch of St. Mark's, and would eventually become a vestryman in the 1930s when he owned his own company. His selection for the post implies a long, continuous, and active association with the church. He took part in Sunday school and in the charitable programs that St. Mark's, like Malta Lodge, sponsored.[11]

Since her remarriage, Dorothy Ford had a special complication in her relation to the church. The position of the early-twentieth-century Episcopal Church was that a divorced person who had remarried was in a state of sin and not permitted to receive communion. That Dorothy continued attending under this condition of second-class membership speaks powerfully to her sense of Christian commitment. Her participation in church activities, and perhaps Junior's, was somewhat restricted, but there was some, and she was well liked in the congregation.[12]

10. Of his father's Masonic activities, GRF stated: "I know of no man, during my lifetime thus far, who was more devoted to Masonry and all for which it stands" (clipping from Empire State Mason, June 1974, in "Freemasonry" vertical file, GRFL). His memberships are recorded in documents on file at the Michigan Masonic Museum in Grand Rapids. On the Masonic Country Club, see *"Your Club and My Club": The Masonic Country Club of Western Michigan*, an illustrated booklet on file in the Masonic Museum. GRF Sr. was captain of the guard at a 32nd degree ceremony as early as 1920 (clipping in L. A. Cornelius Scrapbook, Michigan Historical Collection, GRPL). Details of his activities with Malta Lodge frequently appeared in local newspapers.

11. GRF Sr. become a communicant of the main church when he was elected a vestryman in the mid-1930s (St. Mark's church Register of Communicants, church archives; Allen, *The Story of St. Mark's*, p. 45; Jean Heibel interview).

12. Smith, *Diocese of Western Michigan*, p. 595. GRF Sr. and his three sons appear in church records; DGF and GRF do not. According to one source (Joseph Howell, interview), GRF served as an acolyte at St. Mark's and sang in its famous boy choir, but no photo-

Perhaps because his own father had abandoned the family, making it necessary for him to drop out of school in his teens to help support his mother and sisters, Ford was especially drawn to the kind of charities known then as "boys' work" — programs designed to help younger boys and teenagers develop high moral values, team spirit, and habits of hard work, to prepare them for economic success in life. The Boy Scouts of America, barely ten years old in the early 1920s, seemed like a new and ideal organization for this purpose, taking boys' adventurous spirits and turning them into useful skills, self-discipline, and community awareness. Ford was very active on its council, although his work schedule did not allow him the time to serve as scoutmaster to a local troop. Likewise, he was concerned with developing clubs for local underprivileged boys, an interest that would keep increasing in later years as he became more prosperous. As soon as Junior entered school, both Jerry and Dorothy joined the PTA and participated actively.[13]

No man in Grand Rapids could have been more dedicated to the task of raising a family of boys. By the time the Fords left Union Avenue, there were four: Richard (Dick) had been born in 1924, James (Jim) in 1927. Junior, of course, served as the test bed for the disciplinary system under which all four grew up. His father's "three rules," repeated in maturity by all the brothers, were simple and inflexible: do your best, tell the truth, and come to dinner on time. These were the basics, but there were many others. A son who carelessly left an elbow on the dinner table was sure to have it whacked with a spoon; a boy who failed to clean his plate sat at the table until bedtime. (Except for the elbow-on-the-table routine, Jerry Ford seldom used physical force on his sons; like a progressive parent of the 1920s, he dealt with transgressions verbally, or instrumentally by taking

---

graphs of him with the group have been found. EBF stated in her memoir, *The Times of My Life*, p. 45, that she had heard of GRF all her growing-up years without ever knowing him; yet her family, like the Fords, attended St. Mark's, and she was only five years younger than he. The fact suggests that he had a very low profile at church. He was neither baptized nor confirmed until many years later (Grace Church records).

13. GRF Sr. was on the Troop Council (Ford-Cannon interviews, April 25, 1990, p. 2). Two biographies asserted that he was active with Troop 15, GRF's troop: Schapsmeier and Schapsmeier, *Date with Destiny*, p. 5, say he was a former scoutmaster, and Ter Horst, *Gerald R. Ford*, p. 35, says only that he helped. I have not been able to substantiate either statement. Charles Kindel was scoutmaster while GRF was in the troop; see chapter 4, pp. 47-48. The Youth Commonwealth, on whose board GRF Sr. served from the beginning, was formed in 1938 (*Press*, January 27, 1962, p. 14). Examples of the Fords' activity with the PTA are in the *Herald*, October 31 and December 8, 1926.

away privileges, or both.) They were assigned duties from an early age: they made their beds, cleaned the table after dinner (including dinners when they were guests in other homes), and took turns washing the dishes and cleaning up the kitchen.

As the oldest child, Junior drew the heaviest duties. He cleaned the garage, swept the porch, and cut the lawn in summer. He emptied the drip pan under the icebox every day. When his mother was ill, as she often was, he took care of his younger brothers, including changing diapers — in fact, he would later claim, probably accurately, that he changed more diapers than she did. And since his father, like so many of the other salesmen who lived on the block, was frequently away on sales trips, he was often effectively, even in late boyhood, the responsible man of the house. His photographs from this period often show an expression that seems to go well with this responsibility — a wary, serious look — less than a scowl, but definitely not a smile.[14]

The chore requiring the most responsibility was taking care of the furnace. During the cold season, from October through April, he went down to the cellar every morning between six and six-thirty, removed the ashes, and put in the day's supply of coal, which lay loose in the coal bin. The heat of the furnace came to the upper floors through a system of hot air registers in the floor. There was a certain degree of technique connected with keeping a coal furnace burning evenly all day; variations in the draft, controlled in most houses by a chain from upstairs, could make it burn fast or slow. All this was Junior's responsibility. And every night, once he had learned the technique, which must have been when he was eleven or twelve, he banked the coal in the furnace so that it would burn evenly through the night.[15]

Grand Rapids and America were still very much in the age of coal. The thick, sweetish smell of coal smoke from railways and factories was in the air all year, augmented in the winter by the exhaust from homes. Particles of soot drifted in the air, smudging faces and clothes; a pristine

14. Cannon, *Time and Chance*, pp. 10-11; Vestal, *Jerry Ford, Up Close*, p. 44; Ter Horst, *Gerald R. Ford*, p. 34; Ford, *TTH*, pp. 45-46; Goebel interview, p. 3, Grand Rapids Oral History Collection, GRFL. Richard Ford made the point in an interview ("Family" vertical file, GRFL) that GRF Sr. "wasn't around probably as much as a normal father was" because of his work as a traveling salesman, and mentioned GRF's changing diapers (Ford interview, p. 3).

15. Ford, *TTH*, p. 45; Bennett Ainsworth reminiscences, Grand Rapids Oral History Collection, GRPL.

snowfall was speckled with black within twenty-four hours. Windows became grimy and semi-opaque during the cold months; soot accumulated under the eaves of houses. "You felt that whatever you touched would leave a smear on your fingers," one resident recalled. The coal dealer, with his periodic deliveries rattling down a chute into the basement, was a vital man in the community. Jerry Ford's nephew, Harold Swain, was the manager of the Kentucky–West Virginia Coal Company in Grand Rapids; it was a handy connection, and Ford sometimes supplemented his income by working in the coal company office.[16]

Having a furnace and central heating put the Fords in the upper half of Grand Rapids' population. Probably 50 percent of the city's homes, including those of many of their neighbors, still had the heating system of the previous age: gas heaters in the living room, dining room, and parlor, and no heat at all in the bedrooms. Some still heated their homes with coal or wood stoves. On the other hand, families richer than the Fords had automatic stokers that eliminated the need to adjust the draft and add coal continually. The 1920s were a period of rapid technological change in the household; by locating the Ford household on this technological continuum, one can see how they compared with their neighbors and how the homes of the 1920s compared with those of the present.[17]

The house was clean and well-built. The Fords were so satisfied with it that after a year or two they made arrangements with the owner, an engineer named Burritt Parks, to buy it from him. Built on a base of granite blocks, it had a generous front porch with removable screens, and a smaller porch on the second floor. The first floor had a living room with a bay window, a dining room separated from it by pocket doors, and a kitchen in the spartan style of the early 1900s. The bathroom was on the second floor, along with the master bedroom and a smaller room or

16. Denham, *Growing Up in Grand Rapids*, pp. 66-67; *Pioneer*, March 20, 1930, p. 12; Bennett Ainsworth reminiscences, Robert Davis reminiscences, both in Grand Rapids Oral History Collection, GRPL; Wickenden, *The Wayfarers*, p. 62. Ford, *TTH*, p. 44, mentions Harold Swain, who, according to the city directory, lived next door to the Fords on Madison Avenue and then farther out on the East Side. Occasionally, for example in 1927, the city directory listed GRF Sr. as employed with the Kentucky–West Virginia Coal Company rather than with Grand Rapids Wood Finishing; he evidently had an ongoing arrangement of some kind with Swain.

17. The figure of 50 percent is an estimate based on a 1925 survey of Zanesville, Ohio (Walsh, *Zanesville*, p. 65), and the table in Lynd and Lynd, *Middletown in Transition*, p. 563. Automatic stokers: Bennett Ainsworth reminiscences, Grand Rapids Oral History Collection, GRPL.

two. The third floor, essentially a finished attic, added one more room to the total.[18]

All this was Dorothy Ford's domain, to maintain and to beautify. The ruling thought of the consumer-oriented twenties held that, as the historian Phyllis Palmer put it, "a woman's intelligent choices not only gave the family a good, healthy, moral life at reasonable cost, they expressed to the community the family's social status and her own ability." Dorothy Ford was prepared to undertake that role by both her college education and her genteel upbringing in a leading family of her small Illinois community. Her piano, a symbol of cultural aspirations, stood in the living room near the front door. (She played; none of the men did.) Not too many books were in evidence, but selected antiques from her Ayer forebears, prominent people in New England and early Illinois, made the point that this was a household of heritage and taste, even if the house was small. About the other pieces of furniture few details have survived, except for the large oval Grand Rapids–made dining table, a center of family life, mahogany according to one biographer, oak according to another. Mrs. Ford set a beautiful table when the family entertained.[19]

She had household help, the mark of a middle-class family, even when finances were tight. The 1930 census shows a seventeen-year-old female servant living in the home. By the 1930s, when Jerry Ford was part owner of a manufacturing company and the family lived in East Grand Rapids, they regularly had a maid. With her back problems and high blood pressure, Mrs. Ford really needed help, particularly with heavy jobs like laundry, and there were many young Dutch and German girls available.

18. A deed from Burritt A. Parks and wife, grantors, to GRF Sr. and wife, grantees, was recorded October 2, 1925, in the county courthouse. The sale price was "$1 and other valuable considerations." In the 1920 U.S. Census manuscript Parks was listed as the owner of the property. Nevertheless, the 1930 U.S. Census manuscript, taken when the Fords were in the process of moving to East Grand Rapids, shows that GRF Sr. rented the house for $55 a month. For further discussion, see chapter 6. My description of 649 Union Avenue comes from a tour of the premises, courtesy of Tim England, owner and resident of the house in 1997.

19. Palmer, *Domesticity and Dirt*, p. 22. Piano: England interview. On F. Stuart Chapin's 1928 scale of socioeconomic status ("Socio-Economic Status," p. 584), a piano was one of the highest-ranking cultural artifacts possible for a living room, outranked only by an oriental rug and a bed-davenport. Books: Vestal, *Jerry Ford, Up Close*, p. 48. Several of DGF's antiques are mentioned in B. Ford, *The Times of My Life*, passim, and Ella Koeze Papers, p. 5, Composite Grand Rapids Accessions, GRFL. Dining table: Ter Horst, *Gerald R. Ford*, p. 40 (oak), Vestal, p. 44 (mahogany).

Moreover, she liked to entertain, which gave her still more reason to hire a servant. At first she had a maid come in one or two days a week; many business-class housewives had at least that much domestic help.[20]

Entertaining was an important part of a business-class housewife's duty, but it also appealed to Dorothy Ford because of her warm, effervescent personality. As spontaneous and caring as her husband was serious and stern, she loved having people to the house, whether Junior's playmates or Jerry's business associates and their wives. Her interest in people expressed itself through warm conversations and countless activities; she was "a human dynamo, in a womanly way," as her son described her, visiting sick friends, baking bread and sewing clothes for needy families, sending endless get-well cards, thank-you notes, and gifts on all occasions. She started a bridge club for her women friends, who called her "Doe," which met weekly to play cards and snack on candy and nuts and light refreshments. She delighted in the little holiday rituals of American homes — fudge, cookies, and decorations for Christmas — and belonged to a group called the Santa Claus Girls that made dolls for poorer children at Christmastime. A family friend loved visiting the Fords' home then because it evoked the old-fashioned vision of the holiday.[21]

Dorothy and Jerry Ford belonged to a tight circle of couples their own age who invited each other over for dinner and bridge, as the business-class custom was — in contrast to working-class families, who preferred to go out for social occasions. Most of the men were, like Jerry, in sales or middle management at one of the many Grand Rapids manufacturing companies and lived in the less expensive parts of the East Side. At their

20. 1930 manuscript U.S. Census. Vestal, *Jerry Ford, Up Close*, pp. 53-54, and Paul Ryzy to GRF, May 27, 1975, White House Central Files: Presidential Personal, PP 13, GRFL, document the Fords' use of domestic help in the 1930s. GRF in his interview with Cannon, April 25, 1990, p. 1, mentions a maid one day a week, probably in the 1920s. The general picture of domestic help in Midwestern households in the 1920s can be glimpsed from two studies. Lynd and Lynd, *Middletown*, p. 170, found that in Muncie, Indiana, almost all business-class homes (that is, everyone from the Fords' level on up) had some hired help, and two-thirds of them had it more than one day a week. A 1930-1931 study of middle-income homes (the Fords and a few levels below them) in Lansing, Michigan, cited in Palmer, *Domesticity and Dirt*, p. 11, found that about one-third, including some from the upper working class headed by foremen and machinists, employed servants.

21. Vestal, *Jerry Ford, Up Close*, p. 49; *Detroit Free Press*, May 12, 1974; Buchen interview, p. 6, Goebel interview, pp. 1-2, both in Grand Rapids Oral History Collection, GRFL; Ella Koeze Papers, pp. 4-5, Composite Grand Rapids Accessions, GRFL; Veronica McLachlan manuscript reminiscences, GRPL, pp. 4-5; Hersey, *The President*, p. 86.

dinners, in contrast to those in *Babbitt* or doubtless at some other Grand Rapids homes, there was no surreptitious drinking among the men, no producing a bottle of Canadian Club (illegal because of Prohibition) with much ceremony and snickering. The Fords, like many in the Grand Rapids upper crust, were nondrinkers, and quite firm about it. There was no liquor in their home.[22]

Whether for entertaining or for the daily routine, Dorothy Ford purchased food for the family in a way very different from late-twentieth-century American housewives. Merchandising in America was beginning a transition out of the horse-and-buggy age, but had not yet gotten very far. Many of the familiar brands of canned and packaged food — Campbell's soup, Kellogg's Corn Flakes, Maxwell House coffee — already existed, but they were marketed through a system of small independent neighborhood groceries, like the one down the block from the Fords, at the corner of Franklin. These old-fashioned groceries kept the goods behind the counter; the self-service supermarket was still a decade in the future. In business-class neighborhoods, they typically delivered purchases to the home in a small truck; housewives ordered them by telephone. Often the market had a butcher who sold meat, as well, and usually it carried several kinds of produce, including fruits and vegetables from Florida and California. Dairy products, on the other hand, came to the home early in the morning from the milkman in his horse-drawn wagon. In summer,

22. On social occasions among business-class and working-class people, see Palmer, *Domesticity and Dirt*, pp. 23-24, and Lynd and Lynd, *Middletown*, pp. 281-82. My list of the Fords' close friends comes initially from the names of the men who shared ownership of a summer cottage on the Little Pere Marquette River with Jerry Ford, as explained later in this chapter — J. Hilton Haven, Neil J. Kunst, Charles B. Pearson, Henry Swanson, and Oscar Tandler. All these men and their wives, plus the Fords, are listed among the guests at a dinner and bridge party given by the Havens (*Herald*, December 5, 1926). Their occupations and addresses are from Polk's city directory for these years. Like the Fords, they were mobile, both residentially and occupationally; all but one changed addresses at least once in the twenties and early thirties, and most fluctuated, like Jerry Ford, between management and sales. Three of the men, Haven, Kunst, and Tandler, were Masons (membership records, Michigan Masonic Museum).

Business-class dining and surreptitious drinking are broadly caricatured in Lewis, *Babbitt*, pp. 108-31; but not all Midwestern business-class men were as enthusiastic about illicit liquor as Babbitt and his friends; cf. Bissell, *My Life on the Mississippi*, pp. 33-34, and Lynd and Lynd, *Middletown in Transition*, p. 173 n. 54. A business-class home in Grand Rapids where liquor was served during Prohibition is mentioned in Denham, *Growing Up in Grand Rapids*, p. 98.

farmers from the nearby countryside also drove their wagons around the East Side, calling out seasonal vegetables for sale directly to housewives.[23]

Thus the sounds of a morning on the East Side during the 1920s, in Junior Ford's boyhood world, differed markedly from those later in the century. There was the clip-clop of horses' hooves as the milkman and iceman made their rounds, or on winter mornings the crunch of the wagon wheels in the snow, and the occasional whirring and clicking of a streetcar passing on Franklin. There were no high-horsepower car engines and no car radios — both of these were also a decade in the future — although somewhere on the block there might have been the pops and bangs of a Model T being cranked. Stanton Todd, who lived five blocks northwest of the Fords on Morris Avenue, recalled some other sounds from that era: the furniture factory whistles at 7:00 A.M.; the bells from the nearby hospice of the Little Sisters of the Poor; the loud, guttural cry of the junkman in his horse-drawn wagon; and of course, early-morning birdsong. These were some of the sounds the Fords heard as they breakfasted around seven.[24]

Breakfast for Midwestern families whose breadwinners looked forward to a long day of physical labor was a heavy, fortifying meal, with meat, eggs, potatoes, and hot bread. Some business-class families had gotten away from that tradition, and served one of the popular packaged cereals, hot or cold, but not the Fords, who stuck with the big, hearty breakfast. Citrus fruit like grapefruit or oranges were beginning to be popular as awareness of vitamins spread. At the Fords', the beverages were the standard ones, coffee for the adults, milk for the boys. Junior opened the paper to the sports page and became absorbed in baseball scores (he was an ardent Tigers fan) while his father carefully read the front page and the editorials. When they had eaten, the boys started out for school on foot and Mr. Ford cranked up the car to drive to work.[25]

On a typical day, Dorothy Ford had two meals left to prepare: lunch, when most or all of her menfolk would come home to eat, and dinner, the

23. The grocery at 756 Union, under various managements, was in the city directory from 1920 to 1930. Meijer, *Thrifty Years*, pp. 124-32; Lentz, "Grocery Shopping in the 1930s," p. 128; Manfred, *The Primitive*, p. 82; Stanton Todd, "Let Me Live," Stanton Todd Papers, BHL, p. 3.

24. Todd, "Let Me Live," p. 3.

25. Lynd and Lynd, *Middletown*, p. 158; Walsh, *Zanesville*, p. 87; Manfred, *The Primitive*, p. 440; interview with Richard Ford, May 31, 2012; *Ann Arbor News*, December 7, 1973; Milton Rickman, "Ford's Sports Hero: 'Team Man' Kaline," *Detroit Free Press*, August 9, 1974.

big family meal. She had an ample supply of canned and packaged foods, a gas range, an icebox (electric refrigerators had been invented, but only the wealthy had them), her own skills, and lots of advice from professional homemakers. There was plenty of this in women's magazines and newspapers. Vitamins had been discovered only ten years before, and more continued to be found during the twenties, so that a conscientious mother had to read regularly to provide the best nutrition for her children.[26]

The 1920s on the whole were a rather grim period for American cuisine. Busy housewives, occupied with civic clubs or new work opportunities, relied more and more on canned foods of frankly mediocre quality — canned spinach, canned juices, canned meat. Changing fashions for both men and women dictated slimmer figures and meant fewer rich sauces, more vegetables, and smaller portions at the table, especially for the business class. And Prohibition drastically affected American cooking by eliminating the use of wine.[27]

These changes probably affected Dorothy Ford's kitchen less than others' kitchens. Her specialties were sweets, comfort foods that made people feel good, chocolate caramels for friends at Christmas or molasses cookies for Junior and his friends when they came in the back door. The boys also prized her hand-beaten fudge and her angel food cake with chocolate frosting. Junior was particularly fond of anything involving fresh blueberries, a specialty crop in that part of Michigan. For main dishes, Mrs. Ford set the kind of table that was becoming common nationwide: roast meat, potatoes, a vegetable or two, and bread. Her oldest son adored her pot roast. One good thing about the changing food habits of the period was that when she was ill there were canned soups and packaged foods to take up the slack for the males in the family, who were not expected to know how to cook. Junior, however, silently cooperative as always, did learn basic cooking, hamburgers and the like, well enough not only to win a Boy Scout merit badge but also to hold down a lunch-counter job in high school.[28]

26. Nye, *Electrifying America*, pp. 275-76, 356; Levenstein, *Revolution at the Table*, pp. 147-60; Walsh, *Zanesville*, p. 63.

27. Levenstein, *Revolution at the Table*, pp. 161-69; on canned food, cf. Bissell, *My Life on the Mississippi*, p. 109.

28. Caramels: Ella Koeze recollections, Composite Grand Rapids Accessions, GRFL. Many early accounts mention DGF's molasses cookies: Sheridan, "Portrait of the Next President," p. 20, and Ter Horst, *Gerald R. Ford*, p. 29, to name two. Fudge, angel cake: Schapsmeier and Schapsmeier, *Date with Destiny*, p. 6. Blueberries: clipping from *Petos-*

With all this cooking, Mrs. Ford still found time for a full schedule of clubs, which were held to be an essential part of a business-class woman's life. The DAR, PTA, and Santa Claus Girls all addressed subjects close to her heart. There were also the church women's guild, the garden club, and bridge clubs, often with contests and prizes to add interest.[29]

His mother's outside activities were naturally vague and remote to Junior, who experienced her simply as a warm, loving presence and a good cook — and also as a disciplinarian. Dorothy Ford felt a special responsibility for her eldest son's upbringing. Leslie King had been a man of unusually violent temper — in fact, it was because of his physical attacks that she had left him. Naturally she worried that the same uncontrolled rage would crop up in Leslie Jr. As he grew up, her fears turned out to be true to an alarming degree. Junior had a fierce temper even as a little boy; he would get red in the face and start shouting, or he would push or strike playmates. His mother would give him a pinch on the ear, or mock his expressions to show how silly he was. By the time they lived on Union Avenue, she would simply send him upstairs to his room when he exploded and refuse to talk to him until he was ready to be reasonable. He always cooled down; he was basically good-hearted, but had a very short fuse. Mrs. Ford stressed the value of control; she gave him a poem to memorize, Kipling's inspirational poem for boys, "If":

> If you can keep your head when all about you
> Are losing theirs, and blaming it on you. . . .[30]

Over those years Junior learned some self-control. His last fistfight may have taken place even before the family moved to Union Avenue, although according to one account he bloodied the nose of a boy across the

---

key (Mich.) News-Review, August 14, 1974, in "Childhood and Youth" vertical file, GRFL. Main dishes: Vestal, *Jerry Ford, Up Close,* p. 49. Merit badge: Laackman, *Gerald R. Ford's Scouting Years,* p. 50.

29. DGF's club affiliations are summarized in, e.g., Cannon, *Time and Chance,* p. 10, and Vestal, *Jerry Ford, Up Close,* p. 49. As with her husband, there is a problem distinguishing the activities she participated in at different times of her life. For the 1920s, there is good evidence for the DAR and PTA bridge clubs: Veronica McLachlan manuscript reminiscences, GRPL.

30. Cannon, *Time and Chance,* pp. 9-10; see GRF's kindergarten teacher quoted in www.mlive.com/news/grand-rapids/index.ssf/2009/04/west_michigan_collectors_get _t.html, and a playmate's story in Ter Horst, *Gerald R. Ford,* p. 28.

street when he was twelve and received a black eye in return. (His father was about to get involved when the two boys made up.) But as a rule he was popular and respected by the other children on the block. When he became involved in sports as a teenager, he developed a following among the younger boys. Bill Nichols, five years younger, who also lived across the street, recalled that "when his folks were gone, he'd even show me how to center a football in his living room." They saw in him the same kind of person as his father, strong and fair.[31]

Despite his lurking hot temper, Junior was a popular playmate in the neighborhood. He was not too old to play hide-and-seek with the younger children. He played ball with the Engel twins and other boys, and jacks with Barbara Nichols. In summer he was part of the crowd that hung around the ice wagon as it made its deliveries and took chips of ice, to suck on until they melted or to put down companions' backs. Swimming was a large part of Midwestern summer activity, and Junior swam regularly at the Y or at swimming pools in the public parks. Once in a while he would get on his bike and head for the swimming hole on Plaster Creek, south of town, a couple of miles away. There was a bend in the creek, with a cliff on one side, and a big tree trunk, perfect for diving, that leaned far out over the water. Boys would hang their clothes on the bushes and go skinny-dipping. It was the perfect swimming hole.[32]

On winter days after school, he and his friend Burt Garel would get their ice skates and walk over to Madison Park, a few blocks away. Burt was black, the son of a chauffeur who lived a couple of blocks away on Bates Street. To him, the Ford home felt like a rich family's house, and

31. In an interview with Dick Cavett, GRF stated that his last fistfight was in the first grade, when he was still living on Madison Avenue, but see the account in Sallah, "The Ford Brothers 'Buddies,'" Thomas Ford Scrapbook, GRFL. Other children: interview with Vernon Fox, *Tallahassee Democrat*, August 11, 1974, in vertical file, "Childhood and Youth," GRFL, and with Leigh Nichols, *Jackson City Patriot*, October 28, 1973, in GRF Scrapbook #39.

32. Clipping from *Hemet (Calif.) News*, December 14, 1973, GRF Scrapbook #40, GRFL; Ter Horst, *Gerald R. Ford*, p. 29; Denham, *Growing Up in Grand Rapids*, p. 60. On the South Side of Grand Rapids, just east of Division Avenue, the Gerald R. Ford Nature Center marks the site of what GRF described as "the 'old swimming hole' when I was a boy" (letter to Mrs. Robert H. Amos, March 27, 1975, White House Central Files, Presidential Personal, PP13, GRFL). Contemporaries of GRF who lived nearer the site than he did, however, have expressed doubt that he swam there often (*New Pioneer*, #49 [December 1990], pp. 2-3). Now well within urban Grand Rapids, this site was in the country in the 1920s; cf. the comment of GRF's classmate Dorothy Gray in the *Press*, September 23, 1974.

Junior was "a rich boy — but a regular guy." At the park they would put on their skates and play ice tag, crack the whip, or pom-pom-pullaway with the other kids. Junior had plenty of energy but was not particularly agile, Burt noticed. Out on the ice, his good looks, light blond hair, and steady blue eyes attracted a lot of attention from the girls, even in those prepubescent years, but Junior ignored them. "He was kind of shy," Garel recalled.[33]

When the Fords moved to Union Avenue, Junior was already old enough to go to the movies by himself or with friends. The theater was at Madison Square, the city's oldest commercial neighborhood center, only a few blocks south of the park. He and his friends went on Saturday afternoons, as millions of American children were doing in that decade, to watch silent films — adventure serials or comic shorts — with live piano accompaniment. The young audiences followed them with cheers, laughter, and groans. The serial, as a contemporary observer described it, would break off "tantalizingly at some hair-raising and goose-fleshing point, as when huge iron doors with spikes gradually close[d] in on the hero who remain[ed] peacefully oblivious to his impending danger, with every child in the audience shrieking at him to 'look out,' until the last 100 feet of film when he . . . [made] a desperate jump to safety . . . interrupted in midair by 'Continued at this theater next Saturday.'"[34]

In the 1920s, children dominated daytime movie audiences and for the first time gave American entrepreneurs a hint of a vast new consumer market: juveniles with their own tastes and independent allowances. Junior had an allowance, which he doubtless spent on children's luxuries like penny gum balls and soda pop, but the movies did not fascinate him as they did some children. The same was true of books; he read the tales of King Arthur that his mother gave him, but preferred the Horatio Alger books his father recommended, with their practical moral message.[35]

Play in the street and games in the park led, inevitably, to bruises

33. Ter Horst, *Gerald R. Ford*, p. 29.

34. *Press*, September 13, 1981; Elliott, *Grand Rapids*, p. 74; Denham, *Growing Up in Grand Rapids*, p. 48; Mitchell, *Children and Movies*, p. 35.

35. Hawes, *Children between the Wars*, pp. 4-5; Allowance: Dee Whittington, "Ford's Brother: 'I'm a Much Better Drinker,'" *Palm Beach Post-Times*, May 19, 1978, in Thomas Ford Scrapbook, GRFL. "I'm not a moviegoer; never have been," wrote GRF in an essay for his collaborator on *TTH* ("Movies I've Liked," essay, in "Miscellaneous" vertical file, GRFL). Consistently, asked to name his favorite play or movie in 1976, he answered "none" ("Preferences and favorites" vertical file, GRFL).

and scrapes, but only one major injury: when Junior was fourteen, he broke his collarbone. The sources don't say how, and it may have been related to the team sports he was participating in by that time. He was a remarkably healthy child, with no major illnesses, only accidents. As for the rest, minor injuries and soiled clothes were a normal part of a boy's growing up. Personal cleaning was no problem; although the Fords' single bathroom had no shower (only athletes and the rich had showers in the 1920s), it did have a bathtub — which put it ahead of a sizable portion of Grand Rapids homes, perhaps 30 or 40 percent. Many children in the city, including some of Junior's schoolmates, lived in homes without indoor plumbing, in which bathing was a difficult task and comparatively infrequent. As a consequence, general standards for cleanliness, except among the upper classes, were less exacting than they became later in the century.

Washing clothes for a family of six was a major undertaking. Even with a maid, it took a whole day. Primitive machinery like the mangle for ironing sheets and the early washing machine, consisting of a tub mounted on legs with an electrically driven agitator, lightened the burden a little. A lot of business-class families sent their laundry out, to an individual laundress or a commercial laundry.[36]

In terms of household technology, the Fords stood squarely in the middle of the scale for Midwestern urban families. They had the basic early-twentieth-century conveniences, but only a few of the amenities that were new in the 1920s. Their home life was, as their eldest son later described it, "not an austere, but a moderate life." In their values and activities, they typified the business class. Instead of working, Dorothy Ford managed the home and took part in community affairs; this was the standard business-class arrangement. Equally typical were their regular church attendance and their participation in civic organizations, although the Fords' special interest in charity and doing good to others was unusual. In two ways, however, the Fords were different from most of their neighbors. A 1926 survey of a Midwestern city found that only 3 percent of the families in town owned golfing equipment; the Ford family was part of this small group. Similarly, only 3 percent owned summer

36. "Full Report on Ford's Health," *U.S. News and World Report*, September 9, 1974; Ford, *TTH*, p. 43. Figures for indoor plumbing are estimated from those given in Walsh, *Zanesville*, p. 55, and Lynd and Lynd, *Middletown*, p. 97. The description of techniques for washing clothes is from Lynd and Lynd, pp. 173-74, and Palmer, *Domesticity and Dirt*, pp. 52-53 and passim.

cabins for vacations — and in 1927, Jerry Ford became part owner of a cabin on the Little South Branch of the Pere Marquette River, forty miles north of Grand Rapids.[37]

There are two possible reasons for this interest in golf and summer recreation. First, golf and summer cottages were both part of the lifestyle of affluent Grand Rapids families; Jerry Ford may have chosen to imitate their tastes, perhaps with a view to establishing business or social relations with some of them. Second, the family had a real interest in outdoor recreation.

Probably there are elements of truth in both. Jerry Ford respected riches and rich people; theirs was the style of life he aspired to. He cultivated the friendship of families with money, and he doubtless realized that spending a little extra money on this kind of recreation was a good way of establishing contacts for both business and social purposes. But a much stronger reason was that he genuinely liked outdoor activity and thought it was important. He and Dorothy were both third-generation city people; they had no cousins or grandparents who owned a farm or an old family place suitable for occasional visits. So they took their children to play at city parks, Townsend Park or John Ball Park. In the summer, as often as they could, they got away to the Lake Michigan beaches, only thirty miles west of town, where the boys could swim and play at the water's edge or in the giant sand dunes. A new state park opened at Ottawa Beach in 1928, connected to Grand Rapids by a modern concrete highway. In the dunes behind the park, on what was called the upper and lower boardwalk, prominent Grand Rapids families had owned cozy Victorian "cottages" for a generation (though the richest spent their summers in neighboring Macatawa). Ralph Conger, an old friend of Jerry Ford, and his wife Julia owned a cabin at Ottawa Beach, and from the mid-1920s on the Fords spent some time there every summer. Conger became like a second father to Junior. In the 1930s, the Fords began renting a cabin regularly.[38]

37. Ford quote: Hersey, *The President*, p. 137. The business-class/working-class distinction is from Lynd and Lynd, *Middletown*, pp. 27, 276-77. Average interest in golf and summer recreation: Walsh, *Zanesville*, pp. 104-5. Deed from Lawrence Flanery and wife to Charles B. Pearson, Henry Swanson, Neil J. Kunst, J. Hilton Haven, Oscar Tandler, and GRF Sr., April 27, 1927, Newaygo County Deed Book 146, p. 28. Photographs from the Ford family albums in GRFL, e.g., B-05-058 through B-05-062, suggest that the family may have been using the cabin for a few years before 1927.

38. In describing GRF Sr.'s attitude toward rich people and wealth, I may be going further than the evidence permits. I have only two pieces of evidence, both quite indi-

In April 1927, Jerry Ford was among the signers to the deed for a small summer cabin in the "stump country," on the Little South Branch of the Pere Marquette River. The "stump country" was a vast, impoverished area that began a few miles north of the city; it comprised hundreds of square miles that had been intensively logged during the lumber boom of the 1880s. Its bare hills were covered with stumps, scrub oak, and the spindly second-growth trees known as "popple." It contained no large towns, only scattered small villages connected by unpaved roads that wound through the denuded hills. Broad rivers of dark, pure water, with some of the best trout fishing in Michigan, crossed it from east to west — the Muskegon, the Pere Marquette — and in their valleys there were still stands of pine trees and a feeling of being in the North Woods. Rich families from Grand Rapids owned "cottages" along these streams, some of them very elaborate, with servants, and the Pere Marquette was one of the most popular; from the two-acre property purchased by Ford and his friends, reached by a long drive down a gravel road, they could see other cottages downstream, including one belonging to a fishing club. Their place, however, was only a simple, rambling cabin with plasterboard walls, far up the val-

---

rect. As the next chapter shows, he put his son in a Boy Scout troop led by a rich young man, Charles M. Kindel, an executive at his father's chair company, and established a good relationship with Kindel. Moreover, a friend of GRF in his high school years, Peter Boter, is described as the son of one of the wealthiest men in western Michigan (Winter-Berger, *The Washington Pay-Off*, p. 32; Cannon, *Time and Chance*, pp. 241-42). Yet Boter did not attend South High, and it is not clear how GRF became friends with him if not through his parents.

GRF Sr., in the recollection of his friend Paul Goebel, was not "much of a sportsman" in the sense of outdoor activity (Goebel interview, p. 3), but there is no doubt that he and his wife were committed to giving their boys wholesome outdoor experience (Ter Horst, *Gerald R. Ford*, p. 33; Ford, *TTH*, p. 45). Photographs from family albums in GRFL show the family at Ottawa Beach with the Conger family in the 1920s, e.g., B-05-042 and B-05-73. By the 1930s, they routinely rented a cabin there for six to eight weeks every year on the "Lower Walk" and had a maid to help Dorothy Ford with household duties (Richard A. Ford interview, "Family" vertical file, GRFL; Vestal, *Jerry Ford, Up Close*, p. 52). In the late 1930s, they bought a cottage ("Beach Sign to Carry Name of President," *Press*, March 5, 2002). For background on the area, see Van Reken, *Ottawa Beach and Waukazoo*, especially pp. 122, 127, 139-41; for random glimpses of other Grand Rapids people and their activities, see Mrs. Huntley Russell engagement book, 1928, GRPL; Ralph B. Baldwin, "Highlighted Story of a Long and Unusual Life," computer print, 1993, in Baldwin Papers, Box 1, Local History Collection, GRPL, pp. 10-11; Stanton Todd recollections, p. 32; Manfred, *The Primitive*, p. 272; and Denham, *Growing Up in Grand Rapids*, pp. 94-95. For help with Ottawa Beach questions, I am greatly indebted to Daniel Aument of Grand Rapids.

ley of the Little South Branch, only five miles from its origin in a marl bog bordered by downed trees.[39]

The cabin soon became a place of special attraction for the family. They drove up as often as they could, often bringing friends. They had a canoe — extant photographs show Junior in the bow paddling down the river, with most of the Nichols family aboard and Mr. Nichols in the stern with a paddle. (The Nicholses were social peers and friends of the Fords; Mr. Nichols worked as a buyer for Herpolsheimer's department store.) They took walks in the woods and clearings. Jerry Ford, though no hunter, was a fisherman, and the South Branch had plenty of brown trout and steelhead; he passed his skills and his enjoyment on to his sons.[40]

Apart from trips to the cabin and Ottawa Beach, the Ford family hardly traveled — perhaps occasionally to Chicago, where Mrs. Ford's sister lived. But they did not take off for a couple of weeks in the summer, as quite a few business-class families did, for leisurely automobile trips through the West. Resources were too tight — or rather, they preferred to spend the resources they had on activities close to home.

These summer experiences at the cabin and the beach were blissful interruptions in the main theme of Junior's life, schooling, which occupied most of the cold months of the year, October through April, and had depressing associations like darkness coming on in late afternoon, long underwear, dreary late fall days before the snow started, the galoshes he and his schoolmates had to laboriously buckle on when there was snow on the ground — in other words, virtually every school day — and the crowded cloakrooms full of outer garments that were forever getting mixed up.

He was going into the fifth grade when the family moved back from East Grand Rapids, and reentered the two-story brick school he had attended before, Madison School — one of the oldest elementary schools

39. Newaygo County Deed Book 146: 28. The other purchasers were the Fords' bridge-party friends — Charles B. Pearson, Henry Swanson, Neil J. Kunst, J. Hilton Haven, and Oscar Tandler. Some were also Masons. Descriptive: Kirk, *Confessions of a Bohemian Tory*, p. 8; Bissell, *A Sow's Ear*, pp. 61-65, 149; Grand Rapids, p. 39; Mrs. Stuart Knappen reminiscences, Kent County Council Oral History Collection, GRPL; Stanley Davis interview, tape A, side 1, page 4, Grand Rapids Oral History Collection, GRPL; Supinski, *River Journal*, pp. 11-12; Cassuto, *Cold Running River*, p. 24. A cartoon by Ray Barnes from the *Herald*, April 23, 1933, gives names and locations for many summer cabins of Grand Rapids people, including GRF Sr. (called "Henry Ford").

40. Clipping from *Jackson City Patriot*, October 28, 1973, in GRF Scrapbook #39; clipping from *Hemet News*, December 14, 1973, in GRF Scrapbook #40, both GRFL; Cannon, *Time and Chance*, p. 9; Ter Horst, *Gerald R. Ford*, p. 34; Supinski, *River Journal*, pp. 11-12.

in the city but also one of the best, physically somewhat rundown, with an all-female staff and an excellent woman principal. It was a five- or six-block walk from his house; Grand Rapids elementary schools were planned so that no child would have to walk more than half a mile. He usually walked to school with the Engel twins. Junior was a hardworking, obedient student but not a remarkably good one. He had a problem with stuttering, which he overcame only in the fifth grade when his teacher realized that it was related to the school's efforts to teach him to write using the right-handed Palmer Method. Junior was a natural lefty, at least when seated. He had learned from his father to throw a ball and hold a golf club right-handed, but when eating he still used the left, so much so that the family gave him one side of the dinner table. When the teachers finally gave up on him, he adopted the position called "the hook" by some writers on left-handedness, with his hand arched awkwardly across the top of the paper and curled around to write. The result was a stylized sort of scrawl. But despite his problems with both written and spoken expression, he made decent grades in school. During his difficult elementary-school years, his mother worked unremittingly with him at home, checking his work and enforcing good study habits. By his sixth-grade year, teachers found him quiet, well-behaved, and always prepared; a model student from their viewpoint.[41]

Madison School ran only through the sixth grade; from there, students went on to South High. The Fords lived right on the northern edge of the South High attendance district, and Jerry Ford, if he chose to utilize his contacts, was in a position to get Junior assigned to Central High, which was only a block farther away in the other direction. This was the prestige high school of Grand Rapids, in the heart of the Hill District, and Ralph Conger, its athletic director and basketball coach, had been a close friend of Jerry Ford since boyhood. Ford spoke with him about it, and, as the story has come down, Conger recommended that Junior be allowed to go on to South, with its mixed, working-class, immigrant population

41. Madison School: Ford, *TTH*, p. 43; Ter Horst, *Gerald R. Ford*, p. 29; *Logansport (Ind.) Pharos-Tribune*, undated clipping in "Childhood and Youth" vertical file, GRFL; minutes of informal school board meetings, December 2 and 9, 1926; March 14, 1929; May 6, 1929, Leslie H. Butler Papers, BHL. Cannon, *Time and Chance*, p. 11, says that the struggle over writing right- or left-handed was a brief one, and implies that it was resolved by second grade. The version used in the text is from Schapsmeier and Schapsmeier, *Date with Destiny*, p. 7. Other details: Jim Bell, "A Minority President: Ford, the Left-Hander," *Washington Post*, October 20, 1974.

— "that's where he will learn more about living." Probably an equally convincing point in the eyes of Ford Sr. was that South's principal, Arthur Krause, was a fellow Mason and a longtime brother from Malta Lodge. If Junior ever needed any help at South, he would know how to secure it. So in September of 1925, Junior took a stride toward maturity by entering the junior high division at South High.[42]

The decision had no major effect on the quality of his education — by all accounts, the faculty at South was just as good as the one at Central — but it did affect the quality of his high school experience. At South, he achieved a social standing that probably would have eluded him at Central. His family's economic circumstances, which would have made him socially marginal at Central, put him in the upper class at South; combined with his athletic prowess, they made him a campus hero by his senior year. Ford himself, at the end of his life, had something like this point in mind when he reflected on not having attended Central: "That advice to go to South High was a critical decision. If I had gone to Central, I probably would have been one of those smartass — in the first place I could not afford to do the things that most kids did there." Whether his parents had this in mind when they made their choice about attendance is unknown; it seems unlikely. But it was the most salient result of his attending South; that, and, as Ralph Conger predicted, experience in associating with a wide variety of people.[43]

In the fall of 1925, on the eve of entering junior high school, Junior Ford had already developed the persona he was to retain, largely unchanged, through graduation from South. He was a younger edition of what popular novelists called the "strong, silent man"; a handsome, alert

---

42. Cannon, *Time and Chance*, pp. 11-12; England interview. As GRF told the story to England, there were three high schools in play — South, Central, and the new Ottawa Hills high school, which opened in the fall of 1925, and their attendance lines converged on his block. Ottawa, however, was almost twice as far away as either of the other two, and it seems doubtful that it enrolled many students from Union Avenue. Most likely the Fords were definitely in the South attendance district. Barbara Nichols, who lived across Union Avenue, attended South (clipping from *Hemet News*, December 14, 1973, GRF Scrapbook #40, GRFL), and so did the Engel boys (*Pioneer* yearbook, 1928, p. 76), although they eventually graduated from Ottawa.

43. The quote is from Cannon's interview, April 24, 1990, p. 3, where GRF discussed Conger's advice and his parents' decision. It reads as if he was about to deliver his impression of Central students as a whole, but then, reflecting that his wife and many good friends were Central graduates, he turned his statement in a different, and equally valid, direction.

blond boy, remarkably quiet and undemonstrative. His problem with stuttering had made him less than eager to speak, and his mother's admonitions made him keep his feelings under control. He steered clear of fighting and conflicts, and seemed older than he was, responsible, deliberate, and detached. Acquaintances called him "shy" or "reserved."

Yet what impressed teachers and other adults, despite his uncommunicativeness, was an evident, deep-seated willingness to cooperate. To a remarkable degree, as later chapters will show, even at twelve he had adopted his father's values, his interests, and his goals. He was a friendly, quiet boy, in search of a role model, or role models. Adults sensed this in him and responded warmly. Moreover, he was willing to take on responsibility, even as a boy; he not only did household chores, but he looked after his little brothers and was even kind and understanding to them.

Fundamentally, Junior was not much oriented toward verbal communication at all. What he thrived on was activity — purposeful activity of some kind, preferably physical, but mental would do: canoeing, mowing the yard, swimming, schoolwork, stoking the furnace. At any given time he wanted something to do. He enjoyed getting up early and looking forward to the prospect of a day full of activities. He liked working with others, and equally liked working alone.

Finally, all these qualities were influenced by a factor not sufficiently emphasized so far in this chapter. The Ford household was a religious one, and religious in a way that just suited Junior's temperament. There was grace before meals, daily Bible reading, family devotions led by his father, and prayer at night — no meditation, no discussion, no posturing, just simple nondogmatic action. The feeling and the conviction were there, as they were in the orderly Episcopal service with its hymns and responses. Dorothy Ford's dolls and candy and get-well notes, Jerry Ford's civic clubs and study of political issues, all seemed outgrowths of these beliefs, conviction translated into purposeful activity. "I am most reluctant to speak or write about [my religion]," Jerry Ford Jr. would write in maturity, obviously because in his upbringing religion was not a subject for discussion but an occasion for action. "They didn't talk religion, they just lived it," a family friend said.[44]

In the late years of his boyhood, when he was twelve and thirteen, Junior got into a lot of activities typical for a boy that age. He started a

44. GRF, "What Religion Means to Me?," "Religion" vertical file; Mr. and Mrs. Paul Goebel interview, Grand Rapids Oral History Collection, both in GRFL.

stamp collection, prompted by his father, who had relatives who received letters from Argentina; he ordered assortments of stamps from dealers, always hoping to find a rarity, and affixed them neatly in his album. He sold magazines around the neighborhood, with little brother Tom lugging the magazines door to door for a share of the proceeds. He sang in the boy choir at St. Mark's, according to the memories of some.[45]

But the activity he found most meaningful was the one he became eligible for on his twelfth birthday: he became a Boy Scout.

45. Typical activities of late boyhood in Michigan are listed in Seager, *Amos Berry*, p. 9. GRF did all of them except, apparently, studying piano. Boy choir: Howell interview (but see n. 12 to this chapter). Stamp collecting: compare Denham's account in *Growing Up in Grand Rapids*, p. 49. Magazines: "Today's VIP," clipping in Thomas Ford Scrapbook, GRFL.

GERALD R. FORD SR. (GRFL)

FACTORIES ON THE GRAND RIVER (GRPL)

649 UNION AVENUE, JUNIOR FORD'S BOYHOOD HOME (GRFL)

THE EAGLE SCOUT HONOR GUARD WITH GOVERNOR FRED H. GREEN;
FORD IS IN THE SECOND ROW (GRFL)

SOUTH HIGH SCHOOL, 1929 (GRPL)

JUNIOR FORD WITH HIS MOTHER AND BABY
BROTHER, DICK (GRFL)

THE FORD PAINT AND VARNISH FACTORY (GRFL)

49

RAMONA PARK, 1929 (GRPL)

THE GRAND
RAPIDS
HERALD
ALL-CITY
FOOTBALL
TEAM OF 1930
(GRFL)

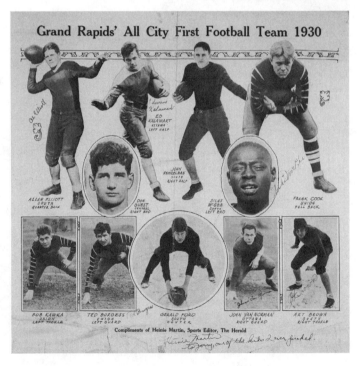

Grand Rapids' All City First Football Team 1930

Compliments of Heinie Martin, Sports Editor, The Herald

CHAPTER 4

To God and My Country

One evening in the fall or early winter of 1925, Junior got into the car and rode with his father several blocks to Trinity Methodist Church on Lake Drive, meeting place for Troop 15 of the Boy Scouts in Grand Rapids. It was not the closest Scout troop to his home — there were some sixty troops in the city, and at least a couple of them were closer to 649 Union Avenue — but it was the one his father had chosen, on the basis of a conversation he had had not long before with Charles Kindel, heir apparent at one of the high-craftsmanship German American furniture manufacturers, just back from two years' study in Europe to help his father with the business. Twenty-seven-year-old Kindel had been one of the earliest American Scouts, had won eleven merit badges, and had become an Eagle; he had just taken over leadership of Troop 15, which needed a scoutmaster, and he inquired if Ford had a son who would be interested in joining. Ford had been involved in the Scouting movement for some time — he served on the board of Camp Shawondossee. His introduction to Kindel may have come through his BSA activities rather than on a business call. In any case, the opportunity was not to be missed; Kindel was a fine young man, committed and experienced, and a connection with an important client could only be good. Ford promised to bring Junior and see if he could sign up other boys in the neighborhood.[1]

1. GRF's Scout troop, numbered 15 at the time of his membership, is now Troop 215; but it has had a continuous existence, and its records are largely intact. My thanks to John Czuhajewski, the current scoutmaster, for help with access and information. GRF told James Cannon that he became a Scout at age twelve (Ford-Cannon interviews, April 25, 1990, GRFL, p. 2), and Troop 215 records show that his name was sent in as a new recruit on December 17, 1925 (1926 charter renewal application, copy at GRFL). The list of

51

Junior doubtless looked at the yellow brick church with attention as they parked and walked up to the door of the fellowship hall, next to the sanctuary. Instead of the stately dignity of St. Mark's, it had the warm, welcoming feel of mainstream 1920s Protestantism; the legend carved over the door read "RECREATION — FELLOWSHIP — CHARACTER," without a mention of specifically Christian doctrine, and the inside was airy and pleasant in a sort of modernized English Tudor style, with oaken beams and wainscoting. The building was only three years old. The big hall to the left, where the troop met, was a multipurpose space where the church showed films for the community on Friday nights; in the basement was a bowling alley. Junior and his father joined Mr. Kindel and perhaps a dozen boys, gathered there to begin the meeting; the usual introductions and handshakes followed; Junior received a copy of the Scout bible, the *Handbook for Boys*, and a list of things to learn for next week.[2]

Conscientious as always with an assignment, Junior returned to the next meeting prepared to recite the Scout oath. Holding his right hand up in the prescribed three-finger position, he slowly intoned,

> On my honor, I will do my best
> To do my duty to God and my country,
> To obey the scout law;
> To help other people at all times;
> To keep myself physically strong, mentally awake, and morally
>   straight.

---

names makes it clear that his was the last name added. Evidently he joined shortly before December 17, 1925. Some writers, and a couple of BSA documents, state that he joined in 1924, but this is impossible; not only was he too young, but the conversation between Kindel and GRF Sr. that led to his joining Troop 15 cannot have taken place before July 1925, when records show another scoutmaster, Clayton Bazuin, in charge of the troop. Bazuin resigned during the summer and Kindel took over (Troop 215 records; Charles J. Kindel taped interview, August 26, 1982, GRFL). For the number of troops in the city, see *Press*, January 1, 1927; for background on Kindel and the Kindel family, see Mary Harvey Kindel interview, Greater Grand Rapids Women's History Council Oral History Collection, GRPL, and Charles J. Kindel interview.

GRF recalled that his father was on the BSA Council in 1926 when he entered Troop 15; BSA records for that era are fragmentary and do not list GRF Sr., but a 1932 brochure, *Shawandossee Camps for Boys*, in the files of the Gerald R. Ford Council stated that he had been on the committee of directors for eleven years.

2. The total number of Scouts in the troop during 1925, as shown by the compilation in GRFL, was twenty-four.

This made him a Tenderfoot, a starter Scout. In addition, over the next few months he brought half a dozen friends into the troop, boys from Madison School or South High. Kindel remembered their names: Junior's backyard neighbors and sports buddies, the blond, cheerful Engel twins, were one pair. Then there were two Franks, Frank Lass and Frank Lusk, Richard Cassada, Ed Ferch, and a boy named White. Cassada was older; the others were Junior's age and probably his classmates in seventh grade, except the Engels, who were a year younger. For the next couple of years they were a tight-knit, energetic group, advancing together from Tenderfoot into higher Scout ranks. They formed a patrol within the troop and elected Junior their leader.[3]

Kindel, with his experience in Scouting, knew how to make the meetings interesting. Every Monday he scheduled a variety of activities: the boys practiced marching together, learned to hoist and handle the American flag, tied knots of different kinds, studied animal tracks and insect nests, played games, or reported on good turns they had done for others during the week. In the time-honored scoutmaster's formula, Kindel limited each activity to twenty minutes or so, to keep the troop focused. He announced participation in city-wide activities, big events in which boys from various troops could meet and fraternize while awing the general populace with their numbers and semimilitary bearing. Scouts often marched in parades and added to the pageantry of civic gatherings with their woolen uniforms, including spats, and banners. City-wide crusades selling Christmas seals, urging citizens to vote, and so forth gave Scouts more occasions to be seen as important.[4]

Scouting was a widespread, surging movement in 1926. Only seven years earlier, its nationwide membership had been slightly above 300,000; in 1926 it was over 800,000. It was growing rapidly particularly among middle-class boys in towns and small cities. What it represented was still not entirely clear. During World War I Scouts, uniformed boys

3. Kindel interview; Boy Scouts of America, *The Official Handbook for Boys*, p. 14. Kindel thought that all of GRF's friends ultimately became Eagle Scouts, and so did GRF himself (Ford-Cannon interviews, April 25, 1990, p. 2); but the records show only Ferch and the Engels at that rank. Ages of the friends are from Troop 215 documents and the 1930 U.S. Census manuscript.

4. Kindel interview; Macleod, *Building Character*, p. 268. Stories in the *Herald* for 1926 mention the participation of all city troops in the centennial "Parade of Progress" (September 29), a get-out-the-vote campaign (October 21), and a very early Christmas parade (November 13). Uniforms: Bob Fraser interview.

from twelve to sixteen years old, had been an active quasi-governmental force, distributing patriotic literature and monitoring participation in government drives. Their association with the outdoors connoted energy and strength, and their leaders still claimed to consider them at the orders of the president or any local authority. "Scouting is not organized for war service," a 1920 article explained, "nor yet exclusively for peace service. It is organized for Service, all service, any service, high or humble." Though their emphasis since the war had changed subtly to the more innocuous goal of "building a sturdy character" through organized outdoor and civic activity, they were still ubiquitous in parades, conventions, and citizens' gatherings of any kind, and often took part in disaster response.

Scouting, thus, could be almost like police duty, but there was relaxation too. Local councils got up holiday events like Halloween powwows; in Grand Rapids, Ramona Park once or twice a summer staged a jamboree for all the troops in the city and gave out free tickets to the rides. When the weather got warm, Kindel would host cookouts for Troop 15.[5]

The most popular warm-weather activity, the one most closely associated with the Scouts in the public mind, was outdoor hiking, the symbolic reconnection with nature that made Scouting so attractive to middle-class urban families. Troop 15 did a lot of that. They would gather at Trinity and hike in uniform, shorts and broad-brimmed hats, beyond the city limits, to the lush flat countryside just beyond the suburban fringe. Kindel recalled camping overnight, probably as early as April, on a "crick" not far from his newly built house and barely a mile beyond elegant new houses under construction. He and the boys erected a tent, built a campfire, cooked pancakes, and told stories. In many ways, this was the real core of Scouting. "Anyone who has witnessed a real camp fire and participated in its fun as well as seriousness," said the *Handbook for Boys*, "will always remember it. The huge fire shooting up its tongue of flame into the darkness of the night, the perfect shower of golden rain, the company of happy boys, and the great background of piny woods, the weird light over all, the singing, the yells, the stories,

5. Murray, *History of the Boy Scouts of America*, p. 137, has membership figures. Macleod, *Building Character*, p. 225, explores the special appeal to towns and smaller cities. Murray, pp. 124-29, discusses activities during World War I. "Sturdy character": Murray, p. 225. "Organized for service": *Muskegon Boy Scout*, quoted in Todish, *Scouting in West Michigan*, p. 68. The *Herald* mentions a Halloween powwow October 31, 1926; a photo is in the Robinson Collection, GRPL.

the fun, and then the serious word at the close, is a happy experience long to be remembered."[6]

As they were having fun, they were building character: this was the idea behind the Scouts. The surging energies of late boyhood, coming into contact with the wholesome toughness of nature, the guidance of an adult male, and the demands of simulated survival, would turn into a set of strong, healthy, masculine attitudes. The promise, everyone recognized, involved some playacting, for as a rule, no real danger or challenge was involved. In the rather jaundiced words of one historian:

> Outdoor life would toughen boys; yet by cloistering the youngsters in pastoral surroundings, camp would also keep them dependent and safe from city vices. Carefully buffered contacts with tame wilderness would enable campers to vent their boyish savagery under close control. Camp programs would encourage boyish activism; yet campfire rituals and natural beauty would encourage mild cases of adolescent romanticism. The hope was to strengthen boys and yet protect them, to keep them boyish and yet reap certain benefits of adolescence.[7]

Junior Ford seems to have been completely indifferent to any issues of independence versus adult control. It was the planned activity of Scouting, and above all of outdoor camping, that suited him. He liked having regular purposeful activity ahead of him from the time he got up in the morning, and he liked being recognized for accomplishment. Membership in a team, with a defined place in the institutional structure, meant a lot to him. Male camaraderie, whether with adult supervisors or fellow Scouts, created an atmosphere congenial to him, where standing rested on performance rather than verbal skills. In camp photographs from these Scouting years, Junior's expression, under the tousled blond mop that made him easy to spot, was nearly always a squint or a scowl; but these were far from denoting dissatisfaction. He really liked the Scouts. The rough exterior was a style this uncommunicative boy adopted at this time of his life, even as he gained recognition from his fellows and advanced in the eyes

6. Kindel interview; Boy Scouts of America, *The Official Handbook for Boys*, pp. 160-61. A 20-acre tract north of the city, Camp Lion, was used by all the troops for outdoor activities. According to BSA records in GRFL, GRF earned his first two merit badges, in cooking and firemanship, in April 1926, probably on one of these pancake-cooking outings.

7. Macleod, *Building Character*, p. 234.

of his superiors. Both groups recognized that his heart was in the hikes, the camps, and the trials of skill.[8]

Summer camp was the essence of Scouting, and Junior and his father looked forward eagerly to its two weeks in the woods, in the company of experienced Scouts, full of games and tests of skill. Camp Shawondossee, named for the goddess of the South Wind in Longfellow's *Song of Hiawatha*, started operations in late June. It was near Port Sheldon, which is on Lake Michigan a few miles north of Ottawa Beach, but the precise location is uncertain. Jerry Ford had been on the board of directors for some years and knew the camp, but had no share in the actual management; that was done by an experienced camp leader, a dark-haired, ramrod-straight man named George Miller, with a small staff. Swimming, always on the buddy system, was a big part of the program, along with archery, hiking, ball games, and nature study. There was a large and proficient band. Around fifty boys attended for a week at a time, organized by troops. They camped in four-man tents around a landmark tree, a big maple. Junior, because of his father's position, was able to attend for two full weeks, and loved it.[9]

Shawondossee was a great place for boys to learn new skills and practice old ones. Activities were scheduled from 6:30 A.M. reveille, including meals, prayers, sports, and instruction in various crafts. The band members carried their instruments around more or less all the time, and doubtless there was a lot of random solo playing in addition to the concert numbers. All boys, band members and others, did a lot of standing and marching in military formation throughout the day. Each troop had a regular time for swimming on the buddy system, and of course, there were classes in lifesaving. Lee Shananaquet, of the camp staff, a member

8. In an interview preserved in the GRFL vertical file under "Preferences and Favorites," GRF identified his favorite time of day as "dawn." An early memory of his younger brother Dick is of GRF's arising in the morning and immediately beginning exercise (interview at GRFL, September 22, 2010). GRFL has about a half-dozen group photographs from Camp Shawondossee, covering mostly the years 1927 and 1928 — in other words, both locations, the "old" and the "new" camp.

9. My account of Camp Shawondossee is from Todish, *Scouting in West Michigan*, pp. 136, 140-46, supplemented by a personal interview with Mr. Todish, December 20, 2011. The camp had two distinct locations during the years of GRF's attendance, 1926-1930: until 1927 it was near Port Sheldon, and from 1928 on it was on Duck Lake, north of Muskegon. The "big maple" at the first camp is mentioned in a letter from Hersch Bayes to GRF, February 15, 1977, on the back of photo AV82-18-P574 in the GRFL Scrapbook. See also *Shawandossee Camps for Boys*, p. 6; this booklet, however, describes only the post-1928 camp. On the band, see Todish, p. 68.

of the Menominee nation and thus a genuine son of the wilderness, did tribal dances at the Council Fire on Friday nights, when the boys sat cross-legged around a natural amphitheater in the woods, "shrouded by blankets of all hues." Boys were urged to write home frequently and remember their prayers. On nature hikes, sometimes at dawn, Junior and his friends learned to identify dozens of different birds and their songs — knowledge that was good for a merit badge in bird study.

Merit badges were awards ideally suited for a personality like young Ford's — concentrated effort followed by a tangible reward, a patch, square rather than round in the 1920s, designed to represent a particular skill, like carpentry or civics. Having become first-class Scouts in the spring by passing basic tests of woodcraft and knot-tying, he and his friends could begin accumulating the badges, which were displayed on a sash in front of the uniform. As early as April they had earned their first badge, cooking, in the course of the troop's hikes in the woods of East Grand Rapids, each Scout taking part in preparing dishes over a campfire he had made. Four more had followed, even before they went to camp. Some badges were essentially tests of verbal knowledge, like firemanship — knowing how to extinguish fires of different kinds — or civics, which meant knowing facts about government. Others were more hands-on. At camp Junior and probably all his patrol began working on a badge in handicraft, which involved such crafts as painting, soldering, hanging curtains, and replacing latches. By the end of 1926 Junior had twelve merit badges. On earning twenty-one he would become an Eagle Scout, the "all-round perfect scout." Eagle Scouts were the elite of the Boy Scouts; there were probably sixty of them in Grand Rapids. They were the boys with brains, self-discipline, and ability, publicly recognized as such. It was a great honor to be an Eagle Scout. Junior attained it in the summer of 1927, when he was at Shawondossee for the second year. He would have agreed with the recollections of another Scout, two years behind him: "Becoming an Eagle Scout was encouraging, but it was not as consequential as living away from home in a wholesome environment, making good friends, having challenging role models, and receiving the affirmation and discipline that a boy of 13 needs."[10]

10. Activities at "old" Camp Shawondossee, *Herald,* July 4, 1926. Photographs of campers in GRFL show many of the boys carrying musical instruments even when no organized band activity is visible. Requirements for the merit badges, including a list of the ones required for an Eagle Scout, are to be found in Boy Scouts of America, *The Official Handbook for Boys,* pp. 24-43. GRF's merit badges are listed by date in the BSA materials in GRFL, and also accessible at the Web site www.lincoln-highway-museum.org/GRF. On merit badges

For two years Junior and his buddies worked on acquiring the skills of good citizens and competent adults, basking in the recognition they received at the periodic Courts of Honor. It was hard, useful work, even if it did have a slightly theatrical quality at times, and it helped them across the bridge between late boyhood and early adolescence, the years of the growth spurt, the so-called pregenital years of body hair and pimples and changes in body chemistry. A certain amount of gross and unruly behavior went with this transition, and Junior no doubt committed his share; but the most visible change was the mop of blond hair he began wearing. As a small boy he had always had neatly combed hair, no doubt at his mother's direction, but from seventh grade through graduation from high school his signature look, so consistent that it had to be deliberate, was tousled, rebellious blondness.[11]

Other camps in the area near the lakeshore belonged to other Boy Scout councils, several as far away as Chicago, and others still were affiliated with the Girl Scouts, Campfire Girls, and various service organizations. Summer camp had become "the customary thing" in raising middle-class children. St. Mark's Church had Camp Roger, operated by the choir director, but there is no record that Junior ever attended it. Camp Manitoulin, closer to Grand Rapids, was connected with the YMCA, where Junior was a devoted member. He spent many hours swimming nude in the pool at the city Y, a modern, well-furnished new headquarters across from the public library, where his father had enrolled him as a small boy and where he had learned to swim well. In high school, wearing the trunks and tank top that were regulation for boys' public swimming in 1930, he would compete on the Y team. Even during his Scouting years he was a strong, enthusiastic swimmer, willing to teach and guide younger boys. The Y and the Boy Scouts worked closely together, in Grand Rapids, at least, and seem to have had an understanding that the Y had a special focus on the workers' boys from the West Side, while the middle-class kids went into Boy Scout troops. No record or recollection connects Junior with Camp Manitoulin, but Shawondossee played a major part in his life.[12]

---

in general, see Macleod, *Building Character*, pp. 250-53, and the Scout quoted in Todish, *Scouting in West Michigan*, p. 253: "I found merit badges interesting and challenging." Square badges: Bob Fraser interview. "Becoming an Eagle Scout": M. Eugene Osterhaven, quoted in Todish, p. 242.

11. Pregenital behavior: Macleod, *Building Character*, p. 236. Photos are in GRFL: see n. 13 below.

12. GRF interview with Gordon Olson, June 30, 2001, transcript in GRPL; letter from

Some half-dozen panoramic photos of the Shawondossee campers exist from the years 1926-1928, and Junior Ford is in most of them, with his unruly fair hair, squinting or scowling at the camera. Like most of the boys, he wore only part of his uniform for the pictures, mixed with other pieces of attire; boys often put together a camp outfit from Army surplus stores that sold items from the world war. More often than not, he was holding the flag or posed in some responsible-looking position. A photo, probably from 1927, refers to him as "Scout Officer of the Day." By 1928, he was on the camp staff, but as early as 1927 he was recognized as outstanding. A picture contributed by Hersch Bayes, another Scout officer and flag bearer, shows a quasi-military formation from which Ford is absent; a note on the picture suggests that he may have been excused to spend a week at Culver Military Academy in Indiana, an honor for a Scout of special ability. An undated snapshot from an older Eagle Scout named Julius Knowlton shows him smiling with a small group of boys, perhaps all Eagles, with a string of fish. To judge by the clothing, it was in cool weather — it may have been a trip for the staff one year after camp was over.[13]

Though several photographs of Junior exist, recollections of him at camp are few and fragmentary; this is surprising, since the experience was so vivid in the minds of most campers. His own most vivid recollection dated from 1928, when he worked on the camp staff. He had had his tonsils removed shortly before camp began, and the cavities on both sides of his throat were still sore when he arrived. One night soon afterward, Junior woke and realized that one side of his throat was bleeding heavily. Confused and alarmed, he couldn't think what to do and didn't want to wake anyone. He ended by going back to sleep and hoping the bleeding would stop, which, fortunately, it did. The camp was thirty miles from the nearest hospital. "That could have been fatal," he noted in old age. "I was damn lucky."[14]

He and other Eagle Scouts made an impression on younger campers. He and Lee Shananaquet made their own headdresses, buckskin boots, and clothing, and danced and whooped in the rain dance and snake dance

Diane Thornton, July 1, 1997; Gleason, "Reflections of Grand Rapids Camps," p. 24, surveys summer camps in the area. On nudity in the Y pool, see Denham, *Growing Up in Grand Rapids*, p. 31, and Arnold Sisson interview. A photo (AV82-18-P118) of the 1931 YMCA swim team is in GRFL. "The customary thing": Schmitt, *Back to Nature*, pp. 96-105.

13. The photos, all in the scrapbook at GRFL, are numbered AV84-230; AV82-216; AV82-18-P573, and accession #2002-NLF-008. T. J. Todish helped me interpret them.

14. Ford-Cannon interviews, April 25, 1990, p. 2, GRFL.

"in frightful manner," according to the tongue-in-cheek story of a Grand Rapids reporter. They were part of the solemn, elaborate Indian pageant enacted on Friday night at the Council Fire. Each Eagle had his own personality and style. William Bradley described Ford as a "big kid," which he had gotten to be: 5 feet 10 inches and muscular, weighing perhaps 140 pounds. Gene Osterhaven of Grand Rapids, thirteen years old, remembered him and several others: "the camping skills and leadership of Jule Knowlton, who knew how to get the best out of a boy by joking, laughing, ribbing and encouraging; the all-around ability of the Engel twins . . . the ruggedness of Kenny Wright, and the character of Jerry Ford." (By 1928 he had begun calling himself "Jerry" instead of "Junior.") Osterhaven didn't define what he meant by "character," but clearly it concerned thoughtfulness about daily decisions of a moral, interpersonal nature, something more fundamental than skills or agility. The years of hiking and crafts had paid off, as they were supposed to, in firm, positive attitudes.[15]

The big event of 1928 was the opening of the new site, some thirty miles north of the old one, north of Muskegon. Purchased with the help of the Lions Club, it was larger than the old camp (240 acres), with newly built rustic-style facilities — rubble-stone fireplaces, wagon-wheel lighting fixtures in the mess hall — capable of serving a hundred campers at one time. It had a large and attractive frontage on Duck Lake, and was within walking distance of Lake Michigan. Camp opened June 28; the formal dedication, with a picnic, bands, and a speech by Grand Rapids' own Senator Arthur Vandenberg, was July 4. A press release announced plans for a fifteen-foot totem pole in front. Junior Ford was one of the four Scouts who made up the color guard, though the hemorrhage in his throat must have taken place only a few days before. He had arrived, with the rest of the staff, a week before the first campers, to help put down the plywood "duck-boards" that went beneath the tents and to police the new site, which meant killing off most of the rattlesnake population before the younger boys arrived. Rattlers or no rattlers, however, the new camp was a wonderful improvement on the old one.[16]

15. Todish, *Scouting in West Michigan*, p. 141 (quoting the *Herald*, August 3, 1930), pp. 242-43 (quotes from Scouts). Newspaper photo captioned "Can You Find President Ford in This Picture?," vertical file, "Miscellaneous"; transcript of Ford-Cannon interviews, April 25, 1990, p. 1, both GRFL. GRF recalled his weight in 1928 as 140, his height as 5 feet 9 inches or 5 feet 10 inches; April 24, 1990, p. 1.

16. *Shawondossee Camps for Boys*, p. 2, describes the new facilities. See also *Herald*, June 28, July 5, and July 8, 1928; *Grand Rapids Spectator*, June 16, 1928; and Todish, *Scouting*

Duck Lake had an outlet into Lake Michigan, so that it was possible to build a twenty-four-man "war canoe," train on the camp waterfront, and then paddle it out into the big lake. The camp organized a branch of the "Sea Scouts," most of whom were Eagle Scouts. Jerry Ford was in it with his fifteen-year-old contemporaries. From canoes they went on to manage even larger craft. As early as 1927, Fred Z. Pantlind, the Fords' Ottawa Beach neighbor, gave the council a two-masted, seventy-two-foot schooner for practice, and the Sea Scouts took it for two short cruises on Lake Michigan, using Lake Macatawa as a home port. This kind of activity was an exciting step beyond camping and crafts, a sort of adventure with overtones of the rich twenties playboy, and it led in the summer of 1928 to two adventurous episodes. Young Ford may not have been a direct participant in either, but he was very much concerned with both. In one, the Sea Scouts were rescuers; in the other they were the rescued.

In late July, as camp was winding down, news came of a terrible accident on Lake Macatawa: a speedboat piloted by a college boy from a rich Holland family, Paul Landwehr, had been buzzing a Chicago ferryboat, a side-wheeler, circling closely, when it was sucked under the steel blades of the right wheel. Four of the young people aboard were lost. The Holland Sea Scout troop joined the search for the bodies; the Grand Rapids Sea Scout schooner, the *Natant,* was by this time based at Duck Lake, but the Sea Scouts there were probably asked to come as well. Jerry may have taken part. Probably he knew some of the missing from his Ottawa Beach summers; in college he would be a close friend of Paul Landwehr's brother. But his name does not appear in any account, and he never discussed the search. All four bodies were shortly found.[17]

A month later, the *Natant* set out on a big lake cruise, bound for the resort island of Mackinac. Most of the Sea Scouts were on board — Art and Ben Engle, Bob Todish, Kenny Wright of Troop 15 — but not Ford, for some reason. They developed engine trouble off Manistee the second day out, and were refueling the dinghy to go ashore when the gas burst into flames,

---

in *Western Michigan,* p. 140. Todish in an interview (December 20, 2011) added the detail about the rattlesnakes.

17. A general description of Sea Scouting is on p. 6 of *Shawondossee Camps for Boys.* See also Todish, *Scouting in Western Michigan,* p. 147. A schooner named the *Matin* is mentioned July 7, 1927 *(Press);* Pantlind's donation is mentioned in Todish, p. 66. The Lake Macatawa accident was covered in *Herald,* July 27 and 28, 1928, but the fullest account is in Van Reken and Vande Water, *Holland Furnace,* pp. 65-75.

which set fire to the vessel. Art Engle, Kenny Wright, and one other Scout suffered major burns fighting the fire, the ship burned to the waterline, and the Coast Guard had to rescue the boys. Real-life danger and injury added a third and somewhat jarring dimension to the Scout experience. Doubtless young Ford pondered more than once what he would have done if he had been there. He hastened to telephone his parents that he was all right and all the boys were safely ashore.[18]

Summer 1928 saw the end of Ford's connection with Troop 15; he remembered his stay in it as "two and a half years," which would have ended in that summer. He was no longer simply a Scout; as an Eagle, he was a successful product of the system, an adept, a role model for others. He may briefly have had some official connection with the Sea Scout unit, but from 1928 on his activity, in a pattern quite common for Eagle Scouts, consisted of working, unpaid, at Shawondossee as a staffer, helping younger boys follow the same path he had taken. When the Eagle Scouts in February 1929 took over the reins of Grand Rapids' city government for a day, to celebrate the Scouts' anniversary, Ford was chosen by his peers to serve as city judge. But the culmination of his honors came in July of that year.[19]

Mackinac, the island popular with millionaires and moneyed families from Michigan and the whole Midwest, had an abandoned federal fort on it, given by the government to the state of Michigan around 1900 and largely ignored thereafter. The old buildings stood untended on a hill; guests from the Grand Hotel and day-trippers wandered through them and scribbled graffiti on the whitewashed walls. A small, haphazard military museum displayed historical artifacts and souvenirs from the world war. In the uprush of historical and patriotic interest that followed the U.S. sesquicentennial in 1926, Roger M. Andrews, the vice chairman of the state commission assigned to Mackinac Island State Park, had the idea of highlighting the historic site with an honor guard of Boy Scouts, outstanding young men with a vaguely military presence who could serve both as guards and guides. It would be a first-class vacation for the boys, who would be the cream of Michigan Scouts: eight Eagles from different regions of the state. They would be formally commissioned as "the Governor's Honor Guard." Rapidly developed, the plan was rushed into effect in

18. *Press*, August 27, 1928; *Manistee News-Advocate*, August 27, 1928; Leroy, *Gerald Ford — Untold Story*, p. 33.

19. Ford-Cannon interviews, August 25, 2000, GRFL, p. 2. *Press*, February 1929.

July 1929, and the West Michigan Council, pressed to name an outstanding Eagle Scout, chose Jerry Ford.

Ford had spent six weeks on the staff at Shawondossee, and his thoughts were probably turning toward high school football, as the next chapter will show; but the honor for him and his family was too great to pass up. The first of August found him suited up in his neatest Scout uniform, hair slicked down and all his merit badges on display, as he was driven to Lansing to meet Governor Fred Green and his seven fellow guardsmen for publicity photos. He made a striking image; big, muscular, blond, good-looking, staring at the lens with a direct gaze, he was often put at the center of the group. The next day they traversed Detroit, city of autos and crime; were entertained by the *Detroit Times* at the Fort Shelby Hotel; and boarded an old Detroit & Cleveland side-wheeler, the *Western States*, for the overnight voyage up Lake Huron to "the cool beauty spot of the world," as promotional literature put it, where they learned the facts about the fort they would present to visitors with Ame Venema, the intense Scout leader from Menominee who had designed the program.[20]

Ford had packed a football with the rest of his gear, and during that first day he was excited to discover that another Eagle was on his school's football team and played the same position, center. Apple-cheeked, bespectacled Joe McIntosh centered for St. Stephen's Catholic High in Port Huron; by the second day, on the *Western States*, he and Ford had paired off and would remain buddies for the rest of the month, talking and practicing football in addition to their Honor Guard duties. Ted Pearson, captain of the guard, was impressed that Ford got up and ran laps around the pedestrian path inside the fort each morning before he started his duties, keeping himself in training for the fall.[21]

The boys slept on folding cots in the deserted fort and demonstrated their skills by cooking their own food. Quick standbys like beans and bacon or hunter's stew predominated. They bugled reveille every morning and raised the American flag (plus the state flag when the governor was on the island), and in pairs of two worked four-hour shifts showing visitors around. At sunset they had the duty of firing the fort's cannon. Cameras were much in evidence: they took photos of each other and posed for pic-

20. Davis, "Mackinac Scout Service Camp," pp. 2-3; Armour, "75 Years of Serving Mackinac," p. 46; *Mackinac Island*, p. 3.

21. "Joe McIntosh's Buddy of '29 Grew Up to Be President in '74," *Port Huron Times Herald*, December 15, 1974; letter from Stanley S. Sowerwine, *Scouting*, November 1975, p. 18; photo of Scouts on *Western States*, Joseph McIntosh Scrapbook, GRFL.

tures with tourists. Their day concluded with taps sounding across the dark water, as it had at Shawondossee.[22]

This schedule left the boys almost as much time for recreation as the vacationers themselves had. McIntosh remembered many activities in detail. (Ford recalled only that the stay was an "honor" and a "thrill.") They dived and swam, quickly in and out, in the icy waters of the Straits of Mackinac, and more leisurely in the figure-eight-shaped pool of the Grand Hotel, where they also occasionally watched silent movies at night. They enjoyed the hotel's theatrical luxury, with its costumed flunkies and elaborate protocol. On the island, where no autos were permitted, they bicycled all over, admiring the limestone cliffs and formations like Arch Rock and Lover's Leap, associated with romantic pseudo-Indian legends, or, in a change of pace for modern city boys, they drove the horse-drawn carriages. On one day off, McIntosh and Ford took the ferry over to St. Ignace on the mainland and had a trout dinner with a family friend of the McIntoshes, a tugboat captain.[23]

In one free-time activity Ford took no part. The Grand Hotel, as a hostelry for the wealthy, had two of "the sportiest, best-kept, and most beautiful golf courses in northern Michigan," where male guests played, discussed affairs, and cemented relationships, as they did at home. For years Jerry and Dorothy Ford, very much aware of this bond between success and golf, had been begging Junior in vain to caddy at the Cascade Country Club east of town, not just for the tips but also for the connections, in the hope that he would come to like the sport and develop some skill at it. Junior had actually caddied for his father at the new Masonic Country Club, built by the joint contributions of the Grand Rapids lodges on the heights northwest of the city. Golf, however, held little interest for him at that time — "I was a lousy caddie," he recalled. In the next ten years his attitude would change, but in 1929 he passed by the Grand Hotel courses without a second glance.[24]

22. Davis, "Mackinac Scout Service Camp," p. 4; Armour, "75 Years of Serving Mackinac," p. 46.

23. "Joe McIntosh's Buddy"; Fuller, *Map and Guide of Mackinac Island*, pp. 19, 27-28, 36-37; Woodfill, *Grand Hotel*, p. 21. Photos from McIntosh's scrapbook, contributed to GRFL, illustrate many of these activities. A photo of the pool is on the back cover of *Mackinac Island*.

24. *Mackinac Island*, p. 15; Ford-Cannon interviews, April 25, 1992, p. 1, GRFL; Ray Barnes, "Razzin' the Rapids," *Herald*, November 16, 1941; GRF, "My Life and Times on the Tour," *Golf Digest*, August 1980.

Another activity he avoided, as far as McIntosh could remember, was dating. Conspicuous in their uniforms, the guards were bound to attract the notice of young female vacationers; there were numerous opportunities at the movies and afternoon dances for the classic American summer vacation-cum-romance explored by Dreiser, Fitzgerald, and others, and the boys were not shy about exploiting them. They all, even McIntosh occasionally, dated the girls from the hotels and cottages, and a couple were real "ladies' men," but Jerry sat these occasions out. He was, from the scoutmaster's viewpoint, the perfect Eagle, immune to "girlitis," still apparently dwelling in a prepubertal bubble. Or perhaps he felt an interest, but his inarticulateness blocked him from making a move; scared of uttering something foolish, he stayed aloof, preferring to run, swim, and dive alone, like one of the mythical Greek heroes he resembled, Actaeon, Adonis, Meleager, in the overpowering freshness and coolness of a Mackinac August.[25]

When Jerry returned to Grand Rapids on September 2 (and promptly wrote Roger Andrews a nice note of thanks for the appointment), he largely left behind the individual athletic, character-building world of Scouting. For the next twelve years the somewhat different world of organized, competitive team sports would dominate his life. But the ideals and precepts of the Scouts had taken lifelong root inside him as they were supposed to do, and in significant ways for the rest of his life he would be a Boy Scout.[26]

---

25. *Mackinac Island*, p. 15; "Joe McIntosh's Buddy"; Macleod, *Building Character*, p. 284.

26. Roger M. Andrews to GRF, September 6, 1929, GRF Scrapbooks, GRFL.

CHAPTER 5

"Hey, Whitey, You're a Center"

A big afternoon for Junior Ford came in the spring of 1927, when eighth-grade boys turned out on the practice field to try out for the next year's football team. They milled around among the bigger, more experienced freshmen, sophomores, and juniors, who already had their playbooks and their uniforms and were forming into squads under the observation of the head coach, Cliff Gettings. Junior knew some of the other eighth-graders, like Allen Elliott and Marsh Reister, but others, like Art Brown, who was to become one of his best friends, he had barely seen before.

Gettings, a big, blond, rangy twenty-four-year-old, three years out of Hillsdale College, with a commanding physical presence, scrutinized the younger boys. He asked them his standard question: "if they'd ever played sandlot ball or what they liked to play best or what they could play." Junior, as he remembered, said that he hadn't played football at all, so Gettings quickly sized him up physically, with a coach's eye; he was "long and lanky and looked [as if] he was going to be big" — clearly a lineman, with some indications of intelligence — maybe worth trying as a center. Gettings passed him a football and told him to start centering.[1]

Ford remembered it more concisely: Gettings looked at him and said, "Hey, Whitey, you're a center." Junior obeyed without comment: "He saw me, and I had white hair, and he needed a center," was the way he put it.[2]

---

1. Gettings interview, pp. 1, 5-6, Art Brown interview, p. 1, both in Grand Rapids Oral History Collection, GRFL. Gettings's obituary is in the *Press*, August 19, 1980.

2. Cannon, *Time and Chance*, p. 12. Red Grange's experience was similar: "I went out for the team as a freshman and on the first day our coach called all the new kids together

But the conclusion of Gettings's story is the most revealing comment about Ford as an athlete: once he was told to play center, "you never saw him without that ball after school and before school, anytime anybody would catch the ball he was over it centering." Joe Russo, the little Sicilian dynamo who played fullback on the varsity, remembered him the same way: "Jerry used to come around me all the time. He was always carrying this football and he wanted to practice passing it to me, even in the hallway outside the gym." The intense focus, the total concentration that Ford's parents and scoutmaster Kindel were already familiar with, prefigured the kind of athlete he was going to become: a natural team player who was willing to practice his part in an operation over and over again until he got it right beyond the possibility of getting it wrong.[3]

One detail of Ford's own recollection deserves notice: the name "Whitey," as in "Hey, Whitey, you're a center." Probably he hadn't used that name for himself before; it was just Gettings's way of identifying him. But Junior Ford's growing dissatisfaction with his name has already been noted, and there are indications that the name "Whitey" appealed to him. Perhaps Gettings kept using the name for him, and the other boys on the team adopted it for a while; at any rate, Junior did too, for a year or so, signing it next to his football picture in the *Pioneer*. That it didn't stick may be just as well — it's hard enough to deal with the confusion between two famous twentieth-century Fords from the same state, without having to add two famous Whitey Fords, the athlete-president and the great Yankee pitcher fifteen years his junior.[4]

If any one thing in these accounts doesn't sound quite right, it's Gettings's assertion that Junior told him he'd never played football before. For a boy from Grand Rapids — indeed, from any city in the Midwest — that was so rare as to be virtually inconceivable. Football was a huge presence in the lives of American boys of the twenties, at least those who lived in cities and small towns. Indeed, Ford remembered football games with other boys, and also his father playing catch with him, teaching him

---

and asked them what they played. He said to me, 'Kid, what do you want to play?' And I said, 'Well, what do you need?' 'We've got ten men back from last year,' he told me. 'All we need is a right end.' 'Well, I'm a right end,' I said, and that was it." Whittingham, *What a Game They Played*, p. 17.

3. "'Good Old Junie' Hosts Thanksgiving Reunion," *Ann Arbor News*, November 28, 1974, in "Football" vertical file, GRFL.

4. GRF autographed Ken Hayes's 1928 yearbook "Whitey." *New Pioneer*, #40, March 1989.

to throw a baseball and a football — basic information for an American business-class male, even one who, like Jerry Ford Sr., had never been to high school. Most boys continued playing until the early teen years, when puberty began revealing what sort of adult body each boy was going to have. Then many slender, lightly built boys began moving away from football into other, more fulfilling pastimes, while big, strong, aggressive ones were more apt to stay with the game.[5]

In some ways, this picture resembles the familiar image of American football for the rest of the twentieth century: a central part of the culture and a vital component of male identity — fathers teaching the basics of the game to their sons, boys playing together enthusiastically but informally, and in high school the bigger and more enthusiastic players moving on to real, organized football, with a coach, uniforms, and popular acclaim. But in the 1920s the picture was different. The football universe was smaller: professional football existed marginally in a few Northern cities, and sports broadcasting was in its infancy. Many immigrant working families in the industrial cities, black Americans in the South, and farm families anywhere in the country were totally unfamiliar with the game. It had a respectable aura, faintly academic, even faintly upper-class. The sport was played only in educational institutions — high schools and colleges — but only about half of all American boys attended high school, and less than 10 percent of college-age males were students. In other words, only a limited portion of them had even a chance for direct involvement.[6]

At every level of the game, football players were smaller in those years than they are today. Many of the big boys and young men who would have played football in the late twentieth century were out earning money in the 1920s, not attending school. The average weight of the 1932 University of Michigan varsity players, selected as much for social class as for size and skill, was just under 180 pounds. The South High team in 1930 averaged 166 pounds — in 1929, 155 pounds, which was small even by the standards of that time. To be sure, the image of the big, dumb college football player

5. Ford, *TTH*, pp. 43, 45.

6. On the state of pro football, see Peterson, *Pigskin*, pp. 83, 104. Broadcasting had begun in 1926, when a network of twenty-three radio stations carried the World Series (Rader, *American Sports*, p. 198). Football is notable by its absence from some of the great social novels of life in the twenties, for instance, Dreiser's obsessively inclusive *An American Tragedy* and Farrell's *Studs Lonigan* — that is, there were great areas of American society in which it was relatively unimportant.

already existed, as did the nickname "Brute" for him; but even the big players were not as large as they would later be.[7]

Because of its lingering image as a game for the best and brightest in American society, football was still associated with intelligence. Percy Houghton, the Harvard coach who published his book *Football and How to Watch It* in 1922 as the game soared in popularity, emphasized this connection. "When properly understood," his book began, "football is both mentally and physically . . . a glorious sport" — or, as he put it later, "a somewhat complicated game of human chess." Naturally the ruling intelligence was that of the coach, who needed "a good intellect, a strong personality, and a thorough understanding of human nature" to produce successful teams. But the player too, in Houghton's words, had to "be taught to think as well as to act, and to do both at high speed, with a consciousness that full responsibility for thinking incorrectly and performing imperfectly is placed on him by thousands of spectators." Football, added a young high school coach from another part of the country, was not just entertainment; it trained players in "quick thinking" and "alertness of action."[8]

Football shared in the surge of popularity that sports experienced in the 1920s — indeed, it led the surge, helped by relentless publicity in city newspapers, whose writers, as one college publication put it, "hippodromed" the sport and made its outstanding performers into instant heroes. Between 1921 and 1930 attendance at college football games doubled, and the receipts from the games tripled. Seating facilities at major colleges went from 929,523 in 1920 to 2,307,850 in 1930. Part of the increase came from football's popularity spreading into immigrant communities and lower social classes, but perhaps the larger part of it came from consolidating its hold on business-class families. A Michigan alumnus commented in 1926 to a football player who had just finished his college career and was going into coaching: "I have watched the development of foot ball [sic] the last fifteen or twenty years and have realized how much stronger hold it is getting on the Alumni. The small boys have always been more or less interested. This fall I have had old men start discussing the team and

7. Weights are calculated from the 1932 University of Michigan official program, "Football" vertical file, and South–Grand Haven game program, October 4, 1930, GRF Scrapbook #1, both in GRFL. On the 1929 team, see the *Reflector*, November 2, 1929, also in GRF Scrapbook #1. See also "Ford Recalls Football Tales," *Ann Arbor News*, October 6, 1994, and Stockwell, *Rudderless*, pp. 79-80.

8. Houghton, *Football and How to Watch It*, pp. xix, 200-201; Bass and Thompson, *Ol' Strom*, p. 38.

its games. But I had not realized that even the young girls had become so interested. . . . Football has come to be more than a mere game. It is an institution." High school boys — socially the upper half of American teenagers — buoyed by their elders' approval, embraced the game even more firmly. In a 1925 survey, tenth-grade boys in Kansas City listed football — not "sports" in general — as their favorite activity.[9]

The sport was even beginning to rival baseball, the national game, in popularity. To Harry Wismer, growing up in Bay City, Michigan, in the 1920s, baseball was the "national pastime," but "college football, Big Ten style, was king in the Midwest." The Wismer boy, like Junior Ford, was a Tigers fan and frequently went to Detroit with his father for baseball games; he recalled, nonetheless, that "I played all sports as a youngster but my favorite was football." A study found that during the twenties coverage of football in Chicago newspapers increased 145 percent, while that of baseball grew only 23 percent. Many spectators found football more interesting to watch, perhaps because of the continuous action and the battle for territory. Some liked the head-to-head conflict; they liked football as "a hard, two-fisted game."[10]

People who looked for deeper meanings in sports found that football had a unique edge over baseball: it was a game more suited to modern industrial America. In baseball nine men stood around in a field, but football perfectly reflected modern industry — a group of specialists, perfectly trained in repetitive activity, under the supervision of a manager, in a game where productivity was measured by numbers and the clock was critical. There was relatively little individual glory in football; the glory lay in teamwork. The game's complexity, as one student put it, "require[d] that its players mold themselves into a perfectly coordinated unit." Most players were, in the words of Michael Oriard, "virtually anonymous, their shapes disguised by masked helmets, and their action often obscured by the massing of other bodies." The heroes of football, thus, were corporate men, players who had learned coordination and self-sacrifice for the good of the team — the kind of young men that the modern state needed. Considerations like these were important to serious-minded people like Jerry Ford, who would attend many father-son banquets while his son was

9. *Michigan Alumnus*, 38:183; Charles F. Delbridge to Bennie G. Oosterbaan, December 9, 1926, Oosterbaan Papers, BHL; Steiner, *Americans at Play*, p. 91; Modell, *Into One's Own*, p. 89.

10. Wismer, *The Public Calls It Sport*, p. 6; Steiner, *Americans at Play*, p. 62; Spring, "Mass Culture and School Sports," p. 494; Tunis, "Gas and the Games," p. 13.

participating and would hear hours of rhetoric about team spirit, character building, and sportsmanship, rhetoric that was inflated but based in solid reality.[11]

Thanks to the boundless capacity of football to mean deeply different things to different people, this analytical view of the game coexisted happily in the 1920s with other equally heartfelt responses: high school girl writers raved about the Friday afternoon exploits of their "paladins," their "knights"; college students and alumni anticipated big football weekends as occasions for spectacle, partying, and illegal drinking; city businessmen enlivened office conversation by laying bets on local teams; small towns in the South and West experienced surges of community feeling as citizens gathered to cheer the local boys and jeer at the visitors; and high school principals across the country observed again what was clearly understood in the twenties, the power of football to pull together a cliquish, socially disparate mass of teenagers into a united, enthusiastic band that evoked the Crusaders, the Pilgrim Fathers, Napoleon's army, or some such legendary heroic group from the past.[12]

With all this welter of symbolism and social activity centering on football, a pertinent question is what the game meant to the players themselves — why thousands of eighth-grade boys like Junior Ford were going out for their high school teams in the spring of 1927. The main cause, clearly, was the sheer boyish enjoyment of playing the game, and the desire to keep playing it at the most challenging level possible. For boys who were good at physical activity and devoted to sports, that was a given. But other factors influenced the decision as well. Football was a key element in high school social structure. "Why don't you play football?" one boy reported his relatives asking him. "You'll never be popular until you do." For high school boys in general, it was far and away the most popular activity they

11. Bernstein, *Football*, pp. 38-39; Oriard, *Dreaming of Heroes*, pp. 61-62; Ross, "Football and Baseball in America," p. 108.

12. Alumni and football weekends: Edwards, *Undergraduates*, pp. 71-72; Stockwell, *Rudderless*, pp. 52-53. Community spirit: McKay, *McKay*, p. 28 (Shinnston, West Virginia); Whittingham, *What a Game They Played*, pp. 170-71 (Temple, Texas). Community spirit, especially in the early years of the century, often involved displays of hostility to the opposing team and to officials who penalized local players. By all accounts, these demonstrations were fading in the 1920s, but incidents like those related in the Michigan High School Athletic Association yearbook, pp. 179, 181, suggest the power that football had over communities. Unifying power of football in schools: Rader, *American Sports*, p. 16; Waller, *The Sociology of Teaching*, pp. 115-16.

could think of, well ahead of movies or dating, to say nothing of study or church; making the school team automatically conferred prestige. It also nurtured the dream entertained by many high school boys of becoming a celebrity on the model of the Frank Merriwell books — enjoying, as one educator of the period tartly put it, "the full and satisfactory life of the school hero, surrounded with every distinction and constantly waited upon by obsequious adults and contemporaries ready to do him every homage."[13]

There is no reason to believe that Junior Ford was immune to this dream, but he may have found another potential benefit of football even more attractive. This was the promise of self-mastery. To achieve the machine-like coordination that serious football demanded, players had to discipline their emotions. "Displays of temper," as Houghton put it, "no matter how provoking the occasion, do no good and generally greatly interfere with the thinking processes of the angered individual." This was essentially what Junior's mother had been telling him for five or ten years, quoting Proverbs 16:32: "He that is slow to anger is better than the mighty; and he that controlleth his spirit than him that taketh a city." Football offered two ways of dealing with anger: it provided a legitimate target for aggression, and at the same time, by constant pressure from the coach and teammates, it made sure that the anger was under control. The personal rewards off the field were palpable: more courtesy and smoothness in dealing with others, more discipline over the explosive force inside. By concentrating on self-mastery, Houghton asserted, "the player becomes introspective; then he begins to see also within others — his own teammates and his opponents. He learns to appraise others, to appreciate their weakness and their strength. In short, he has made a great stride in his understanding of human nature." It seems likely that this promise of self-mastery had a special appeal for young Ford.[14]

Naturally, one wants to know whether football delivered on this promise, whether it actually helped Ford control his temper. The answer seems

---

13. Boorman, *Personality in Its Teens*, pp. 68, 129; Waller, *The Sociology of Teaching*, p. 187. On the image purveyed by the Frank Merriwell books, see Oriard, *Dreaming of Heroes*, pp. 28-36.

14. Houghton, *Football and How to Watch It*, pp. 205-6. It was a common assertion among coaches that women teachers told them that playing on the team often improved a boy's behavior and attitude in academic classes (Mercer, "Special Values in Football," p. 286). The character-building aspect of football also appealed to GRF's parents (Ford, *TTH*, p. 47).

to be yes, but only gradually. Paul Goebel, the Michigan football star of the twenties who came back to Grand Rapids and opened a sporting goods store, a great friend of the Ford family who helped young Jerry out at several crucial times, recalled a high school game in the late twenties that he officiated. Ford was having a problem with an opponent, and both boys were getting angry. Goebel warned them, but in a pileup the other player did something Ford didn't like; Ford got up and knocked the other player down with a "good, hard belt in the chops." "You're out of this game," Goebel shouted at him, and Ford walked off the field without argument. This was early in his high school career, however; he was still learning.[15]

Something of a reputation for temper followed Ford through high school, despite the claim of his friend and teammate Art Brown that he never lost control of himself in anger. In senior year Tena Sikkema, his observant classmate, wrote a story for the school literary magazine in which she described a football captain, "George Fulton," with the same physical appearance and personality as Ford (not to mention the same initials), endowing him with a temper she described as "savage" and "fiendish." The rest of her details were accurate enough to suggest that this detail too was drawn from life, but she gave no indication of where this temper was displayed — on or off the gridiron — and may have been drawing on a reputation based on events that were one or two years old. During senior year, it appears, there were no angry outbursts, even in a year that had its share of frustrating moments.[16]

By college, Ford had developed into the impassive athlete whose emotions were under near-complete control — capable, to be sure, of deliberately savaging an opponent during a game, but only in the context of "game reasoning," which justified the action. He fought hard where fighting was called for, but otherwise seemed to have no feelings. He had learned an athlete's most challenging lesson, how to deal with losing a game; "to walk off the playing field as a sorehead or with a public display,"

---

15. Vestal, *Jerry Ford, Up Close*, p. 6. I haven't definitely identified this game. Marshall Reister (interview) thought it was a Muskegon game, probably in 1928, sophomore year. It probably is not identical with the 1928 or 1929 Union game mentioned in Sheridan, "Portrait of the Next President," p. 22, in which GRF was thrown out for allegedly kneeing an opponent in the ribs; in that case, Joe Russo, Sheridan's informant, was sure that the referee was mistaken. But it was definitely not a game in his senior year, and probably not in his junior year, when he played relatively little because of knee trouble. It could have been a junior varsity game.

16. Art Brown interview, p. 7; "Darel — Coxswain," *Pioneer*, October 20, 1934, pp. 3-4.

his code ran, "is bad for one's conscience and for one's reputation." One Grand Rapidian who came to know him as an adult praised him for "the quality of insensitivity which is essential to succeeding politically." He had also by that time, as the Houghton book promised, begun acquiring some insight into the strengths, weaknesses, and motivations of others. Football had delivered on its promise.[17]

A recurrent note in Ford's memories of his high school years is his distaste for the rivalries and feuds between fellow students, even between teammates, over things like girls' favors or recognition of athletic performance. His own response to such situations — learned from his parents, he claimed — was not to demonize his opponents but to try to find something good in everybody. His comments give no details about these high school vendettas ("several of my classmates hated each other"), but they seem to say that in high school he was very conscious of the destructive potential of his temper and took particular care to stay out of conflicts — which may be an additional reason why so many fellow students described him as "reserved," "quiet," "shy," or "silent."[18]

Center, the position for which Gettings had designated him, was what he played, almost exclusively, for the next eight years. It was a position where the responsibility far outweighed the glamor. In the wing formations popular in the twenties, the center initiated every offensive play, not by handing the ball to the quarterback as in contemporary football, but by passing it back between his legs a substantial distance, often to a back who was in motion. In addition, since substitution was very limited and each player had to play both offensively and defensively, he played the entire game, often serving as the key defensive lineman. "The center had to think in those days," recalled a college teammate. "On defense he was a linebacker or what we called 'roving center.' On offense he had to know where to pass the ball, do it accurately and with exact timing." But in the

17. On "game reasoning," see Miracle and Rees, *Lessons of the Locker Room*, p. 92. Examples of GRF's deliberately hitting hard and to hurt, which will be covered later in the chapters on his college career, are in, e.g., Vestal, *Jerry Ford, Up Close*, p. 60. GRF's own assessment in an interview was, "There were some who thought that I played very hard, and enjoyed the combat, which I did" (President Ford Committee interview, p. 12, Grand Rapids Oral History Collection, GRFL). Insensitivity: "To Benjamin Clough a synopsis of my experience in Republican politics," Stanton Todd Papers, MHC. There are hints that at a very personal level his temper remained volatile some years longer; cf. the incident cited in Cannon, *Time and Chance*, p. 29.

18. Ford, *TTH*, p. 46; Hersey, *The President*, p. 87.

1920s, as later, ball carriers got most of the spectators' attention and most of the glory.[19]

To be effective, a center had to memorize a number of routines. Different plays required different kinds of passes, as Junior was to learn — "leading the tailback a step in the direction he was going to run, putting it high and soft for a fullback coming into the line, getting it on the right hip for the punter," he recalled. "And then after you centered the ball, you had to be quick to block the opposing lineman who had the jump on you." Coach Gettings taught him these moves in rigorous repetition; he was "a stern taskmaster," Ford remembered. That was a coach's job, of course: to instill accurate performance of these physical responses so deeply that it became subconscious, mechanical. The coach wanted a performance so automatic and accurate that it would hold up against excitement, noise, or physical exhaustion. It was an ideal expressed in Houghton's satisfied report that "players have been known to have no recollection of the last part of a bitterly contested game, yet they played in perfect form until the final whistle blew."[20]

Houghton's account to some extent undercut his earlier assertion that football was a game requiring intelligence. Intelligence was important in football, to be sure — on the coach's part. But players were supposed to use primarily the noncognitive part of their minds, operating without thinking. For most purposes in football, intelligence was not an asset — nor was it a handicap; it was simply irrelevant. What was important was motivation, persistence, and practice. The Ford boy's constant practice on and off the field, therefore, was more than just another example of his ability to impress adult supervisors with his willingness and commitment; it was the recipe for becoming a good player.

So far as motivation and attitude were concerned, then, Gettings had nothing to teach young Ford. But he did have a lot of technical knowledge to share, what coaches called the fundamentals of football, matters of stance and grip, where to put your feet, how to hold the ball, how to hit with maximum effectiveness, how to avoid getting hurt unnecessarily. It was a lot like ballet or acrobatics — the careful placement of each limb,

19. On the importance of the center, see Houghton, *Football and How to Watch It*, pp. 38-39, 151, 153, and "Fundamentals — Center Play and Pass Receiving," reprint from the *Athletic Journal*, in GRF Scrapbook #1, GRFL. The quote is from Willis Ward, cited in Vestal, *Jerry Ford, Up Close*, pp. 61-62.

20. Cannon, *Time and Chance*, p. 12; "Fundamentals — Center Play and Pass Receiving"; Houghton, *Football and How to Watch It*, p. 106.

each muscle — with the additional challenge that it took place in an environment of rough physical contact. The center's stance, for instance: a center had to stand with legs wide apart, butt down, weight evenly distributed, one foot back to stabilize his stance and to be able to charge as soon as the ball was passed. Lore like this was probably the most valuable information the coach had to impart to a committed player. It was fairly standardized throughout the game, but every coach, because of his own training, had a slightly different approach, and every player adapted the coach's training — as one said, "You do what the hell your coach says if you're smart" — modifying it to his own physique. Junior Ford, for instance, either because of Gettings's method or through his own experimenting, ended up developing an unusual splay-fingered grip on the ball.[21]

After a busy summer at camp, Junior returned with the other ninth-grade football players to take a place on the second team, coached by "Pop" Churm, a well-liked history teacher and administrator who had been responsible for all the interscholastic teams before Gettings was hired. Varsity and second team practiced together on the Garfield Park practice field, doing exercises, running laps around the swimming pool, blocking and tackling, covering punts, and especially the all-important calisthenics — "arms flung out, stretched high, knees lifted, legs kicked out, straining backs, perspiring bodies," in the words of an eyewitness. Gettings worked them hard, especially early in the season when there was more light after school. Sometimes the players didn't get home until eight o'clock.[22]

The idea of playing football by artificial light was still remote for Michigan high schools in the 1920s, although some Lansing schools would begin experimenting with night football in 1930. For South players, football games were Saturday afternoon affairs, usually at 2:30 unless South was playing half of a doubleheader. Daytime football was only one of many ways in which the game of the 1920s differed from the game played later in the century. It was still the era of the round ball; not until 1934 was the ball's diameter slimmed down to its present size. There were no hash marks on the field; every down began where the previous play had ended, even if it was only a yard from the sidelines. Scoreboards, where they existed, were manual, not electric; only the scorekeeper knew how much

21. "Fundamentals — Center Play and Pass Receiving"; Luckman, *Luckman at Quarterback*, pp. 3-4; Whittingham, *What a Game They Played*, p. 224.
22. Garfield Park field: Marshall Reister interview. The description of practice is actually from South's great rival, Union High (*Unionite*, October 1927, p. 20); I assume it is equally applicable to South. Late practice: Art Brown interview, p. 4.

time was left in a period. The equipment itself was much simpler: leather helmets ("you could sure feel it if you got rapped pretty hard on the head"), no face masks (Ford's teammate Russ Koepnick would become one of innumerable high school boys to break his nose playing football), no tape, and little protective gear of any kind beyond the basic hip and shoulder pads.[23]

The game, despite its growing popularity, still did not command the automatic prestige that it would later in the century, and communities did not feel obliged to spend a great deal of money on it. Facilities, by later standards, were primitive. South High, for example, did not have a playing field of its own until 1930 — the team practiced a few blocks away at Garfield Park and, like most Grand Rapids high school teams, played their games at Island Park, a centrally located, "pebble-filled, rough, muddy" field in which the last three yards at one end were uphill. Other communities where South played had similar fields; at one Holland game in wet weather there were six inches of water on the last ten yards at one end, and the referee had to hold the ball in place. The red-and-blue South High uniforms were a similar problem; there were never enough to go around, and some were in really bad condition. At the beginning of the 1929 season, their appearance became so scandalous that the problem came before the school board.[24]

Ford's performance in the fall of 1927 was almost invisible to the public eye and even to many South students. The second team, about half of whose members were ninth-graders, or freshmen as they were sometimes called in imitation of the four-year colleges, operated in the shadow of the varsity. It went where the varsity went, week to week, and staged a contest against the opponents' second team, usually before the main game. Often the second-team game was not written up at all by the newspapermen who covered high school sports in the city; when it was, only the score and a few other details were given. But Gettings and the other coaches paid close attention to their games, because the second team was the nursery for the next year's varsity. Churm, impressed by the Ford boy's intelligence and drive, experimented with using him as a linebacker on defense, but he worked best as a center. By the end of the season he had established

23. *Herald,* August 31 and September 27, 1930; Rader, *American Sports,* p. 211; Whittingham, *What a Game They Played,* pp. 54, 71, 134; Harold Bosscher interview.

24. *The Reflector,* GRF Scrapbook #1, p. 35; Harold Bosscher interview; Cannon, *Time and Chance,* p. 12; Minutes of Informal Committee Meetings, September 16, 1929, October 6, 1930, Leslie H. Butler Papers, MHC. These problems were not unique to Grand Rapids; compare the experience of Paul Brown in Massillon, Ohio (Brown, *PB,* p. 43).

himself as the best on the team, with an unusual capacity for energizing and leading his teammates. He earned his reserve letter and a likely spot on the varsity for the next year.[25]

He had also acquired a new nickname — not "Whitey" (which he might have preferred) but "Junie." Short for "Junior," it was the product of his teammates, who called him "Junie" throughout his high school football career. He was glad to have the name from a group he liked belonging to, and also glad not to be called "Junior." High school was a good time for changing names and assuming a new identity closer to adulthood; beginning in the tenth grade, he tried to convince teachers and new friends to call him "Jerry" like his father. Off the field, however, he was still "Junior" to most of his old friends. Evidence from high school publications and classmates' memories suggests that the results were thoroughly mixed. To some at South he was Gerald, to some Jerry, to some Junior. He signed his classmate James McNitt's annual both "Gerald" and "Jr." In a fashion not too uncommon for adolescents, he had several slightly different identities, corresponding to different groups in his life. This narrative, for the rest of his years at South, will refer to him as Junie, the name used by the group to whom he felt closest, his fellow athletes.[26]

Ninth grade was the year in which the high school experience really began, because only in that year were all the members of the class finally together in one place. Several feeder schools sent students on to South High — some, like Madison, in the seventh grade, others in the eighth, and still others, like Burton Junior High, in the ninth. For that matter, seventh and eighth grades at South High, technically speaking, were South Junior High School, housed in the same building, with the same principal. At the beginning of the ninth-grade year, then, the class of 1931 came together for the first time, some four hundred strong. Not all of them would graduate

25. A typical schedule is in the announcement of the 1930 South–Ottawa Hills game in GRF Scrapbook #1, p. 31, GRFL. The varsity played at 2:30, the second team at 1:30. Sometimes the fortunes of the second team were covered in the South High yearbook, as in the 1931 *Pioneer*, p. 88, and sometimes they were ignored, as in 1929. Leadership on second team: Leroy, *Gerald Ford — Untold Story*, pp. 42, 44.

26. One could summarize it this way: "Junior" was Ford's family nickname; "Jerry" was the adult identity he wanted; and "Junie" was his high school persona. "Junie" was what most people at South called him most of the time. One classmate remembered, "Even Mr. Krause called him Junie" (Kenneth Hayes, in the *New Pioneer*, #40). On the importance of nicknames in high school, see Ralph Keyes, *Is There Life after High School?* pp. 35-36. The McNitt yearbook is mentioned in James H. McNitt, "Men of South High School, On to Victory," in Composite Grand Rapids File, GRFL, p. 1.

from South — only about half would — but in their numbers, together with the three upper classes, they formed part of a relatively new American phenomenon, the large urban public high school, mass education for adulthood.[27]

It is remarkable how early in its existence the comprehensive high school assumed the features that would characterize it for the rest of the twentieth century — the big square buildings; the dominance of athletics, with enormous gyms and big pep rallies; the students rushing through crowded hallways from class to class; the numbingly familiar sequence of subjects: English, biology, chemistry, algebra, geometry, Latin, American history; and most of all, its distinctive atmosphere of a world dominated by adolescent concerns, where daily dramas of love, rivalry, and ambition were enacted amid the total unawareness of the adult custodians who were supposed to be guiding the process. Students of the institution have come to agree with the casual comment of a college senior quoted by one of them: "High school is always the same."[28]

As a token of how little the high school experience, in some respects, changed from 1925 to 1995, consider some reminiscent lines by Sid Nadolsky, a classmate of Junie Ford, on the smells that permeated the halls of South High in the early 1930s — an olfactory history that could be written about any twentieth-century American high school:

> Remember those exotic smells
> They weren't those of Taco Bells.
> Past rooms of test tubes filled with dregs
> Of stuff that smelled like rotten eggs.
> And from the locker room and gym
> Those sweet aromas never dim,
> 'Cause we were healthy, sweaty jocks

27. Marshall Reister, in an interview, said that all seventh-graders north of Stewart Street went to South, and all south of Stewart went to Burton Junior High for two years. James McNitt notes the separate administrative existence of South Junior High in "Men of South High School," p. 1.

28. The senior was, oddly enough, named P. J. O'Rourke; see Keyes, *Is There Life after High School?* p. 240. Other instances of the same conclusion abound in Keyes's book: James S. Coleman, in a study, cited the "striking . . . similarity of all the schools in the importance attached to athletics" (p. 234); Keyes himself (p. 206) had no difficulty reading the motivations of a 1920s high school graduate in terms of a conceptual model derived mostly from the 1950s and 1960s.

Who seldom ever changed our sox.
And that peculiar smell of smoke
Came from the forge of burning coke,
In which cold steel was soon turned hot
And hammered into Lord knows what.
But from Home Ec. a sweet surprise,
Mouth-watering smells of cakes and pies.
However the cafeteria fare,
The menu had a certain air:
From green beans to baking pike,
Everything would smell alike.[29]

The features of the high school experience that loomed largest to students were largely unintended consequences of the efforts of a small group of educators in the early years of the twentieth century. These men, advocates of "social efficiency" or "education for life," had argued that high school should not be just for those middle-class children who intended to go on to college, but should also teach skills useful in industry, home-making, and citizenship; high school should be "comprehensive," taking in the nonacademically inclined. This vision entailed larger buildings and more courses; it meant coursework that separated the vocational from the college-bound; but most of all it meant herding together an unprecedented number of fourteen-to-seventeen-year-olds, seven hours a day, under the more or less effective supervision of a few adults. It called into being an essentially all-adolescent world, in which adolescent values were supreme, which would shortly acquire a distinctive name — the "peer group."[30]

Traditionally, American society had integrated its young people into adult life one or two at a time, as clerks and apprentices, operators and secretaries, hands on the family farm or on a neighbor's farm. Formal education, the grouping of children for learning basic information, ended

29. Nadolsky, "High School '31," in *New Pioneer*, #42 (October 1989). I have changed spelling and punctuation in some cases for clarity.

30. Krug, *Shaping of the American High School, 1880-1920*, chap. 11, especially pp. 273-83; Kett, *Rites of Passage*, pp. 235-36. Kett also observes (p. 254), in a remark that has clear implications for a working-class high school like South, "In a real sense, a youth who dropped out of high school ceased being an adolescent [or, as one could rephrase it, a member of the peer group]. Instead, he became a young adult." The first *OED* citation for "peer group" is 1943; the phrase probably was coined in the 1930s.

at fourteen, if not before; from then on, the young person was on his or her own, part of an adult group, learning by observing older people and striving to acquire their skills, meeting other members of his or her own age group only occasionally, after hours. The few exceptions to this pattern had to do with institutions like the army and the church, in which young men were preparing for a specialized adult role and had a lot of additional learning to master.

Many American families in the 1920s continued to prefer this traditional model to the new glittering promise of high school. Particularly in a working-class district like that of South High, and often at the request of the students themselves, parents let their children leave school after age fourteen, when they were no longer covered by the compulsory attendance law, and begin earning money. Boys and girls who stayed in South after fourteen, even if they were motivated by the hope of increasing their lifetime earning power and their social status, often took part-time jobs immediately after school to get a toehold in the adult world. By doing so, they missed out on many of the extracurricular activities, like pep rallies and after-school dances, that gave adolescent social life its special flavor. The high school experience at South was pallid compared to that at its business-class rivals, Central and Ottawa, whose students created almost an adolescent country-club environment with their social clubs and lavish spending. Nonetheless, it was essentially the same: an institutional world dominated by the peer group, rapidly maturing in physique, social skill, and intelligence but stuck in a period of prolonged tutelage. As Joseph Kett suggested, the high school experience defined and validated the term "adolescent."[31]

The main topic of thought and a recurrent topic of conversation, for these hundreds of young people going through puberty, was what could be called either, according to the person and the occasion, romance or sex. "To touch a girl, to dance with her, to have one take my arm, to say goodnight, are just about the things that are most wonderful to me," confessed one high school boy. "If I am talking to a girl at a dance, and I touch her hand, or happen to lean against her when I am talking, I am moved and excited, although I don't mean uncontrolled." Most of his male peers were "girl-crazy" like him, although they did not express it in such naive, minute language; but the striking thing about all these urges is that the great majority of them were unconsummated — and, for that reason, all the

31. Kett, *Rites of Passage*, p. 254.

more obsessive. A cartoon, "'Tis Educashion," in the South High *Pioneer*, showed, in traditional fashion, a South boy stumbling through his classes and making stupid errors, haunted by the vision of a girl with bobbed hair and pouting lips. For high school boys, adolescence meant some furtive experimentation and a great deal of frustration, in contrast to the experience of their contemporaries who had entered the workplace. In that adult milieu, conversation about sex was practical, graphic, based on reality, and slightly disgusting — at least that was the feeling of boys who experienced both worlds. High school, in contrast, was an idyll.[32]

With sex a constant but mostly unexpressed presence, the perpetual themes in student lives were acceptance and exclusion, associated for each boy and girl with the painful process of coming out from the protective cocoon of family identity into a larger society in which their bodies, their interests, their clothes, their habits, their money or lack of it were subjects of scrutiny in a way that mimicked the values of adult society, but in a peculiar context. High school became a search for allies, for people of similar dress, interests, and manners, with whom one could band together and achieve some sort of social status — because, as one student of the process put it, "life as a member of the undifferentiated mass is unbearable." Students formed cliques based first, usually, on grade and gender, then on interests — "athletics, dating, music, and scholastic success" being four of the most common. Acceptance versus exclusion from the clique of one's choice became the overriding fact of life; writing of a typical high school student of the 1930s, one teacher said, "Those who populate these groups are the real people of earth for him. The activities of these groups are vivid and interesting, and all else is dull by comparison. The loyalties of this world are paramount, and they exclude others. Adults do not enter this world."[33]

The dramas of this world, at South High, were played out on a variety of stages: the "session room," a sort of combination homeroom and study hall for over a hundred students, usually all male or all female, where students assembled at the beginning and end of the school day; the steps of the school, or of the student hangouts across the street, Nye's drugstore and Bill's sandwich shop, during lunch hour; the after-school dances in

---

32. Boorman, *Personality in Its Teens*, pp. 110, 187. For similar contrast in the conversational atmosphere between school and work, see Stockwell, *Rudderless*, p. 134.

33. Keyes, *Is There Life after High School?* pp. 34-36, 191-92; Gordon, *The Social System of the High School*, pp. 23-25; Waller, *The Sociology of Teaching*, 181.

the gym; the off-campus social affairs of groups like the band and the Hi-Y Club. Girls agonized over their complexions and their hair, boys over basic things like clean hands and buttoned flies. Friends got together to discuss events of the day, to plan activities together, and, implicitly, to comment on other groups in their social universe. In contrast to its business-class rivals, Central and Ottawa, South did not have social fraternities and sororities sponsored by adults in the community, so that one kind of exclusiveness was lacking; but one can be sure that cliques, an inseparable part of high school life, existed just the same. ("We can say with pride that we haven't any cliques," claimed the senior class history in the 1931 annual — Ford's class; but the context made it clear that the writer was referring to ethnic-based cliques, especially old-stock Americans versus immigrants' children, which very likely existed at Central and Ottawa but not at multiethnic South.)[34]

Junie Ford took the line of least resistance as cliques began solidifying in ninth grade. Like many athletes, he hung out mainly with other athletes, in a sort of separate caste. Doubtless his shyness had something to do with this. Football and basketball players, and members of the track team — the three "major" sports at South, as at most high schools — pretty much constituted his social universe. (They were not "jocks" yet; that term, with its slightly daring allusion to male anatomy, would come into use a generation later.) When Fielding Yost, the legendary head coach at the state university, addressed the student body in February 1928, accompanied by a phalanx of ex–football greats from Grand Rapids, including the Fords' friend Paul Goebel, Junie listened closely — this was his immediate future. When his schoolmates remembered him later, it was nearly always in an athletic context. Even the nonathletic recollections were apt to have a sort of dumb-jock quality about them, as in the case of the tenth-grade girl who remembered Junie and a couple of his buddies, just for fun, blocking her way down an aisle in English class.[35]

In terms of status among his classmates as a whole, he had some obvious strong points. His blond good looks attracted the attention of others and made him popular. As he grew taller, his height alone — which finally reached 6 feet 1 inch — gave him authority among other boys. His parents' social status may have given him extra cachet with some students, as a

34. 1931 *Pioneer*, p. 42.
35. *Herald*, February 2, 1928. The *OED*'s earliest citation for "jock" in anything like the late-twentieth-century sense of "dedicated athlete" is 1956.

"rich boy" in terms of the South social order. Working against him was his reticence, his quietness; he was likable, but not fun. But the characteristic that trumped all others, and assured him a high place in the class pecking order, was his football prowess. Without needing to strive, he was a social success. And as the 1928 season progressed, he went from a handsome, likable football player to a certified School Hero.[36]

Luck played a part. The starting center from the 1927 team had graduated, and for 1928 his place was supposed to be filled by a senior, Orris Burghdorf. Shortly before the season started, however, Burghdorf was injured, and Junie Ford with his good record from the junior varsity seemed the next best bet. Ford played the first few games, and by the time Burghdorf had recovered, the sophomore had established himself. Ford started the rest of the season.[37]

But his luck did not end there. Gettings's record in his short career at South had been less than stellar. He was just out of college and still feeling his way. His 1927 varsity had won three games and lost six. But in the 1928 season the fortunes of the Red and Blue started to change. When they played Davis Technical School, one of their rivals for the city championship, on September 15, it looked at first like the start of another mediocre season. Neither team had its game together; the first half was marked by "sloppy football" and pathetic fumbles. In the third quarter, Ford made a bad snap from center, the halfback dropped the ball, and Davis scored. But in the fourth quarter, just in time, the South team found its passing game, made two touchdowns, and won, 12-7. Likewise, the second game against Creston, another city rival, was a scoreless tie for three quarters and most of the fourth, but then the South quarterback, thanks to a good snap from Ford, faked a punt and threw a long forward pass with only three minutes to go. South scored the only touchdown of the game and seemed to have a chance at the city championship.[38]

The same pattern recurred in two later games of the season: a scoreless tie in the first half in which the teams seemed evenly matched, followed by a second half in which South won by a single touchdown. As the victories

36. On height and status, see Keyes, *Is There Life after High School?* p. 233.

37. This is the story in Cannon, *Time and Chance*, p. 12. It lacks detail; one does not learn what Burghdorf's injury was, or how long he was unable to play. Burghdorf played most of the final game, on Thanksgiving, after GRF was thrown out (*Herald*, November 30, 1928). He may also have substituted in earlier games; newspaper reports often fail to list substitutions.

38. 1928 *Pioneer*; 1929 *Pioneer*; *Herald*, September 16, 23, 1928.

piled up, sports reporters began taking Gettings's team more seriously and extolling the ball carriers in the flowery language of the twenties. Lester Nelson, the light-skinned African American track star who played halfback, became "Lightning Les," and squat Joe Russo, the fullback, was likened to an "infuriated ox." Crowds turned out at Island Park to follow their progress toward the city championship. [39]

Progress was not uninterrupted. On October 13 the Red and Blue were manhandled by the team from the neighboring city of Muskegon, a gritty industrial town where football was taken very seriously. Even so, the score was only 19-12, and South's passing game continued to be impressive. By the middle of November, with two weeks to go in the season, South had a 7-1 record, and Junie Ford was experiencing the rush of being part of a star football team — the buzz in the school corridors, the friendly comments downtown. Dorothy Ford began keeping a scrapbook to record her son's exploits. [40]

The last two games were a bit of a letdown. Both were matches against traditional rivals. Holland, the little Dutch city on the shore of Lake Michigan, was generally an easy opponent for South, but not this year. The game was played at Holland in a pouring rain that eventually drove away all the spectators except a few diehards from Grand Rapids and completely neutralized Gettings's passing attack. Covered in mud that obscured their uniforms, the teams struggled back and forth through great ponds of standing water on the field, raising fears among the spectators of a drowning before the game was over. The play was "indifferent," according to sports reporters, and the outcome a 6-6 tie. [41]

There was dry weather for the final game at Island Park against South's traditional crosstown rival, Union, the working-class high school from the West Side whose stars had names like Bozo Brzowski and Eddie Piechocki. South had already won the city championship by defeating all its other city rivals, but a Thanksgiving victory over Union would be especially sweet; in its thirteen years of existence, South's football team had defeated Union only once. City football fans in general were anticipating a major clash, a

39. *Herald*, October 28 and November 11, 1928.

40. *Herald*, October 14, 1928. Scrapbook #1 in the GRF Papers begins in 1928; a summary of South's season is on p. 8. Several clippings in it have handwritten comments by DGF. Internal evidence, however, suggests that GRF, around his senior year at South, took over responsibility for keeping it current.

41. *Herald*, November 18, 1928. This is undoubtedly the Holland game mentioned by Bosscher in his interview, when ten inches of water were on parts of the field.

"spectacular encounter," as the *Herald* put it; more than 10,000 jammed Island Park and watched from neighboring rooftops and boxcars. But, except to Union fans, the game was a disappointment. The West Siders dominated the field all afternoon, even into the dusk that closed the game. None of Gettings's plays worked as they were supposed to. South couldn't seem to get together, and lost 12-0.[42]

Junie Ford watched most of the game from the bench. In the first quarter an official sent him off the field for kneeing a Union player in the ribs, and Burghdorf played the rest of the game. Ford was adamant, even years later, that it was a bad call, that he hadn't done anything, but he was keenly embarrassed at being on the sidelines while his teammates were hard pressed in the center of the field. (One wonders how much his reputation for temper influenced the referee's call.) As twilight thickened, he ended the season with a bitter taste in his mouth.[43]

Or so he thought. But the real end of the season came two days later, when the *Herald* announced its selections for the all-city high school team. Ford's luck continued to hold. Union's outstanding center, Tony Dauksza, had been out much of the season; so had Bert Koning of Central. Weighing all the factors, Heinie Martin of the *Herald* judged Ford the year's best center, for "his hard, earnest, and aggressive work all season." The selection meant a photo on the front page of the Sunday sports section, duly clipped and pasted into his scrapbook, another on a special page in the South High *Pioneer* that June, and a first taste of wide public recognition. "Earnest and aggressive" was different from becoming an Eagle Scout; it marked Junie as someone peers and perhaps adults would have to reckon with. It was not the last time either word would be applied to him.

---

42. *Herald*, November 29 and 30, 1928. The stats for the Union-South rivalry come from *Herald*, "Union's Title Dreams Shattered as South Passes Way to 12-7 Victory," 1929.

43. *Herald*, November 30, 1928. Sheridan, "Portrait of Our Next President," p. 22, mentions a conversation with Joe Russo years later in which GRF was still denying any wrongdoing; clearly, his absence from the rest of the game weighed on him. Harold Bosscher, interview, mentioned a similar incident but thought it took place in a game against Davis Tech.

CHAPTER 6

Brainy Jerry Ford

Junie Ford's dream season took place against the backdrop of a highly unusual national presidential election. President Coolidge had unexpectedly decided to step down, and the contest to succeed him was between his talented Commerce secretary Herbert Hoover for the Republicans and Al Smith, the Catholic governor of New York, for the Democrats — the first Catholic ever nominated for that office by a major party. Prohibition and religion were underlying issues as the candidates argued social and economic policy. On November 6, 1928, the Tuesday before South's game with Catholic, Grand Rapidians, like the rest of the nation, went to the polls. A campaign to increase turnout, led by several civic and women's organizations, was in progress; "Get Out the Vote" banners, many held by serious-faced women, reminded citizens of their civic duty. Grand Rapids voters as a whole were religious, civic-minded, and dependable supporters of the Michigan Republican Party. Most of them voted for Hoover, who won the national election by about 55 percent, but in Kent County his vote topped Smith's by about three to one. Even on the Catholic West Side, Hoover had significant support; students in Union High's speech and debate class, for example, favored him by three to one as well.[1]

In the aftermath of the election, the *Grand Rapids Herald* ran interviews with a group of representative citizens on the new president's administration and the figures he ought to name to his cabinet. Someone suggested Gerald Ford Jr. to them as a high school student who knew something about public affairs, and sure enough, the sophomore center responded

1. Gitlow, *The Big Vote*, p. 137; *Unionite*, October 1928, p. 14.

with a plausible list of cabinet appointments — ex-president Coolidge for secretary of state, Senator Borah for Interior, General Pershing for War, ex-governor Lowden for Agriculture. The names were reasonable — they were not the men Hoover actually chose, but all were well-known Republicans. The boy clearly was up to date on politics. It was not the only time he surprised people with a depth of knowledge unexpected in a football lineman.

To people who knew the family, it was obvious where Jerry Jr. had gotten his information: Jerry Sr., who followed public affairs closely. Like almost everyone in the Grand Rapids business establishment, he supported Republican values, without being active in politics to any degree — he had no time. He talked about political news regularly at the dinner table — not like a Joe Kennedy or a Will Buckley, to prepare his sons for government, but simply to express his own sense of community duty. Practical politics had no attraction for him, but questions of right and wrong did. Like any Michigan Republican, he went for fiscal prudence and self-restraint in foreign policy.[2]

To all his judgments his eldest boy was an attentive listener. They chatted about city problems occasionally, and they talked about people. "We got into a discussion about somebody one time," Junie remembered, "and I said, 'Oh, he's no good. He does this, or he does that.' And he said, 'Well, but he also does this, which I like — and you ought to like.'" Jerry Ford used adult realism and tolerance to temper his son's judgments.[3]

Taciturn in most of his classes at school — perhaps a legacy of his childhood fear of stuttering — young Ford spoke up frequently in classes related to history or civics, where he felt that the information gained from his father gave him something to contribute. Classmates at South

---

2. "If I Were a Hoover," without a date, is pasted into GRF Scrapbook #1A, GRFL. "Ford, Senior, was always interested in politics," remembers a neighbor of earlier days (clipping from *The Almanac*, December 13, 1967, Thomas Ford Scrapbook, GRFL, p. 27). But a story from a few years later makes it clear that his interest was ideological and not practical. In 1940 he sent GRF, home from Yale and afire with enthusiasm for Wendell Willkie's candidacy, to talk with the Republican boss Frank McKay about speaking in the campaign. But McKay, uninterested in chatting with a law school student who had nothing substantive to offer him, kept GRF waiting in his office three hours and then dismissed him after a cursory interview. GRF Sr. clearly understood little about McKay's style of politics (Cannon, *Time and Chance*, p. 30) and admitted the fact when, in 1944, he told a group of Republican Party reformers trying to recruit him that "he had never been in politics [and] knew nothing about it" (Ter Horst, *Gerald R. Ford*, p. 11). See also Vestal, *Jerry Ford, Up Close*, p. 48; Arthur Brown interview, Grand Rapids Oral History Collection, GRFL, p. 5; Ortquist, *Depression Politics in Michigan, 1929-1933*, p. 18.

3. Hersey, *The President*, p. 91.

who studied history or economics with Junie were apt to think of him as a good student. In Miss MacLennan's American history class senior year, other students who wanted a distraction would often try to get a debate going between him and Tena Sikkema, his brilliant, awesomely articulate Dutch-born classmate. Tena, who embodied European realism, matched her Dutch-accented flights of argument against Junie's stolid recitation of facts in a fairly even battle. Looking back years later, she recalled his views as "provincial" and "business-oriented" — as of course they were, being essentially his father's. Other classmates too remembered him as a "conservative Republican." But conservatism was no handicap in Grand Rapids, and in history — European, modern, or American — he made straight A's — his best subject next to physical education.[4]

In other subjects his grades were not so high. And he was less verbal; Lucy Reed, his favorite English teacher, who had him in both seventh and tenth grade, described him, fairly typically, as "quiet, attentive, and always prepared." Other teachers might have agreed with Cynthia Stocking, who taught math: "an average student, but an excellent athlete." But after an undistinguished year in ninth grade, his grade-point average hovered pretty consistently around 3.0, or 90 on a 100-point scale. He was definitely in the top third of his class throughout high school, and hence eligible for the National Honor Society. Dorothy Gray, the "brains of the class," as one student called her, remembered being initiated together with him as a senior. For a football player, such academic prowess was enough to win him a reputation as "Brainy Jerry."[5]

4. Interviews with Florence Johnson Moore, 1997; Arlene Loverin Willison, 1997; Tena Sikkema Streeter, 1997. James H. McNitt, "Men of South High School, On to Victory," in Composite Grand Rapids File, GRFL.

5. His four-year grade-point average was 89.6, according to a World War II report from the Office of Naval Intelligence, GRFL. Reed: *Logansport (Ind.) Pharos Tribune*, no date, clipping in "Childhood and Youth" file, GRFL; William Schuiling interview, 1997; Dorothy Gray Guck to author, September 25, 1997. Stocking: *New Pioneer*, #74, June 1996. His official transcript, or "Grand Rapids High School Scholarship Record Card," is also in GRFL.

GRF's selection to the National Honor Society (NHS) has led to some misleading inferences. Some (Schapsmeier and Schapsmeier, *Date with Destiny*, p. 10) have used it to claim that he was in the top 5 percent of his class scholastically; others (Clifford Gettings interview transcript, Grand Rapids Oral History Collection, GRFL, p. 12) have settled for 10 percent. In fact, the only academic requirement for admission to the NHS was being in the top third of the class; only 15 percent of the class could be admitted, but their selection was made by the principal and faculty based on nonacademic considerations (Parker, "A Comparison," p. 7). Dorothy Gray: Don Daverman interview, 1997.

Secrets of his success were simple. Like many successful athletes, he had the ability to focus on a single activity and exclude everything else from his mind. He used it to good advantage in his schoolwork; he could spread his books all over the dining table while his little brothers played on the floor, and not lose his concentration. Most important, he had been drilled in good study habits by his mother, who had supervised his work in grade school every night and had taught him the importance of uninterrupted work. He had the ability to master a large body of facts, and as a rule came to class prepared. In history and football, genuine interest led him on; in other subjects, discipline and hard work.[6]

He had the best of motivations to study hard in high school. His friend Allen Elliott, who would be starting quarterback in their senior year, put it this way: "Not many of us harbored a thought of entering college, consequently most of us selected courses of study that would get us through high school. Not Jerry — he knew what he wanted to do and what he needed to do to reach his goal: the University of Michigan and a law degree." As early as the eighth grade, at the same time he began calling himself "Jerry" rather than "Junior," he showed that he had his eyes set on college. When he selected his courses for ninth grade, he chose Latin I and algebra; both were part of the standard college requirements in the 1920s, and there was no other reason for studying Latin. He sweated over four years of the language, which he found difficult, and four years of math, because they were part of the preparation of a college man. His parents knew of, and encouraged, his ambition. His stepfather, according to Ford, "was very influential in stimulating me to go to college," and his college-educated mother naturally supported him.[7]

But the idea of law school was most likely Junie's own, although one of his younger brothers was convinced that "Jerry became a lawyer . . . because of Dad's direction." It was a strange choice for a youngster who had difficulty with verbal expression. An aspiring lawyer was supposed

6. Schafer, "Salute to a Native Son"; GRF interview with Cannon, April 25, 1990, pp. 1-2: "They expected high performance, and monitored it." Charles M. Kindel, in his 1982 interview, GRFL, referred to GRF's remarkable memory for names.

7. Leroy, *Gerald Ford — Untold Story*, p. 44; Potter, "A Legacy of Leadership," p. 30; Vestal, *Jerry Ford, Up Close*, p. 45. The deposition of Dorothy G. King, October 10, 1930, Douglas County, NE, District Court records, *King v. King*, at GRFL, confirms his career intentions. On the question of parental influence, compare Harvey Graff's observations (*Conflicting Paths*, p. 313) on middle-class fathers' influencing their sons in this era toward political interests and a desire for power.

to be a fluent speaker, and many young people chose to study law precisely because they had a talent with words and hoped to use it to gain a living and even show off their rhetorical skill. This profile was not Junie's, though he tried to cultivate his verbal ability. In tenth grade he tried out for South's well-regarded debating team, which made it to the state finals that year. But, articulate as he was in history class, the words just would not come in a more formal setting. Miss Joanna Allaben, who coached the team, finally told him he was just not cut out to be a debater, and other incidents from his high school years seemed to bear her out. His speech on formal occasions was halting even for an athlete; at the 1930 football banquet, when Junie, the new captain, was called on for a speech, he got up, gulped, and sat down without a word. But this problem did not make him rethink his career choice; he seemed to assume that at some point, somehow, he would overcome it.[8]

In his autobiography Ford gave a different motivation for pursuing a law degree. He had no vision of himself as a trial lawyer, he said; he saw himself as a conciliator, an office lawyer who would meet with all the parties and use his knowledge to help them settle their differences for their own and society's benefit. This concept fit the mold of his earlier childhood experiences: his stepfather's three rules of conduct, his mother's unremitting insistence on study, the Scout path to merit badges and Eagle rank, the rules that provided a framework for competitive sport. Human affairs, his experience seemed to say, were governed by rules, and a person who knew the rules and helped others obey them was doing good for both the participants and society. This characteristic, "playing the game according to the rules," was singled out as one of Ford's strengths by "Pop" Churm, counselor of the South High senior class and Ford's track coach. It was a view some physical education teachers promoted strongly as a step to good citizenship, and Junie may have heard it from them in his early school years, but it resonated strongly with his own outlook.[9]

8. "Jerry became a lawyer": Vestal, *Jerry Ford, Up Close*, p. 45. GRF recalled being one of six members on the debate team in junior and senior year (Cannon interview, April 25, 1990, GRFL). Art Brown (interview transcript, GRFL, p. 9) also asserted that he was on it, but he is not listed with the team in any of the South High yearbooks for 1929, 1930, and 1931. *Miami Herald*, "Treasure Coast" section, March 8, 1989, is the source for the story about Miss Allaben. The football banquet was reported in the *Grand Rapids Herald*, December 24, 1930.

9. Ford, *TTH*, pp. 53-54; Doris Berglund, "Jerry's Ex-Teachers Recall His School Days with Particular Pride," *Press*, August 13, 1974. A 1922-1923 Michigan educational periodical

One other characteristic was desirable for a lawyer: competitiveness. In his junior year he was one of the two best students in "Modern History," the kind of class he liked, with a wealth of facts and clear rules for performance; the other was a fifteen-year-old sophomore, Virginia Berry, who was taking extra courses to graduate early. "Our teacher gave weekly exams," she remembered later, "and the way it went one week I would get a ninety-six and Jerry a ninety-three, next week he'd get a ninety-seven and I'd get a ninety-four. I sat in the back of the room and Jerry up front, and every time exams were returned he would come back to ask what my grade was. He didn't resent it if I got a better grade, he was just checking. We both got A's in that subject, the only two in the class."[10]

Occasionally his performance slipped; in those cases, he learned, personal contacts could sometimes help. Ken Hayes, who was on the track team with him, was also in Miss Wilson's tiny Latin IV class senior year, slogging his way through the *Aeneid*. Good, ambitious students, Junie and Ken shared a lonely distinction: they were the only boys in the class. Ken was president of the Sodalitas Latina second semester, and Junie showed up for the yearbook photo wearing a coat, tie, and vest, complete with watch chain and fob. On the day of the semester exam, Ken mistook the time of the test and arrived seriously late. Miss Wilson would not let him take the test: there was no way he could complete it and pass, she said, but he could try to talk with Mr. Krause the next day. The next day Ken and his normally stern mother, now in tears, had a tense interview with Krause, who said he could do nothing, and that Ken would have to take an F on the exam. As they were leaving the office, a big man brushed by Ken going in. It was Jerry Ford, with Junie in tow. Junie, it turned out, had also mistaken the time of the exam, and had had the same experience as Ken. Addressing Krause, his Masonic brother, as "Arthur or Art," Ford Sr. demanded to know if the problem couldn't be fixed, and after pondering a bit, Krause decided it could. Both Junie and

made the connection this way: "It is not too much to say that the most educative thing for good government is our school athletics. The rules are first made by those who play and then the referee sees that the game is played according to the rules" (quoted in Mitchell, "The Growth of Physical Education and Allied Movements," p. 262).

10. Vestal, *Jerry Ford, Up Close*, p. 59. Berry remembered it as an American history class, but at South, American history was a twelfth-grade subject. She also recalled her age, fifteen, and the fact that it was GRF's junior year. Since she appears in the 1930 annual but not in 1931, I assume that she got the school year (1929-1930) right and the class wrong.

Ken could make up the exam the next day at 3 P.M. The Latin credit Junie needed for college was safe.[11]

College would cost money — several hundred dollars a year, which in the 1920s was a considerable amount. But in 1929, at the beginning of young Ford's junior year, the family's financial picture seemed brighter than it had ever been. Ford Sr.'s hard work over the past few years had paid off spectacularly, and he was about to become head of his own business.

Since joining Grand Rapids Wood Finishing in 1923, Jerry had made rapid progress at work, earning $75 a week plus expenses by 1927, which put him well in the upper half of American wage earners. Albert Simpson, the boss, was a good man and a fellow Mason — they belonged to the same lodge, Malta — who admired Jerry's character and sales skills, and helped him get involved in Scottish Rite Masonry with its dramas and public presentations. Toward the end of the 1920s, Simpson, like most Grand Rapids manufacturers, was forced to deal with fundamental changes in the nature of the furniture industry. The first part of the decade had been excellent, with customers looking for high-end specialty and custom finishes; but beginning around 1924, Grand Rapids found itself threatened in the lower-end lines by competitors in Southern states, where wages were lower. Furniture production stagnated, and from 1927 some factories began cutting back or closing.[12]

Simpson, looking for some way to counteract the decline in varnish orders, decided to open a division that would make wall paint and sell it wholesale to the trade in western Michigan — decorators, painters, and institutions like hospitals and hotels. Jerry Ford, with his experience in that line, seemed the man to head it. Simpson bought a concrete block factory on the West Side in late 1927, on the Pere Marquette railroad, and began installing paint-making machinery. Then, on further consideration, he

11. Interview with Kenneth Hayes, 1997. The photo of the Sodalitas Latina is in the 1931 *Pioneer*.

12. For the furniture industry in the twenties, see Carron, *Grand Rapids Furniture*, pp. 81-82, and Ransom, *City Built on Wood*, pp. 68-74. A biographical sketch of Simpson appeared in the *Grand Rapids Spectator*, February 11, 1928, p. 5. The records of the DeWitt Clinton Consistory in the Michigan Masonic Museum contain GRF Sr.'s application for the Scottish Rite Lodge, sponsored by Simpson and another Mason, August 11, 1924. *Press*, October 20, 1928, carried the announcement of the "Masonic drama" *Darius*, with GRF Sr. in the title role. Grand Rapids Wood Finishing Company records, Public Museum of Grand Rapids, Ledger 12, give GRF Sr.'s salary; figures on income during the twenties are in Lynd and Lynd, *Middletown*, pp. 84ff.

decided to spin it off as a separate company if Jerry could raise the money to buy the factory. Simpson would retain a minority interest in it, but the concern would be Ford Paint and Varnish.

By the late twenties, Jerry Ford had a reputation in Grand Rapids for integrity and energy. He was recognized by his peers; he was just about to serve a term as Grand Exalted Ruler of the Elks. Comic as the title sounded, it carried real status in the business community. He not only raised the money, he also found a partner with technical credentials — Dr. Carl L. Schuman, Simpson's plant manager, a chemist who had worked for Pratt and Lambert and held several patents. The new firm at 604 Crosby Street was a minnow among the big fish of the industry — "the lowest bracket of 'little business,'" in the words of a retrospective article nine years later, with capital of $50,000 and only four employees on the factory floor. With Ford as president, Schuman as vice president, and Simpson as treasurer, it opened for business on a date that seems ominous only in retrospect — October 30, 1929.[13]

More than once that fall, doubtless, the Ford family hopped into the family auto, a LaSalle or a Chandler — Jerry drove good cars as part of his job — and motored across the river to see the unassuming little concrete-block factory that represented success and status. Junie was the only one of the boys old enough yet to work there, but it was a certainty that, come summer, he would be an employee. Summer was the busy season for house painters, and Ford Paint was going to be very much a family concern.

That fall, his mind was on football and the follow-up to South High's glorious season of 1928. As things turned out, however, South's 1929 season was a disappointment, with frustration both for the team and particularly for Junie.

It began with a shock. The season's first game, at Island Park on Sep-

13. Simpson's acquisition of the Crosby Street property is mentioned in the *Spectator* article cited in the previous note. That property appears in the 1927 city directory under the name of Spruit Bros., cement block manufacturers. The transition from a branch of Simpson's company to a stand-alone enterprise is nowhere spelled out, but it can be followed through the ledgers of Grand Rapids Wood Finishing Co. in the Grand Rapids Public Museum, Ledgers 7, 11, and 12, and Journal volume 125. A distorted reminiscence of it survives in the recollections of Veronica McLachlan, a relative of Simpson's, p. 11, in the Local History Department, GRPL. Public announcements of the opening are in *Michigan Tradesman*, October 30, 1929; *Press*, October 31, 1929; and an unidentified clipping in the Ford Paint and Varnish Scrapbook, GRFL. See also *Grand Rapids Mirror*, Summer 1938, p. 15, in the scrapbook. Benevolent Protective Order of Elks, *Golden Jubilee*, p. 14.

tember 21, was against Ottawa Hills, a new high school on the far east side of Grand Rapids, where affluent families from the Hill District were building comfortable homes. It was the first time the two schools had met, but Ottawa already had an image — a junior version of Central High, attended by socially privileged kids, with no talent for football. Their team belied the school's image. Led by an African American who happened to live within the new district's boundaries, halfback Aurelius Douglas, whom the *Herald* referred to as a "diminutive colored chap," Ottawa upset South, 10-6. The problem, as reporters saw it, was South's backfield. Ford and the rest of the line played a strong defense; but South had no offense. In their primitive dressing room after the game, the South players cried, as players do after a losing game, partly from sheer physical exhaustion, more from disappointment. It was a bitter bonding experience.[14]

A week later they were back at Island Park on "a miserable wet afternoon, with the field a virtual morass," according to a seventeen-year-old cub reporter watching damply from the sidelines (Island Park had no press box), playing Davis Technical. Gettings, in the intervening days, had managed to get some performance out of the backfield, while Ford and the line played another fine game. The South team ended mud-caked and victorious by a score of 13-0.[15]

Practice every afternoon was the time to build up bodies and spirits through endless repetition, running plays, and blocking. "I wouldn't say Mr. Gettings was a driver, but he wanted perfection," a teammate of Junie's recalled. Besides the drill, the daily sessions generated team spirit and camaraderie through activities like those described by a Union student reporter: "When practice has ended you will find that the weary day's work has not quenched the fire of mischief that runs rampant in these boys. There are vocal renditions that stir the emotions (of disgust most likely), wisecracking and repartee galore, and horse play. The fight for showers is always a spectacular battle."[16]

In a practice shortly after the Davis game, Junie Ford got hit from two sides and suffered "the most distressing common injury in football": displaced cartilage, which went by a dozen names, like "floating cartilage" and "trick knee." Two small, almost circular, pads of cartilage in

14. *Herald*, September 22, 1929; Wood, *What Price Football?* p. 41; Mercer, "Special Values in Football," p. 284, in Conklin, *Aims and Methods in School Athletics*.

15. W. B. Wolfan, "I Covered Jerry Ford's First Game Plan — Football," clipping in GRF Scrapbook #1, GRFL.

16. Art Brown interview transcript, GRFL, p. 4; *Unionite*, October 1927.

the knee joint that normally functioned to cushion contact between the two leg bones were torn loose by a strain on one of the ligaments. They floated within the joint and occasionally locked it, preventing it from closing, inducing a muscular contraction and great pain. Any coach or trainer with some experience knew how to handle the case. Young Ford, writhing in pain, was carried off the field, and the leg (the right leg, as it happened) was carefully maneuvered to open one side of the joint and let the disc escape; then gentle massage restored it to place. Next day he was fine.[17]

The worst feature of a trick knee was that, with the cartilage loose and floating about, it could recur at any time. A player could suddenly lose strength in the joint, or in the worst case, it could lock again. There is evidence that that was Junie Ford's experience. He played in later games that season, and often played well: his performance against Central was spectacular; he was in the season's last game, a loss to Union at Island Park on a raw, wintry day; and he and the rest of the line were splendid in the most crucial game of the season, the loss to Creston in which a South player muffed a catch in the end zone and cost the team its city championship. But Gettings decided not to use him in out-of-town games, relying instead on his backup, Pete Dood. Maybe he figured that an hour's bumpy ride over country roads was taking one chance too many. So Junie ended the season having played in only six games; despite that fact, he was still named to the second all-city team for that year. After his taste of stardom the year before, that was no consolation.[18]

Joe Russo had to retire on reaching age twenty after the Central game. The team chose Junie as its captain for the rest of the season, and for 1930 as well. Despite that fact, his football career, at least his career as a star player, was over unless he could find some way to deal with his knee. Sur-

17. The clearest, most detailed contemporary description of dislocated cartilage I have found was by a basketball coach: Meanwell and Rockne, *Training, Conditioning, and the Care of Injuries*, pp. 123-31. The *Pioneer* yearbook for 1930, p. 124, reported that GRF's injury occurred at practice prior to the Muskegon game; but the sports section for that year was indifferently edited and has the sequence of games confused, so that it is hard to fix a specific week. Doris Deakin, "Ford's Knee Trouble Dates to High School," *Washington Post*, June 4, 1975, states that it was the left knee; "Full Report on Ford's Health," *U.S. News and World Report*, September 9, 1974, and GRF's FBI special agent application, 1941, GRFL, call it the right knee.

18. 1930 *Pioneer*, p. 122; Tom LaBelle, "South High School, We're for You," *Press*, December 6, 1970; Wolfan, "I Covered Jerry Ford's First Game Plan"; Heinie Martin, "Union, Creston, and Ottawa Each Awarded Two Berths," GRF Scrapbook #1, GRFL.

gery, the obvious answer, traditionally had a bad name among coaches as too risky. Certainly a good orthopedic surgeon could remove the cartilage readily, the argument ran, but the incision might become infected and lead to permanent stiffness of the joint. If he escaped that, a couple of weeks in a plaster cast might weaken his muscles, perhaps permanently. In the late twenties, opinion on this score was starting to change: during World War I, American surgeons had learned a lot about keeping incisions sterile, and the time spent in a cast had become shorter; at major universities, athletic directors, trainers, and surgeons were collaborating to create the new profession of sports medicine. Gettings, however, coming from a small college, likely had learned the traditional view and discounted surgery as a solution.[19]

Fortunately for Junie, he had a source of more up-to-date information. There was a new basketball coach at South High that year, who also worked as an assistant in football — Danny Rose, the bright, assertive son of an Italian immigrant family in Rogers City, Michigan. Rose, a physical education major, taught biology and health and was just out of the University of Michigan, where he had starred on the basketball team despite his 5 feet 8 inch height. He assured Gettings and Ford that successful operations for dislocated cartilage were almost routine at Ann Arbor, and offered to drive Junie over there himself for a personal examination.[20]

The fullest source on the episode states that Junie Ford's right knee was successfully operated on "during a school vacation during or after his junior year" by Dr. Carl Badgley, a leading orthopedic surgeon at Michigan and a pioneer in sports medicine, but leaves the exact date uncertain. University Hospital records, which could answer the question, still exist but are closed for privacy reasons; one is left with a range from December 1929 to June 1930. An earlier date seems more likely, because the high-cost operation would have been at family expense; but another report places it in the summer. For the procedure itself, surgeons usually charged a sliding fee proportioned to what they considered the family's ability to pay. Hospital costs, however, were inelastic and could have been considerable if Junie's stay stretched over several days. Jerry Ford, in the euphoria of opening a new business, might have been more inclined early in 1930 to overlook the signs of a gathering economic crisis and write checks total-

19. Meanwell and Rockne, *Training, Conditioning, and the Care of Injuries*, p. 131; Frantz, "Doctor, Where Were You?" p. 146 n. 295.

20. Dinse, *Mr. C.M.U.*, pp. 27-34.

ing several hundred dollars to salvage his son's dreams. It was a smarter investment than he knew.[21]

Junie, then, made the four-hour drive to Ann Arbor at least twice that semester, one weekend with Coach Rose for examination and getting acquainted, the other, probably with his parents, for the operation itself. He had probably been there before for track meets, or with the Boy Scouts. Grand Rapids Scout troops sometimes were called on to usher at Michigan's home games, where they learned to deal with the crowds of football enthusiasts, sober and otherwise, at Michigan Stadium (one of the many instances where Scouting was more educational than its founders intended). The Scouts of Troop 15 may have taken their turn, although there is no record of it. As they passed the massive, stately academic buildings of the university, Coach Rose explained the landmarks.[22]

Junie and his knee were on display that day. He spoke little as he was taken around massive, academic-Romanesque Waterman Gym with its dozens of small windows. He met the head trainer, Charles Hoyt, later to become head coach of the track team, and George Veenker, who, like Rose, doubled as head basketball and assistant football coach. It was his first glimpse of a modern athletic establishment and first hint of the money even then connected with it. Perhaps he met Dr. Badgley; certainly he took a good look at the large, modern hospital, not suspecting how thoroughly he would get to know it over the next five years. Junie had no fear of hospitals. He had been hospitalized twice; when he was five he had his appendix removed (unnecessarily, as it proved), and he broke his collarbone in junior high. Hospitals, to him, were associated not with illness, but with repair.[23]

Whatever the date of the actual surgery, it was completely successful:

21. Deakin, "Ford's Knee Trouble." A story by sports columnist Heinie Martin in the *Herald*, August 31, 1930, reported that the treatment took place in the summer. On Badgley, see Davenport, *Not Just Any Medical School*, p. 207. On costs at that time, see Roberts, "Comparison of Medical and Hospital Costs," pp. 24-25. Thanks to Dr. Howard Markel for giving me perspective on this question.

22. Dinse, *Mr. C.M.U.*, p. 34. Denham, *Growing Up in Grand Rapids*, pp. 77-78, recounts the experience of one Grand Rapids Scout troop at Michigan Stadium in these years.

23. Images of Waterman Gymnasium are easily found online through, e.g., Google. Most are uncredited. One that is, is in *Michigan Alumnus* 26 (1919): 119. A letter from Hoyt, in GRF's FBI special agent application, 1941, GRFL, recalls the consultation; Harry Kipke to Arthur W. Krause, May 11, 1931 (Board of Control of Intercollegiate Athletics, Correspondence, Box 14, BHL), establishes that GRF met Veenker on his 1930 visit. "Full Report on Ford's Health," clipping in Scrapbook #1, GRFL. The appendectomy is from Ford, *TTH*, p. 43

the cartilage was removed, and the convalescence was evidently short and uncomplicated, for all the information about Ford in this spring involves physical activity — in the summer of 1930 he worked at three jobs, two of them involving heavy physical labor, and in the spring he threw shot put and discus on the track team. That spring, too, was the time of his encounter with his biological father — but apart from that odd episode, the predominating tone was hopefulness and satisfaction. His knee was fixed, he had seen a little of the professional athletic world and was curious to see more, and he was more and more comfortable with the fellows with whom he shared football and track.

Gettings, like most football coaches, liked to see that his players kept in condition outside football season, and one easy way to accomplish that goal was by putting them on the track team. Those who didn't have work or family obligations were usually happy to take the hint; they, too, wanted to stay in shape and enjoyed the exercise. Junie had been on the team since ninth grade, specializing in the weight events — discus and shot put. At track practice, he found himself beside most of his football teammates — tall, handsome Allen Elliott, who was to become his closest friend; the irrepressible Siki (pronounced "Psyche") McGee, a fast runner, an impromptu dancer, and a great mimic, one of the few African Americans in the school; Archie Ross, his partner in the line; little Johnny Heintzelman, the halfback, another speedy runner; and a dozen others. These boys were to be his constant companions for the next year, on the track team, the 1930 football team, and the school social organization for athletes, the Varsity Club. They were companions outside school as well, all but McGee; American mores in the thirties made social contact between blacks and whites difficult almost anywhere.[24]

The South High athletes were a different sort of group from any that Junie had associated with before. They had a collective image of themselves as lower-middle-class dead-end kids; when the 1930 football team held its reunion at the White House in 1975, Al Elliott remarked that he thought it more likely in high school that they would be having their forty-fourth reunion in Sing Sing prison than in the nation's capital. They were "a real melting pot," according to another player, and included boys from poor families who wore patched clothes to school because that was all they

24. Heintzelman: Clifford Gettings interview transcript, GRFL. Elliott and Brown are both described in Sheridan, "Portrait of the Next President," pp. 22-23. A class of 1931 publication recalled McGee "with his wide grin and ORANGUTANG walk."

had. Gettings saw them as foul-mouthed tough guys in need of discipline, and worked hard at getting them to clean up their speech, punishing them with a lap around the track for every obscenity at practice. They were, in his recollection, troublemakers, with no more than three or four players who never talked back (Ford and Elliott would have to have been two of them). From time to time he gave them motivational talks. Once he noticed some of the streetwise players ignoring his words and whispering to each other; annoyed, he "ordered them all off the field and into the gymnasium," as he told a reporter in 1973, "with the remark that they didn't deserve to win an important game coming up that Saturday." Fifteen minutes later, the whole team, headed by Junie Ford, showed up in his office to apologize. Ford had talked them into listening to the coach as they were supposed to. Just how tough these kids actually were is uncertain; the surviving evidence is pretty innocuous, but there could be buried instances of rowdyism and minor criminal behavior. One can say for sure that they were quite unlike the boys of Troop 15 or Camp Shawondossee.[25]

Socializing with these friends meant hanging out at Fletcher's Drugstore in the Italian neighborhood on South Division, where football teammates gathered to talk over the previous week's game, help Joe Russo with his schoolwork, and kick around ideas for future plays. It meant driving aimlessly around the South Side if someone had his father's car; cruising slowly past girls' houses, well-known taverns, and whorehouses; joking and swapping stories; waiting for something exciting to happen. Smoking and drinking were doubtless discussed as they rode, but not practiced much, at least not during football season. The biggest topic by far was the dates each one had had, girls and their mysterious attitudes; they compared notes on what they tried to do on dates and how much of it the girl permitted them. That was the best thing about access to a car in 1930 — it was the passport to serious dating. A car, particularly a new, good-looking one, was "quite an advantage" with girls, as one of the gang put it. "The flashier the car, the more they look."[26]

25. Gettings interview, GRFL; "'Good Old Junie' Hosts Thanksgiving Reunion," *Ann Arbor News*, November 28, 1974; Dan Troutman, "33 Years between Visits," *Marquette Mining Journal*, October 16, 1974; *Boston Globe*, December 7, 1973.

26. Dating: interview with Art Brown in Jim Mencarelli, "Life Has Changed for Ford's Pal from South High," *Press*, June 30, 1974; Art Brown interview, GRFL. For boys' attitudes, cf. the views expressed in Boorman, *Personality in Its Teens*, pp. 179-89, and also pp. 216-18 in Hynes, *The Growing Season*, a great evocation of lower-middle-class adolescent life in a Midwestern city in the 1930s.

The boys of the 1930 football team — the Trojans, as the school had decided to call its sports teams — stuck together in dating as they did on the field. Typically, they double- or triple-dated, for practical reasons like the cost of gas, and because few had cars of their own. Girls too liked double-dating, for reasons of their own: it made them feel less isolated. So two or three couples would go bowling together, to a movie, to a moonlight cruise on Reeds Lake, or, best of all from the boy's standpoint, to a school dance or public dance hall, where a dance floor offered the promise of achieving the momentous goal that preoccupied many sixteen- and seventeen-year-old males, football players and ordinary mortals alike — contact with female flesh. That experience was so satisfactory that it made correct dress, learning the dance steps, and cultivating social conversation almost worthwhile.[27]

Dating was a new way of structuring boy-girl relationships, and was hardly more than ten years old in most places. It had soared to popularity just after the Great War, especially in urban areas, as part of the conscious movement toward liberating youth from the stifling piety and hypocritical conventions of their parents' generation. It replaced the older arrangement by which the boy called at the girl's home and cultivated an acquaintance under the more or less vigilant eyes of her parents. The basic premise of dating was simple: the boy offered cash, transportation, and the promise of a good time in return for a limited amount of physical contact, during the activity itself and sometimes also on the way home, when the boy could park for a few minutes in a secluded area for some mutual exploration. This was another reason, an adolescent of that period explained, why girls favored double dates: "numbers inhibited passionate actions, and protected both girls and their dates from the scary mysteries of below-the-waist."[28]

Junie had not dated much, to the intense frustration of the young women in the class of 1931, who avidly watched this blond god in the halls

27. The name "Trojans" was actually chosen by the Varsity Club: *Pioneer*, March 20, 1930, p. 29. Double-dating: Marsh Reister interview; Sharon Bohn, "Zylstra Remembers School Days with Ford," *Sun Journal*, July 10, 1975, GRF Scrapbook #1, p. 40, GRFL. Destinations: Tena Sikkema's poem in "Fifty-First Reunion/South High School/Class '31/ Book of Poetry," p. 14, mentions several destinations for dates. Dorothy Gray in her letter stressed the centrality of dances: "I loved dances. Of course we danced fox trots, waltzes, etc., partnered with girls or boys" (Gray to author, September 25, 1997).

28. Modell, "Dating Becomes the Way of American Youth," pp. 93-96; Hynes, *The Growing Season*, p. 228; Betty Ford, *The Times of My Life*, pp. 19-20.

of South High, trying to capture his attention. He realized their interest, even writing some doggerel verses that found their way into his scrapbook about himself, "a young wolf named Junie / who drove all the women folk looney," but was too shy to make a move. Virginia Berry, the smart girl in his American history class, recalled: "I tried to get Jerry to visit my home. No success. He never would come. I got the impression of a fellow with the mind of a child in a man's body, a big St. Bernard."[29]

Now, however, he needed a girl for full participation in this part of his friends' lives, and in the course of his junior year he found her, though there is no record of when or how it happened. Her name was Mary Hondorp, and she was a senior — that is, one class ahead of him. For her he would dress well and slick down his hair with Vaseline in the approved male manner, as his friends Brown and Elliott did, instead of leaving it "in prickles, just to keep the girls away," as he put it in his verses. Mary shared several characteristics with the other women with whom he would become seriously involved in the course of his life: she was cute, cheerful, and sociable, and she was physically active, competing in high school swimming. Although she was definitely working-class and from that point of view an unlikely girlfriend, she was just right for the social milieu he was in. She and Jerry hit it off so well that they remained a couple for the rest of his high school career — that is, for nearly two years — and for some time afterward. From that winter on, Jerry's female classmates looked on enviously with the knowledge that Mary was, in the words of one, "cared for enough to keep him from dating the rest of us." At the same time, the conventions of dating made it clear to all that going steady did not necessarily lead to marriage. Jerry's parents might have had reservations otherwise. Dorothy Ford cheerfully pasted Mary's picture into the football scrapbook she maintained.[30]

---

29. Ter Horst, *Gerald R. Ford*, p. 37; GRF Scrapbook #1, GRFL; Vestal, *Jerry Ford, Up Close*, p. 59.

30. Hondorp's picture is on p. 71 of Scrapbook #1, GRFL. Richard Ford (interview, May 31, 2013) recalled seeing her with GRF as late as 1933, when the family lived on Santa Cruz Drive in East Grand Rapids. GRF's teammates thought her good-looking ("He didn't waste time on the homely ones," his friend Marshall Reister said), and the *Herald*, August 15, 1926, reported that a Mary Hondorp, possibly the same girl, won a swimming competition. Most of GRF's classmates, interviewed in 1997, carefully avoided mentioning her by name, but Bill Schuiling confirmed her identity. "Cared for enough," etc., is a phrase of Dorothy Gray Guck (letter, September 25, 1997). On the distinction between going steady and courting, see Modell, "Dating Becomes the Way of American Youth," pp. 121-23.

The Hondorps lived in the heavily Dutch southwestern part of town, on Grandville Avenue, so Junie needed a car for a visit or a friend's car for dating. Art Brown related that once his football buddies, driving around one night, spotted Junie's father's car parked in front of Mary's house. They got out and used their combined strength to pick it up and move it around a corner. Concealed, they guffawed as they watched him come out, panic at the disappearance of the car, search, and eventually find it. The next day they kidded him, and may have gotten a few swear words out of the normally clean-spoken Ford.[31]

By his junior year, then, Junie had learned to drive. Presumably his father taught him; there is no record. Learning to drive felt momentous. "Knowing that I could drive made me feel mature and capable of taking a girl out on a date," remembered a friend of Junie's from East Grand Rapids. A Midwestern boy of that era put it more tersely: "you can't do anything without a car." The driver's license ratified this power; in Michigan, you had to be fourteen to get one, and each city or county devised its own driving test, though the actual license was issued by the secretary of state. Applicants in Grand Rapids had to demonstrate basic driving skills, including knowledge of the hand signals, to a Traffic Squad policeman to get the four-inch-by-four-inch cardboard square with their height, weight, and description, and their signature on the right edge.[32]

Licensed to drive, a young man needed to master techniques of wheedling the car out of his father or other male relative when he wanted to date. (The use of the male pronoun here reflects not only Ford's gender but also the reality of the time: four out of every five drivers were male, and among adolescents the proportion may well have been higher.) Once he had the keys, the initial structure of the date — parking in front of the girl's house — was essentially that of horse-and-buggy days; but once she was in the car, the power of the motor allowed him to whisk her off to a school dance, a roadhouse outside the city, a downtown movie, or a popular wooded area on the far side of Reeds Lake with equal ease.[33]

Speed was the key, but only in a comparative sense. Popularly priced

31. Art Brown interview, GRFL, pp. 9-10.

32. Denham, *Growing Up in Grand Rapids*, p. 87; Hynes, *The Growing Season*, p. 216; Whitney, *Man and the Motor Car*, pp. 78-79; *Public Acts of the Legislature of the State of Michigan, 1931* (Lansing: Secretary of State, 1931), pp. 141-43. Items in the *Press*, March 8 and September 23, 1922, give details of the licensing process. A Michigan driver's license of the era is in the Alfred James Palmer Scrapbook, BHL.

33. Blanke, *Hell on Wheels*, p. 46.

automobiles made to go fast had not yet come on the market; that would happen two years later, when Ford introduced the V-8 engine. Downtown traffic in 1930 moved at an average of fifteen miles an hour, reflecting the congestion of streetcars, horse-drawn wagons, and autos that clogged the center of most cities. In the residential areas and the outskirts, one could go faster. Twenty or thirty miles an hour, the official speed limit, was disregarded by most drivers. (For that matter, so were stop signs and, often, traffic lights. Enforcement of traffic regulations was a brand-new idea in 1930; the first traffic police were added in 1929.) On the open road, speeds of forty and higher were possible. A South High student writing in the school magazine rhapsodized about the thrill of traveling seventy-five miles an hour in his (fictional) roadster.[34]

That sort of speed would happen beyond Grand Rapids, where the real excitement began — the prospect of traveling to the lake and its beaches, and the freedom they represented, in only an hour, for instance, or of traveling U.S. 16, now paved all the way to Detroit, and sampling the new culture that had sprung up along the highways — tourist cabins, roadhouses, truck stops, all of them brand-new institutions. The two-lane concrete ribbon crossed the flat Michigan landscape, going straight through the center of each little town and county seat. New kinds of vehicles, trucks and intercity buses, vied for room with farm wagons. Rules for passing were flexible and, like speed limits, rarely observed. The resulting high accident rate and death toll were beginning to catch the eye of insurance companies, which would begin a massive push for auto safety in the following decade. But for the moment auto owners boldly took to the highways to enjoy the benefits of technology and trusted their wits to avert disaster. Grand Rapids to Ann Arbor, 132 miles, in one's own vehicle, was now only a four-hour trip.[35]

Thrills like these, however, were unavailable to a young man driving his father's car. For a high school boy, obtaining a driver's license almost

34. McCutcheon, *The Writer's Guide*, pp. 142, 145; Barrett, *Automobile and Urban Transit*, p. 161; Blanke, *Hell on Wheels*, pp. 171-72; *Herald*, March 15, 1931 (disregard of traffic laws); 75 mph: *Pioneer*, April 10, 1930.

35. As early as 1928, a Grand Rapids business publication boasted that U.S. 16 was paved all the way to Detroit, 150 miles (*Grand Rapids Spectator*, August 11, 1928), p. 3. Manfred, *The Primitive*, pp. 57-61, offers an evocative picture of travel on a major highway in 1930 as a group of boys drives from the Plains States to Grand Rapids. On the death toll, Blanke, *Hell on Wheels*, p. 51. Driving time between Ann Arbor and Grand Rapids is from Helen Loomis to her parents, November 25, 1932, Helen M. Loomis Letters, BHL.

immediately created the desire for his own vehicle. Some achieved that goal rapidly. Rich boys at Central, Ottawa, and East Grand Rapids drove cars purchased for them by their families, but boys from less free-spending households had to negotiate parental permission and then come up with the money on their own. The sums were not large — one could buy some kind of "jillappie," as a South student spelled it, for under fifty dollars — and, beginning in the late twenties, student-owned cars in small numbers, belonging to juniors and seniors, appeared parked on Hall and Jefferson, the streets adjoining the school, or behind local businesses, beside the teachers' vehicles. They were still the flat-topped, box-like sedans of the twenties; streamlining would not come into fashion until 1934 — but increasingly, they came in distinctive colors. A student survey for the literary magazine in spring 1931 discovered five parked cars in various shades of green, with three blue ones and a yellow roadster. Some belonged to the faculty, but a Ford behind Bill's Place, "with a broken window patched very artistically with adhesive tape" and a pair of gym shoes inside, was clearly the property of a student athlete, as was an open car on Jefferson, "one of those 'Fresh Air Taxis' which looks accustomed to carrying an over abundant number of passengers," with "a sticker of two listening dogs on the windshield."[36]

Junie Ford occasionally drove his father's LaSalle to the high school — a friend recalled his backing it into a phone pole on Hall Avenue — but probably to dances and after-school affairs rather than for the school day. The arrangement was convenient for dating, but lacked the charm of ownership. Students developed quasi-personal relationships to the cars they owned, giving them pet names, decorating them with words and pictures, calling them "the old bitch" when they refused to perform. One boy claimed he could tell the make of any auto just by listening to it on the street.[37]

Junie, thus, was already nursing the desire to own a car in the spring of 1930 when a shift in circumstances made ownership not only possible but almost a necessity: his father announced they were moving that summer to East Grand Rapids. The move was connected with his new status

36. "Jillappie": *Pioneer*, March 20, 1930; parked cars, May 21, 1931, pp. 27-32. The Great Depression, officially under way by summer 1930, had little effect on auto sales in Grand Rapids, especially used car sales; see, for instance, the auto section of the *Herald* for July 6 of that year. Gasoline consumption in Michigan hit a new high in 1930 (*Herald*, March 26, 1931).

37. *Pioneer*, April 10 and May 22, 1930; Manfred, *The Primitive*, p. 215.

as president of his own firm, and 2163 Lake Drive, a big frame house on the main thoroughfare, with a den, a modern kitchen, and four large bedrooms upstairs, was clearly more appropriate. The house was in disrepair, and the family would have to spend evenings and weekends refurbishing it before moving in, but it was a clear step up. It was also in the East Grand Rapids school district, however, very close to Ramona Park and East Grand Rapids High School, where Junie, according to regulations, should expect to enroll as a senior. But as incoming captain of the South football team, he had no intention of doing so, and his father, with Mr. Krause and other influential friends, had no trouble persuading district officials that Junie should stay at South. It was an amicable arrangement; Junie himself called Reed Waterman, athletic director at East, to explain how much he would have liked to play football for them if the situation had been different. Waterman was impressed, as grown-ups often were, by Junie's sincerity and courtesy.[38]

However, 2163 Lake Drive was nowhere near within walking distance of South; to attend school there, Junie would need a car of his own, which he expected to buy with his own earnings. That meant finding a third job — he already had two: flipping burgers and washing dishes for Bill Skougis one night a week, and supplying seasonal labor at the paint factory Monday to Friday. Now he needed a weekend job as well. Fortunately Junie, like his father, was not afraid to work hard, long hours. The prospect was worth it: a fall of football with his knee in good shape, a car of his own, and the adolescent glory of senior year ahead.

38. GRF himself in *TTH*, p. 48, referred to the Lake Drive house merely as "an old house," whereas his first biographer, Ter Horst, *Gerald R. Ford*, p. 35, who knew Grand Rapids well, called it "a fine big home." Ter Horst's judgment is nearer the truth: GRF was doubtless influenced by all the arduous cleanup work he had to do. The house was torn down in the sixties to enable expansion of the high school parking lot, but a card in the Grand Rapids Real Estate Files, GRPL, describes it in detail as of 1955, with a photo. The Reed Waterman story is from Bill Wolfan, "I Covered Jerry Ford's First Game Plan — Football," *CTA News*, p. 10, in Scrapbook #1, GRFL.

CHAPTER 7

The Thirty-Thirties

The summer job that Junie took to earn money for a jalopy of his own gave rise to one of the classic Jerry Ford stories.

Ramona Park, the big East Side amusement park, within a few blocks of the Fords' new home, was a natural place to look for summer work. It was thronged from May to September with families from all over the area, with kids enjoying the roller coaster, the fun house, and the adorable miniature steam railroad that carried small children around the grounds. There were games in the ballpark; vaudeville shows all day in the old-fashioned frame theater, something of a firetrap really with its many wooden stairs; and at night some of the best bands in the state for dancing. Balloon ascensions and special shows took place against the backdrop of Reeds Lake, with its two little steamboats and flotilla of rented rowboats cruising the waves.

Junie, with two other South High boys, got a job working on weekends for Alex Demar, the Greek American who ran the concessions, for three dollars a day plus snacks. Demar especially liked Junie, "a Greek Adonis with the build of Hercules" who was respectful, called him "Mr. Demar," and asked questions about things he didn't understand. On weekends when the park was jammed with visitors — on Kiddies Day in 1929 they had 30,000 children — they carried crates of sodas and cases of Cracker Jack and hot dog buns pretty constantly, earning their pay with sweaty work. Fourth of July weekend, naturally, was the high point.

That Fourth of July, amid the widespread public consciousness of a looming economic crisis, the park was full. Demar recalled making his way through the holiday crowds, the noise, and the smells of food to check on the stands and how they were doing that busy day. He recalled seeing young Ford in motion almost constantly, carrying supplies and getting rid of empties, but not the two other boys. He asked Ford where they were; Ford didn't know. At last he located them in the back row of the vaudeville theater, blissfully absorbed in the Marcus Girls Review, dragged them out, and put them to work. The difference stuck in his mind — Ford, the blond football star, with every reason to have a bit of a privileged attitude, working in the heat while his two comrades goofed off. Demar, who recognized character when he saw it, in later years became one of Jerry Ford's strongest political supporters in western Michigan.[1]

Demar's story goes far to explain why Ford made such a strong impression on most adults who knew him, and got such glowing recommendations. Adults who worked with teenagers, used to making allowances for immaturity, for adolescent moodiness and attitude, found that with Junie Ford allowances were not necessary. The good manners he had learned from his parents, the responsibility he had acquired as an Eagle Scout and role model for younger boys, his self-discipline, and his even temperament seemed to say that he had already worked out solutions to the problems of youth and was ready to get on with the challenges of adult life. To some degree, his maturity was an illusion produced by an excellent upbringing, but the comfort and security it brought to adults were palpable.

That summer of 1930, he did more than simply display adult competence and self-control; he actually took on the leadership role of an adult in influencing sports events. He may have been influenced by Danny Rose, the bright, hard-driving basketball coach, to a vision of how preparation and planning could lead to athletic victory. As team captain, Ford wanted a winning season in 1930. So did his teammates, and, importantly, they wanted to start by avenging last season's loss to Ottawa Hills in the first game. Suppose he and the team held a football camp to get into fighting trim before the first game, with Ottawa? They could work on basic passing, blocking, and getting in shape; they could even run plays, since Junie knew the playbook by heart. Gettings couldn't organize it; he was prohibited by high school association rules. But Ford, as a player, could; and

1. Demar told this story himself in an interview in GRFL, #110. Much of the language used here is borrowed from Demar's telling, including the link with the coming Depression. GRF's recollection is in the Cannon interview, April 25, 1990, p. 4. Details about Ramona Park are from *Trolley Topics*, the newsletter of the Grand Rapids Street Railway, which owned the park, June 1928; April, May, and June 1929, GRPL; *Grand Rapids Spectator*, June 30, 1928, p. 1; Denham, *Growing Up in Grand Rapids*, p. 91; Frantz, "Doctor, Where Were You?" pp. 229-30; and Blanco, *Then Sings My Soul*, p. 29.

the idea came up either during bull sessions at Fletcher's Drugstore or in lunch-break conversation at the paint factory between Junie and Al Elliott. They needed a site, somewhere other than the school, somewhere remote enough so that Gettings wouldn't stumble across it by chance. Here Ford made the contribution that put his stamp on the whole idea — he offered the fishing cabin on the South Branch as a site. They would have to clear a playing space for themselves, but it was surely remote enough, and Ford's dad could chaperone.

The camp was a complete success. A majority of the guys were able to get away for a week and find their way up to the isolated North Woods property; they brought their own food, and Junie, using his experience on the Camp Shawondossee staff, organized them into work details to handle dishwashing, garbage, and chores. The same animal spirits visible at practice were in evidence at the cabin — the first night two groups got to horsing around, someone put his fist through a plasterboard wall, and Art Brown got a fragment of plaster in his eye that Junie's dad had to remove. Junie worried that the property damage would have consequences, but Mr. Ford was understanding. Practice went forward, with days full of intensive running, passing, and blocking, orchestrated by Junie, who drove his buddies like a coach. Someone had a camera and documented the scene. "When they came out of there," Gettings was later to say, "brother, they were MEAN."[2]

That would have been around the beginning of September, when Junie gathered his summer's wages and bought a 1924 Ford coupe, with rumble seat, for seventy-five dollars. It was not in the best of shape — Gettings called it an "old beat up Ford" — and his schoolmates and teammates vied in deriding it, then and later: "not much of a car," Bill Schuiling recalled. It spent considerable time that fall in Mr. Mulder's auto mechanics class at South, as an exhibit; Junie also brought it in when there were night sessions. (Ford once recalled Henry Mulder as "the man who taught me to crank a Model T without breaking my arm.") He brought it proudly to football practice and conveyed members of the team to the practice field, "Fresh Air Taxi" style, as many as twelve at a time hanging on to the running boards and rumble seat. Afterward he drove it home to East Grand Rapids and parked conspicuously in the driveway, a sign that one of

2. Art Brown interview, GRFL; Sheridan, "Portrait of the Next President," p. 23; Sharon Bohn, "Zylstra Remembers School Days with Ford," *Sun Journal*, July 10, 1975, GRF Scrapbook #1, p. 40, GRFL; Harold Bosscher and William Schuiling interviews; Gettings interview, GRFL; "A Not-So-Instant Replay at Junie's White House," *People*, December 16, 1974.

the summer's goals was accomplished. Now the other remained: beating Ottawa Hills.

The game was to be September 19, not at Island Park but at South's new home field next to the school, which had been finished just that summer after two years' planning. The school district had purchased the property, but the equipment and stands were paid for with money raised from South alumni, following the model of college fans. Rumor in local papers had it that Coach Gettings planned to move Junie Ford to the backfield, on the theory that a player with that much intelligence ought to be a ball carrier, and in fact, Ford recalled, such an arrangement was tried out in practice, "but I wasn't very agile, so I went back to the line." On the morning of the game, the first football pep rally of the year introduced the team to the student body, and each player "gave a word of encouragement," leading a writer for the South literary magazine to comment, "We wonder why the best football players make the worst speeches on Friday mornings."[3]

The Trojans took their revenge that afternoon, a "balmy September afternoon" as the *Herald* called it, before an overflow crowd, many of whom had come to see the new field as well as the game. The South band with its legendary seven-foot bass drum was there to urge them on. After a scoreless first quarter, South scored two touchdowns, both by Elliott, in the second, and "outplayed, outgained, and occasionally outclassed" Ottawa for the rest of the afternoon. The line was outstanding, led by Ford until he had to be carried off the field in the last quarter with a leg cramp. The final score, 18-6, told the tale. So disappointed were the Ottawa fans that, when the existence of the North Woods training camp became known, an outraged parent or administrator filed a protest with the state high school athletic association, and Gettings had to go to Lansing to explain, where he managed to convince the regulators that it had all happened behind his back.[4]

Indeed, the *Herald* sports editor, Heinie Martin, who wrote up the game, praising the Trojans' "clock-like precision," made a startlingly di-

3. Ford, *TTH*, p. 49; Gettings interview, GRFL; William Schuiling interview, 1997; Harold Bosscher interview, 1998; Tom Labelle, "Labelle at Large," *Press*, October 15, 1975. On the building and financing of South's football field, see *Herald*, October 7 and 9, 1930.

4. Heinie Martin, "South High Beats Ottawa Hills . . . ," *Herald*, September 20, 1930; Fred Girard, "This Year, Old Grid Cronies Will Meet at the White House," *Detroit Free Press*, November 24, 1974. Sports reporters initially thought GRF was having knee trouble again, but *Herald*, September 25, 1930, identified the cause as a leg cramp. Bass drum: James McNitt, "Men of South High School, On to Victory," in Composite Grand Rapids File, GRFL, p. 3.

rect statement about who was running the team. "Jerry Ford," he said, "was their master and leader. He cracked the whip on the field for three periods and a half." It sounds as if Martin had somehow learned of Junie's extreme competence in organizing the camp, knowing all the plays and all the positions. His verdict harmonizes with a rather odd statement made by Principal Krause ten years later, recommending Ford as a naval officer: "The Coach at that time was not very good. . . . I made Subject [Ford] responsible for much of the training and discipline of the team, and [Ford] fulfilled his duties admirably." No other source calls Gettings "not very good," but it is true that he was not very experienced, an earnest young man — not the gruff veteran some biographers portray — only a few years out of college. To older observers, the novice coach and the remarkably adult lineman formed a matched pair — not too different from Gettings's own formulation when he said that "having Junie on the team was like having another coach on the field."[5]

Under this dual leadership, if one can call it that, the Trojans moved forward the next few weeks, defeating their opponents and very rarely even being scored on, in a near replay of the 1928 season. This year, however, it was not just the city championship at stake. By the middle of October, when they defeated a determined Creston team 13-0 on a wintry afternoon with snow flurries, the team was one of a rapidly dwindling number of undefeated high school teams in the state of Michigan, and a real contender for the state title. The boys of the team bonded more tightly. Around this time they began calling themselves the Thirty-Thirties: twenty-seven varsity players, two student managers, and Coach Gettings made a group of thirty, and it was the fall of 1930. There was a whiff of predestination about the name.[6]

Grand Rapidians began to realize how good this team really was. It was not just Elliott and Ford. Little Johnny Heintzelman, the halfback, was fast and nimble. Siki McGee and Leon Joslin, the ends, were great runners who moved the ball effectively. Art Brown was a pillar of strength on the line. But Junie Ford, over and above his abilities at motivating and coordinating the team, was both a great center ("an ideal center," one official called

5. *Herald*, September 21, 1930; this quotation marks the first use of "Jerry Ford" in a public context to refer to GRF rather than his father. U.S. Department of the Navy, Office of Naval Intelligence, investigatory information on GRF, January 10, 1942, GRFL; Gettings interview, GRFL, p. 3; Leroy, *Gerald Ford — Untold Story*, p. 37.

6. *Herald*, October 19, 1930; Ter Horst, *Gerald R. Ford*, p. 37n. The yearbook photo of the varsity team on p. 86 of the 1931 *Pioneer* annual shows thirty-one faces — the people named plus "Pop" Churm, the assistant coach.

him) and a great blocker. In those years before offensive and defensive specialization — and with limited substitution — he played both offense and defense. He placed the ball accurately on offense. On defense he excelled as linebacker, which was called "roving center" at the time. "One of the main things about Jerry," Art Brown recalled, "was that he could never find enough guys to throw a block at. He'd knock down his assigned man and then jump up and look for somebody else." "He was all over the field making tackles," Coach Gettings said. "He seemed to be able to run faster when he was chasing somebody than he could when they were chasing him." Jim Trimpe, the backup halfback, put it this way: "When I was on defense, it was always great to see Ford up ahead as linebacker. By the time I got up to the play, he usually had the ball carrier flattened." Gettings called him "one of the toughest players I ever saw."[7]

South's opponents, well aware of Ford's importance, concentrated their defense against him. "They recognized his ability," recalled the *Herald*'s sports editor, "and in every game they were out to 'get' him. Perhaps we should stay 'stop' him. . . . They believed that with Jerry out of the game, they could get places." Their pressure made his performance that much more impressive.[8]

In the next-to-the-last game of the season, against a determined Holland team, it was Ford who opened a hole in the Holland line big enough for Elliott to sneak through and score South's only touchdown. It was also Ford who, late in the game, intercepted a Holland pass in the end zone and saved the 7-0 victory for South. The outcome left the Trojans one of four undefeated, untied football teams in Michigan. One of the others, as it happened, was also from Grand Rapids: South's archrival, Union High School, led by its 198-pound fullback Frank Cook, a letterman in several sports, "very fast and a wonderful line plunger," in the words of a Michigan official. The final game of the season, the meeting of the undefeated rivals on Thanksgiving afternoon at South's new field, suddenly acquired epic dimensions; it might settle the state championship.[9]

With public interest high, the Hi-Y Club at South decided to capitalize on it and publish a special souvenir program for the game, selling space

7. "Flint Northern Given Two Berths," GRF Scrapbook #1, p. 51, GRFL; Ter Horst, *Gerald R. Ford*, p. 37; John G. Rogers, "His Old Teammates Are Still Betting on Jerry Ford," *Parade*, May 9, 1974; *Boston Globe*, December 7, 1973.

8. "Sport Chatter," *Herald*, May 15, 1932.

9. The description of Cook is in "Flint Northern Given Two Berths," GRF Scrapbook #1, p. 51.

to downtown merchants and sharing the proceeds with their Union counterparts. One advertiser, the men's clothing store Houseman and Jones, asked the two teams to let their captains be photographed wearing the store's merchandise, so Junie appeared on a page looking like a prosperous young city businessman in hat and heavy overcoat, opposite Ted Burgess of the Union team. It seemed a first step toward the sports stardom so common in the journalism of the 1920s. The South athletic department, meanwhile, raised the cost of a ticket to one dollar, an unheard-of price for a high school game, especially in the face of an economic crisis. But they had no difficulty selling twelve thousand tickets, which represented a capacity crowd. Dorothy Ford reacted to the occasion in her own way, planning a big party after the contest for the South team, its coaches, and the captains of all other high school teams in the city.[10]

After this buildup, the actual game had overtones of farce — or maybe it was just a reminder that the story took place in 1930 and not in any later year. The night before, it began snowing, and by Thanksgiving afternoon six inches were on the ground and more was falling rapidly in near-blizzard conditions. It was also the coldest Thanksgiving on record in the city, sixteen above at noon. Twelve thousand spectators, looking, as a newspaper story said, like animated ice cream cones, shivered expectantly as the teams took the field. The South High band tried vainly to make its instruments play. Stories about this game abound — how the lines on the field disappeared, and bottles of laundry bluing were brought out to mark them; how Gettings had the team constantly changing footwear in the hopes of getting some traction on the frozen surface; how Elliott, punting, had the ball blown back in his face by the wind; how the ball was coated with ice. "The snow was up to your butt," Heintzelman recalled. In the circumstances, there were five fumbles and only one first down in the entire first half. Ford, like most of the line, spent most of the game on his face or sliding down the field on his rear. But this was 1930, and no one, apparently, suggested postponement of the ridiculous spectacle. You accepted the conditions you were given. The teams fought doggedly through four blinding quarters — at one point Union nearly scored, at one point South — to a scoreless tie, which knocked both out of the running for the state

10. Most of the sources for this paragraph are in GRF's Scrapbook #1A, GRFL: the souvenir program for the South-Union game, DGF's invitation to the postgame party, and undated clippings entitled "South and Union to Enter Grid Classic on Even Terms" and "Entertain at Dancing Party on Thanksgiving." The admission charge of one dollar is noted in the Art Brown interview transcript, p. 7, GRFL.

championship. It was a unique experience, to be remembered for years; perhaps for that reason, the Fords' after-game party at Aunt Marjory's dance studio was a great success.[11]

The final twist, however, came a couple of months later. In January, it was revealed that Frank Cook, the previous summer, had signed a memorandum of understanding with the Cleveland Browns, after a scout assured him it would not affect his amateur status. No money changed hands, but the signature under High School Association rules was enough to make Cook a professional and therefore ineligible to play high school football. All Union's games were automatically forfeited under the rule; South High School was the state champion after all.

If one could imagine a less satisfactory ending to the season than the Blizzard Game, this was it. No one liked to lose, or win, purely on a technicality, especially after a series of banquets and dinners around Christmas in which representatives of both schools had jointly accepted the city championship and lauded each other's sportsmanship and abilities. Ted Burgess, the Union football captain, wrote a letter to the *Herald* denouncing the ruling as a "joke," which was perhaps predictable, but even Arthur Krause stated that he thought the association was too strict. Letter writers from both sides denounced the decision in the newspapers. In the opinion of Heinie Martin, the *Herald* sports editor, Cook had been "naïve," but that was no reason to penalize his school. Junie Ford, at the Elks' father-son banquet in February, which both teams attended, was in tune with public sentiment when he said: "If it were left to the members of the South squad, the name of Union would be inscribed on this cup as 1930 cochampions." In time, even this ambiguous end of the season would become part of the Thirty-Thirties' legend, a remarkably durable one, celebrated with annual Thanksgiving meetings for over fifty years.[12]

By February, basketball season was in full swing, in fact getting near its end, and the football championship was already a thing of the past for South High students. Somewhat surprisingly, Junie was on the first five —

11. Roscoe D. Bennett, "Giants of Gridiron Unable to Score," *Press*, November 28, 1930; "South and Union Tie," *Herald*, November 28, 1930. Anecdotes: *New Pioneer*, #43, p. 2. DGF's note on the cover of the game program, which she sent to a friend, read "Party a huge success." GRF Scrapbook #1, GRFL.

12. *Herald*, November 30, 1930; January 23 and 25, 1931; February 5 and 8, 1931; Tom LaBelle, "They'll Warmly Toast That Chill Game of Yore," *Press*, November 30, 1985. The 1974 meeting was held in the Executive Mansion; "A Not-So-Instant Replay at Junie's White House," *People*, December 16, 1974.

not that he was not a superior athlete, but he was not a ball handler or a goal maker. His skill set, centered on strength, stamina, and discipline, did not seem like a good fit for basketball. Coach Rose, however, had lost the best players on the previous year's team by graduation and had a lot of gaps to fill. He asked Ford and the halfback Louis Cooley to go out for the team, and both agreed, Ford perhaps feeling that he owed Rose a lot for setting up the knee surgery that had enabled him to become center on the 1930 all-state high school football team. To Rose, it was a fascinating challenge to work with this intelligent, competitive kid with the lurking hot temper and see to what degree he could transform him into a decent right guard.[13]

The experience of learning competitive high school basketball with Rose turned out to be, as Ford described it looking back, "most fortunate." "Even then," he recalled, "Dan was an unusual coach as the relationships were serious and demanding on the one hand but relaxed and personal on the other. He definitely expected the most from his athletes as he sincerely believed that each of us had something unique and valuable to give for the team and each other." Rose clearly sensed something unusual in Ford and worked hard to motivate him and focus his abilities. One weekend they drove to Ann Arbor to take in a U of M basketball game, talking all the way about college, athletics, and the other challenges of life. Junie found that they had "the same basic concepts as to citizenship and character," and came to feel in retrospect that "there was something magical about the man behind the coach."[14]

This language, unusual for any time of Ford's life, shows how strongly Coach Rose's transformative performance must have impressed him. Rose realized that Junie's combative, persistent style of playing worked best on defense and praised his play in that area, but also used the full range of his friendly, intelligent personality to take him further, kidding him constantly about accuracy in shooting. From the time practice started in November, Ford spent hours in the gym practicing free throws and taking the ball off the backboard. His motivation and Rose's encouragement did not make him a star, but they did make him a respectable basketball player, who would go on to be on the varsity at Michigan.

The process can be traced in the sports columns of school and city papers that winter. Basketball season began after Thanksgiving, and by December 12 Ford had established himself as a good defensive player, whose

13. *Pioneer*, November 13, 1930; *Herald*, December 23, 1930.
14. Dinse, *Mr. C.M.U.* foreword, p. v.

style was to guard closely and hassle opponents constantly. In the game with Grand Haven on December 20, he had three fouls called on him and scored no points. In the words of the *Herald*'s reporter, he and Cooley, the other guard, "possess[ed] a world of scrap but little experience and [had] much to learn." In early January, the sportswriters still praised his "good defensive game," and on January 11 he scored his first point, a free throw, against Catholic Central. (The scores of these games, incidentally, seem absurdly low to modern fans — the score in the South-Catholic game was 32-22, in the South-Union game 10-9.)

As the season went on, Ford maintained his intensity on defense — he racked up four fouls in the January 24 game with Central and fouled out of the Ottawa game two weeks later — but he also began to score more regularly: a field goal in the Davis game on January 18, a free throw against Ottawa. Against Union on February 14, the *Herald* reported, "Ford, who doesn't score very often," put in the decisive field goal. He moved the ball more readily — a classmate recalled seeing him charge red-faced down the court, dribbling. Against Davis again on February 18 he scored both a field goal and a free throw. In the Catholic game near the end of the season, he scored a field goal and three free throws, over a fourth of the Trojans' eighteen points. At the team dinner in April (where, as the school reporter carefully noted, "lots of food" was served), he received a well-deserved letter in basketball.[15]

Basketball season saw the end of the saga of Junie's Ford. One December night, when the temperature was predicted to drop below zero for the first time that winter, he drove home after practice and parked in the driveway. He noticed steam coming from under the hood. Looking underneath, he saw that the engine block was glowing a dull red. Model T's were known to run hot in cold weather, but this was worrisome, and Junie, thinking about the low temperatures predicted later that night, felt vaguely that the engine needed protection. He had seen other car owners put blankets over the hood on cold nights. Deciding to go them one better, he got some old blankets from the garage and laid them directly on the engine.

An hour or so later, as the family was finishing dinner, younger brother Tom looked out the front window and exclaimed that the car was on fire. Junie rushed out the front door and heard sirens; a neighbor had called the fire department, because the car was wrapped in flames. It was already too late; the Ford burned to a shell in the driveway. To add to Junie's embar-

---

15. *Herald*, December 12, 13, 21, and 23, 1930; January 4, 11, 18, and 24, 1931; February 8, 14, 18, and 21, 1931; March 7, 1931; *Pioneer*, April 23, 1931; Arnold Sisson interview.

rassment, he had ignored his father's advice to insure the car and could not afford to replace it. For the rest of the year, he had to take a streetcar downtown and then transfer to the Division Avenue line to get to school. His classmates kidded him mercilessly. But he had unintentionally created a family legend — from then on, events in those years were dated by whether they took place before or after the night young Jerry's car burned up.[16]

He had other automotive misadventures that final year in high school. In April, South's track team was invited to a three-way meet at Grand Haven, thirty-five miles away, on the lake. Parents generally supplied transportation to out-of-town meets — there was no athletic bus — and Junie got permission to drive his father's snazzy new six-passenger Chandler, and got himself and five teammates there on time. They won the meet and headed homeward. "That's where my troubles began," Ford recalled.

> Leaving the parking area, I backed the Chandler into a tree. The impact broke the clamp that attached the spare tire to the back of the car. We couldn't put the tire inside because six of us from the track team were packed in the car. No problem, I thought; I would simply tie the tire on the back. Not until I returned home did I realize my mistake. The heat from the exhaust had burned a hole in the tire and my stepfather let me have it. "Why did you back up without looking?" he fumed. "Look at all the damage you caused." Insurance paid the bill to repair the car, but the policy didn't cover the ruined tire. I had to pay for that.[17]

Ford was probably no more unfortunate than the average teenager learning to drive. He just remembered his mistakes better and admitted them more openly.

Track season, which lasted into May, was the last and in some ways the least important part of the sports year at South High. Churm was esteemed a good coach, and South regularly produced winning teams; but track and field attracted few spectators, and it mostly lacked the excitement of face-to-face, moment-to-moment competition that was so much a part of other contests. Ford rarely spoke about it when he was recalling his athletic career, perhaps because it was the one sport in which he did not excel, although he was on the varsity three years. Leon Joslin consistently threw

16. Vestal, *Jerry Ford, Up Close*, pp. 46-48; Ford, *TTH*, p. 49.
17. Ford, *TTH*, p. 49. Melvin Barclay, captain of the track team, recalled that parents provided transportation (interview with author).

the discus farther than he, and Archie Ross was the school record holder in shot put. Ford was generally second or third in track meets, behind Joslin in one event or Ross in the other, and sometimes behind the number-one man on the other team. In ninth grade, at a meet with Central, he was beaten in the discus throw by a Central boy named Olsen, normally a runner, who was filling in for the regular starter. But he seems to have liked being on the team; he went out for track all four years. Maybe he just enjoyed hanging out with his friends — the few memories he shared were social, like the one above. He may also have liked the way track contests led him to new places outside western Michigan: the High School Invitational Meet at Ann Arbor, and the yearly High School Championship Meet on the Michigan State campus in East Lansing — where Athletic Director Ralph White had noted his ability and kept writing him letters urging him to attend State, and to play football while he was at it.[18]

Similar in some ways was the final sport he competed in that spring: swimming, where he swam freestyle for the YMCA team, not for South. (Most Grand Rapids high schools did not have swimming pools, though East Grand Rapids High did.) With Al Elliott and a couple of other friends from South, he was part of the twenty-man team, coached by Budd Carr. Swimming, an activity he loved for itself, had long been part of Ford's life; to be able to pursue it competitively was a real treat. As with track, some contests were held outside western Michigan — a tri-state contest at Fort Wayne, Indiana, for instance, or the state championship, which they won, at the Detroit Y in mid-March. Sports offered a way to see more of the world. This pattern would hold for Ford over the next ten years, as athletics took him to New England and the West Coast.[19]

The last track meet of 1931 marked the end of Ford's athletic career in high school — which, taken as a whole, was decidedly a success story. In fact, for a biographer, it was unnervingly similar to the archetypal image of the high school sports hero in the reams of popular fiction analyzed by Michael Oriard in *Dreaming of Heroes*. Like Oriard's composite, Ford's story was about a hero who was handsome and a good student, "fair, always modest, committed to his duty and loyal to his team, friends, and school," who began his career with a "minor triumph" — Ford's lucky

18. On GRF's performance, see, for instance, the report in the *Pioneer*, May 7, 1931, p. 24. The story about the Central meet is retold in a letter from Harvey E. Olsen to GRF, June 4, 1998, GRFL. Ford's scrapbook #1 in GRFL contains several letters from Ralph White.

19. Harold Bosscher interview. A photo of the championship team is in Leroy, *Gerald Ford — Untold Story*, p. 41. The 1930-1931 season schedule is in GRF Scrapbook #1, p. 71.

showing as center his sophomore year. He met adversity (in the form of his knee injury) but overcame it with the support of "kind, understanding" parents and his friends on the team. Ford's circle contained all the requisite characters: Elliott was the Best Friend, Brown the Sidekick, McGee the comic relief. In Oriard's words, "The greatest responsibility for the success of the team [was] given to the hero. . . . the hero [was] explicitly entrusted with primary responsibility by the coach." Like the classic football hero's story, Ford's culminated in the Big Game. The only major departure was the Thanksgiving snowstorm.[20]

The resemblance is so striking that the biographer wants to look for hints of literary influence, of conscious reshaping of Ford's story. But the effort is in vain. Too many independent variables fed into Ford's high school career to make contrivance possible. This heroic narrative was the way it actually happened. That conclusion, however, leads to another set of reflections about athletic success. In Oriard's words:

> For all his benevolent virtues he [the heroic athlete] is essentially a self-centered hero. . . . No real maturity is achieved in his allegory of maturity — the athlete-hero remains a child. The prototypical athlete-hero celebrates unlimited human achievement and potential, but at the point where his virtues should transform him from a pedestrian "star" to a mythic godlike hero, he fails. His accomplishments are self-directed and not other-directed as are those of the heroes of myth.[21]

Ford the high school star was still within the unreal bubble of high school athletics as understood in the 1930s. His experiences as a college athlete were to be quite different, less like inspirational fiction, with more ambiguity.

As the athletic year ended in May 1931, even before graduation, the strains of the deepening Depression were beginning to pull apart the legendary unity of the Thirty-Thirties. Joslin's family lacked the money for a suit, and he chose to pass up graduation. Art Brown had to leave school to support his family. Siki McGee simply disappeared. Even brainy Jerry Ford, captain of the team, saw his dream of college and law school flickering.[22]

20. Oriard, *Dreaming of Heroes*, pp. 30-35.

21. Oriard, *Dreaming of Heroes*, p. 39.

22. Brown and Joslin: Marshall Reister/Florence Johnson interview; McGee: Arnold Sisson interview.

CHAPTER 8

Getting to College

The school year of 1930-1931 began "just before the real pinch of the Depression set in." That was the estimate of Edmund G. Love, whose memoir *Hanging On*, about the Depression years in Michigan, is an essential guide to understanding Gerald Ford's path through college. Two years older than Ford, Love was from Flint, from a business-class family a bit wealthier than the Fords. Love and Ford pledged fraternities at Michigan, and knew each other slightly in Ford's senior year. The rich collection of stories and reminiscences in *Hanging On* shows vividly how the unfolding economic calamity affected young men's career strategies.[1]

Here is Love's evocation of the summer of 1930, when Ford worked at Ramona Park. It was as true for Grand Rapids as it was for Flint:

> That summer of 1930 was the perfect example of the philosophy of "hanging on." All over the country people were living off the fat they had accumulated in good times. Savings were slowly used up. Investments were liquidated. . . . Even my father, for all the financial disaster he had encountered, had a little fat left. He had good stocks of lumber and coal and he could sell them off for enough cash to keep a dribble of money coming in. Moreover, his credit was still good enough so that he could replenish these stocks. He had a sizable file of accounts receivable and money trickled in from this source. It never seems to

---

1. Love, *Hanging On*, p. 54. Almost as good a guide, but dealing with the later thirties, is a memoir by GRF's friend and political adviser Jack Stiles, "With the Coin We Blew (An American Goes to College)."

have entered his mind to cut down his expenses during this period. The important thing was to keep his organization intact and busy until they were needed again in the coming era of prosperity.[2]

Families like the Fords, too, were waiting for "the coming era of prosperity," which was to them not just an inane phrase of President Hoover's, but a firm reality. Like most Americans, they accepted prosperity as a normal condition.

In one way, Grand Rapids that summer was different from other Michigan cities. The furniture industry had been in decline since 1927 — a couple of large companies had closed or been sold — and for two or three years the streets, especially on the West Side, had been full of unemployed men. In 1929 the voters had elected a dynamic new Republican mayor, George Welch, who had promised to tackle the unemployment problem energetically in the progressive Grand Rapids fashion, and 1930 saw him putting into action an elaborate plan of shelters for the homeless, city jobs for the jobless, and city-issued paper credits ("scrip") to help workers pay for basic food items. The process of setting up the local relief system was so interesting — and generally so effective — that citizens could easily ignore or minimize the signs of a downturn about to affect the entire country.

To quite a few Grand Rapidians, not directly involved in the furniture industry's troubles, prosperity still seemed a reality. The city was no longer a one-industry town, and other manufactures, from carpet sweepers and metal products to refrigerators, continued making money. Construction jobs, many of them public, were still conspicuous all over the city: South High, in addition to the new football field, was adding a large new auditorium on the other side of the school. In opening Ford Paint and Varnish, Jerry Ford Sr. counted on the new suburban developments that continued to spring up on the East Side, and up to the fall of 1930 it seemed he had calculated right.[3]

The South High seniors who reported in September for classes, most of them from working-class families, were less confident. The opening issue of the student magazine noted that students seemed glad to be in

2. Love, *Hanging On*, p. 50.
3. Ransom, *City Built on Wood*, pp. 68, 73-74. Harms, "Paid in Scrip," pp. 37-43, tells the story of Welch's relief program. A letter to the editor in the *Herald* of September 26, 1930, pointed out that metals, not furniture, had become the city's leading industry.

school again, but guessed that it was because they foresaw nothing but unemployment in the outside world. Over two hundred seniors were slated
to graduate in June. Ominously, the picnic to welcome them back was held
on a dismal day of wind and rain.[4]

On the day of the first football game, against Ottawa Hills, national
stock prices, which had been improving since the previous year's crash,
stalled and began falling again. It seemed that economic difficulties
were not over yet. That Sunday night, city leaders held a mass meeting
at All Souls Universalist Church downtown to consider the possible consequences for Grand Rapids and possible measures to take. The church
was packed; Jerry Ford was undoubtedly present. Mayor Welch reminded
the audience of the city's successful efforts to help the unemployed, and
School Superintendent Leslie Butler pointed to the high rate of home ownership in Grand Rapids as a barrier to economic want. Fred Stiles, one of
the city's leading businessmen, guessed that 1930 was a "pause" before a
new era of prosperity. Hang on a bit longer, in other words, and the economy might come right.[5] The Trojans' long, tortuous march to the state
championship, and Junie Ford's to the all-state high school football team,
took place in this uncertain atmosphere.

The seniors' year began with a practical lesson in civics. "Pop" Churm,
a respected history and political science teacher besides his athletic responsibilities, was forever urging democratic procedures — committees
and elections — on his students, especially seniors, since most of them
were assigned to his session room. The class elections, which chose four
members to be responsible, as the class annual of 1928 put it, "for further-
ing school enthusiasm and social activities," provided a perfect occasion
for hands-on democracy, and in 1930 Churm managed to secure the use
of a real voting machine as a prop, through a student whose father was in
city government. He invited the seniors, beginning with his session room,
to organize political parties for the class election.[6]

The student leaders frustrated his plans by all getting together on a
single ticket, with Junie Ford for class president, Dorothy Gray for vice
president, and Allen Elliott for treasurer. In junior year, Junie and Dorothy had run against one another for class president, and she had won
by "a couple of votes." Now their vote-getting skills would be joined, as

4. *Pioneer,* September 25, 1930, p. 12; 1931 *Pioneer,* p. 42.
5. *Herald,* September 20 and 22, 1930.
6. 1928 *Pioneer,* p. 46; *Herald,* October 23, 1930.

candidates of the "Progressive Party" — no one recalls how the name was chosen.[7] The only difficulty was in finding someone to run against them. The candidate who finally stepped forward was a complete outsider — Bill Schuiling, a serious Dutch kid who always wore a suit to school, who never took part in school activities because he had to go straight to work after classes. He had friends, though, who met with him outside school and decided to call themselves the "Republican Party," borrowing the most popular political label in Grand Rapids. He had one of the most popular boys in the school as his manager — Clarke Veneman, a friendly, smooth-talking fellow whom some in the class thought of as a natural politician.[8] (Ford's campaign manager, Paul Duyser, was an equally smooth operator, but his line of gab had a cutting edge absent from Veneman's.)[9] At the last moment a third group appeared on the scene, the "Universal Party," headed by Leo Van Tassel, the bright, energetic editor of the literary magazine, who also managed the football team.[10] The exercise in democracy turned into an exhibition of political theatrics: three mad weeks of mobilizing friends, backbiting opponents, making allegiances, and planning strategies, with a formal debate every week.

The outcome surprised everyone: Gray and Elliott won their offices easily, but Junie lost to Bill Schuiling by a margin of three to one. Participants' explanations of the results varied widely. Many students, for years after, believed Ford lost because Paul Duyser crossed some unspecified line in his comments about other candidates, and Ford paid for the mistake. Ford's own explanation centered on Van Tassel and the third party that robbed him of support, but it was clearly wrong: Ford and Van Tassel together did not have the votes to defeat Schuiling. Schuiling maintained that he won because his party label, "Republican," corresponded to most students' political views. What was almost certainly the real reason for Ford's defeat came out years later in a remark by Coach Gettings: the coaches, worried that the formalities of student government would take up too much of their captain's attention and keep South from the state championship, passed the word among their

7. Dorothy Gray Guck to author, September 25, 1997.
8. Interviews: Marshall Reister, Florence Johnson Moore, Arnie Sisson, Don Daverman, Bill Schuiling.
9. The *Herald* story on the election, October 23, 1930, gives Duyser as the Universal Party campaign manager, but this was the reporter's error. All the students interviewed agreed that Duyser was Ford's campaign manager.
10. McNitt, "Men of South High School," p. 2.

senior students to vote against Ford; the seniors understood and pulled the levers accordingly.[11]

It is difficult to believe that Ford would have known nothing of these efforts; but it is even harder to believe that, personally competitive as he was, he would have consented to throw an election for the football team's benefit. If Bill Schuiling's recollection is correct that Junie was a "good debater" in their joint appearances before the class, then he must also have been deeply engaged in the campaign and trying to win. He was an effective speaker only on subjects he really cared about and had prepared for. As a practical matter, the loss did no damage to his status in the class, and immediately after the election he was back in student government affairs, when Schuiling named him to head the important photo committee, responsible for choosing the photographer to make seniors' portraits for the annual, and having the pictures back in time for any dissatisfied students to request a second shooting. But the margin of his defeat stung, perhaps more than the defeat itself, and within a few months he would wage another hard — and successful — campaign to be elected.[12]

Since the summer, the national paint business had been "dragging bottom" in sales volume; during the fall of 1930, the bottom fell out of the national varnish and lacquer trade. The business picture in Grand Rapids followed these trends. Building permits fell dramatically, although some fancy suburban homes were still under construction. Ford Paint and Varnish, then, would be operating on a reduced scale until business conditions improved, and the money needed to send Jerry Jr. to college was going to be short. This much must have been clear as early as October.[13]

Both parents were determined, however, that he should go. So was

11. Moore, Reister, Sisson, and Schuiling all mentioned Duyser's "mud-slinging" as contributing to GRF's defeat. The term also occurs in Tena Sikkema's class history in the 1931 *Pioneer*, p. 42. Schuiling, in addition, referred to Duyser's "cynical attitude." But none of the students interviewed remembered, or cared to repeat, exactly what Duyser said. Coaches' story: Clifford Gettings interview, GRFL, pp. 12-13. Schuiling's "Republican" explanation was quoted by James McNitt in "Men of South High School, On to Victory," Composite Grand Rapids Accessions, GRFL, p. 1. GRF's explanation is in the Cannon interviews, GRFL, April 24, 1990.

12. Schuiling interview. Photo committee: "Rings, Pictures Arrive Early," South High *Star-tler*, GRF Scrapbook #1, GRFL; *Pioneer*, January 15, 1931, p. 17.

13. *Proceedings of the 43rd Convention of the National Paint, Oil, and Varnish Association, October 14-17, 1930*; *Herald*, December 28, 1930. Manfred, *The Primitive*, p. 197, notes homes under construction in East Grand Rapids in late 1930, and cf. the reminiscences of Virginia Peck, Grand Rapids Women's History Collection, GRPL.

Junie himself: the only question was how. Using the Nebraska courts to pry some money out of Leslie King, who could certainly spare it, was not an option, because King had moved to Wyoming, out of their legal reach.[14] That left one obvious recourse: using Junie's football talent as a way to get the necessary financial support.

That course was as obvious in 1930 as it would become in the America of 2015, but the ideas and moral values surrounding it were completely different. College football had begun as a game for gentlemen, to build moral fiber in the sons of the American elite. To many Americans, particularly those born before the world war, college football was the classic amateur sport, to be played for love of the game and the institution. Money should have no connection with it. To put football in the same class with professional sports like boxing and horse racing, the province of gamblers and other semicriminal types, was offensive and degrading.[15]

The nature of college football had changed during the twenties, but the values changed more slowly. As the game grew in popularity, ticket sales and newspaper attention increased and competition became keener. In a time of prosperity like the New Era, it was natural to want to use money to improve one's team — better facilities, better training, and "encouragement" for players of talent — but direct pay still seemed a violation of the amateur ideal. The debate about money in football, passionate and constant through the decade, culminated in the "Carnegie Report" of 1929 condemning "subsidization" of college football players. Big Ten policy, reiterated in 1927, was that it was "illegitimate to give or loan money to athletes."[16]

Both Ford men, Junie and his father, given their values and aspirations, were doubtless concerned about the question of money in football. Junie certainly was. When a letter to the *Herald* criticized his appearing as a model for Houseman and Jones in the Thanksgiving game program and

14. A court order in the case of *King v. King*, dated April 10, 1931 (GRFL), shows that DGF requested, and the Nebraska court ordered, that King pay $100 per month for his son's college education, but according to Cannon, *Time and Chance*, pp. 15-16, the judgment could not be served because he had moved out of state.

15. Rader, *American Sports*, p. 147; Peterson, *Pigskin*, p. 23.

16. Rader, *American Sports*, pp. 196-98; Savage, *American College Athletics*. A good account of this debate in the Big Ten is in Soderstrom, *The Big House*, pp. 121-30. Watterson, *College Football*, pp. 183-86, gives an excellent brief summary of the national picture in the early 1930s and points out that the Big Ten was by far the strictest conference. See also Sponberg, "Evolution of Athletic Subsidization," pp. 36-39.

wondered how much he had been paid for it, he fired back an indignant letter to the sports editor, breathless but clear, which is worth reproducing in full as a sample of his writing style, as a high school senior, on a topic that engaged him:

Dear Mr. Martin: Since there seems to be some question as to whether the football captains accepted a reward for having our pictures in the Houseman & Jones ad in the fall, I wish to state emphatically that I accepted nothing whatever from them, except their offer to us of agreeing to take a large ad to accompany the said pictures in the South and Union program in order to help the Hi-Y finance the printing of their program.

They also wanted the right to use the picture in an ad in the school paper. Hoping that that this will explain my status in the minds of the doubters, I remain

Yours truly,

GERALD FORD, JR.[17]

Around the same time, scholarly, serious James McNitt, who shared a public-speaking class with Ford at South, chose as his subject for one speech "the hypocrisy of 'amateur' tennis, with its under-the-table payments to outstanding netters. Ford," he recalled, "possibly interpreting it as an attack on sports in general, took issue with my stand." In fact, amateur-professional issues in sports were an area Junie was sensitive to, as his sudden, articulate response to McNitt showed.[18]

Junie and his parents, then, hoped to get financial help for college, but only in an ethical way. In practice, that meant looking for the support of an alumnus. Colleges were prohibited by the rules of their associations from offering football scholarships, but rich alumni, singly or in groups, could offer as much aid as they pleased. For them to do so seemed like a continuation of the familiar Horatio Alger tradition in which a rich man helped a deserving youngster to rise in the world. In Junie's case, one soon materialized. A wealthy Harvard alumnus in Grand Rapids, not named in the reminiscences but almost certainly the lumber company president Fred Stiles, who had graduated from Harvard Law in 1913 and whose son

17. *Herald*, February 12, 1931. The revelations about Frank Cook's status were still fresh, and clearly GRF was anxious to free himself from any taint of professionalism that might affect the South High championship.

18. McNitt, "Men of South High School," p. 4.

Jack later became Ford's closest friend, offered him substantial aid to attend the Massachusetts school. Ford, in his reminiscences, did not spell out the exact offer, but it probably included travel and living expenses. All Junie had to do was be admitted, which meant getting his application in by March 15 and passing the College Board entrance exams, given in mid-June. He had months to prepare, and he would need all the time he could spare, because the exams were heavy in Latin, his weakest subject.[19]

Young Ford doubtless studied with some seriousness, for he took the College Board in June; but he did not make an adequate grade, and considering his heavy activity that winter and spring in basketball, track, and student government, it seems fair to say that at some point he decided not to make an all-out effort to enter Harvard and began concentrating on other possibilities.[20]

19. On alumni financial aid, see Canham, *From the Inside*, pp. 7-8; "What Football Players Are Earning This Fall," *Literary Digest*, November 15, 1930, p. 28; Stockwell, *Rudderless*, pp. 141-42; Savage, *American College Athletics*, p. 251. Over two dozen Harvard alumni lived in Grand Rapids in 1930. The 1919 *Alumni Directory* lists the older, more affluent alumni more likely to have made GRF such an offer; of the names on the list, Stiles's stands out for the reasons given in the text. More uncertain, in my view, than the identity of the Harvard man is the exact nature of what was offered. GRF recalled the offer in Ford-Cannon interview transcripts, April 24, 1990, p. 9, GRFL, and it is also mentioned in a contemporary source, Paul Goebel to Harry Kipke, May 4, 1931, Athletic Department Correspondence, BHL. (In the same place, GRF also mentioned being offered the same kind of aid by a Northwestern alumnus, but gave fewer details concerning it.) Both sources mention some sort of "scholarship" Harvard was offering GRF, which, in GRF's account, he had to pass a written test to receive. It is on record that he took the College Entrance Examination, the original version of the SAT, in June; see the next note. I conjecture that, unfamiliar with the concept of entrance examinations, he confused this test in memory with a qualifying test for the scholarship, and that most or all of the aid he was being offered would have come not from Harvard but directly from Stiles. After 1933, to be sure, Harvard offered a generous "National Scholarship" intended for students who lived outside the Middle Atlantic states, and for which the SAT was a qualifying examination; but before that year it offered few scholarships of any kind (Jerome Karabel, *The Chosen* [Boston: Houghton Mifflin, 2005], pp. 139, 176). For Harvard entrance requirements, see College Entrance Examination Board, *Annual Handbook, 1941* (Boston: Ginn and Co., 1941), p. 38. GRF took the "Plan A" examinations; see the following note.

20. College Entrance Examination Board, *Thirty-First Annual Report of the Secretary, 1931* (New York: Published by the Board, 1931), p. 141. Only five Grand Rapids students took the test; only one, clearly GRF, was from South High. (He also was required to take the recently invented Scholastic Aptitude Test, which had not yet achieved the prominence it would have in post–World War II American life.) Test scores are not given in the report; GRF recalled that his grade was not high enough without giving specifics.

Like many a high school senior, Junie found that school affairs dominated his time. It was not just his lettering in three major sports and being
admitted to the National Honor Society, "practically the highest honor
that can be awarded to a student," as the yearbook said (he was one of
only six boys admitted). In addition, he, Dorothy Gray, and Leo Van Tassel
served on the Inter-High Student Council, representing South in meetings
with other city high schools. He was proud of being in student government, and dressed up in coat, tie, and vest, complete with watch chain and
fob, for his yearbook photo — a far cry from the tousled athlete look. When
the student government decided to institute a system of hall monitoring,
Junie was among those seniors checking student passes during class hours;
when his athletic buddies on the Varsity Club put on a show or a dance,
he was generally on the arrangements committee, and he never missed
Varsity Club dinners ("feasts") held outside town at some rustic restaurant
like the Lone Pine in Lowell.[21]

For a couple of months in late winter, he also engaged in a personal
campaign to win an all-city popularity contest. The Majestic theater downtown announced a promotion in February: a competition among the most
popular students from city high schools for a free trip to the nation's capital, courtesy of Amerop Travel Service. Similar contests were under way
in other Midwestern cities, and one winner from each city would make up
the Washington-bound group. Possibly smarting from his loss in the senior class election, Junie made a real effort to win this one, urging friends
to see lots of movies, and to vote often by depositing their ballots for him
in the Majestic lobby when they went. The contest lasted seven weeks and
attracted other South students, including Dorothy Gray and Siki McGee.
Vote totals carried in the *Herald*, which was cosponsoring the promotion,
showed that the race was between Ford and John Prendergast of Central
High. Unrealistically high numbers as the final date neared suggested eager, not to say systematic, multiple voting on both sides — 19,975 for Ford
to 18,765 for Prendergast was the final tally. Junie got his picture in the
paper, hair properly slicked down, with the promise of a trip to Washington when school ended in June.[22]

21. 1931 *Pioneer*, p. 43 (student government), p. 108 (NHS), p. 116 (Varsity Club), p. 118
(student government); *Pioneer*, December 4, 1930, p. 19; January 15, 1931, pp. 18, 29, 30;
April 23, 1931, p. 17. *Herald*, October 22, 1930; Doris Berglund, "Jerry's Ex-Teachers Recall
His Student Days with Particular Pride," *Press*, August 13, 1974.

22. *Herald*, February 6, 1931; March 5, 26, 31, 1931. An unprocessed interview of
Thomas Ford in GRFL states, according to Donald Holloway of the GRF Museum, that

Meanwhile, Grand Rapids had entered 1931 — with the customary steam whistles from all the furniture factories sounding at midnight on New Year's Eve — still waiting for what its residents had learned to call "the business depression" or simply "the depression" to be over. Periodically, headlines in the *Herald* proclaimed that its end was in sight: late in February, when the stock market climbed back to its October level, the paper announced, "Growing Conviction Depression Is Past Seen as Stimulating Speculators," and on April 17 it noted that the economist Roger Babson believed business had "turned the corner." But the employment figures read differently: in January, 30 percent of Grand Rapids wage earners had only part-time work, and 24 percent were entirely jobless. Beginning in February, a disquieting series of armed robberies by individual bandits, targeting gas stations ("oil stations," they were called) and neighborhood markets, spread unease throughout the city. In the Hill District, some of the remaining wealthy families began quietly barricading the doors of their mansions. A Lake Drive house, two blocks from the Fords, was broken into and ransacked while its owners were vacationing in Florida. The pattern behind these events was clear: some people in Grand Rapids were without money, and others had a great deal.[23]

The contrast weighed on the minds of many in the city. Letters to the editor condemned "the menace of the unequal distribution of wealth." A prominent woman refrained from appearing downtown in her new Pierce-Arrow, fearing to provoke hostility. Local Communists began rallying at City Hall to demand free food for the unemployed and to extol life in the Soviet Union. Most were from the Russian-Jewish neighborhood on South Division; some were related to Junie's classmates. Their message attracted more attention than usual from citizens, but the fact that it was usually coupled with aggressive atheist propaganda made it hard for most Grand Rapidians to endorse wholesale. One speech to the Advertising Club suggested accepting "whatever is good in Communism."[24]

---

he and GRF stuffed the ballot box with votes for their side. The totals would indicate that Prendergast and his friends did likewise. The contest was announced to end March 15 but was extended two weeks because of the interest it generated.

23. *Herald:* all dates 1930: January 26 (employment), 29 (robbery); February 3 (robbery), 5 (robberies), 22 (stock market), 24 (break-in), 27 (robbery), 28 (robberies); March 1 (robbery), 4 (robberies), 5 (robbery), 15 (robberies), 20, 29 (robberies); April 17 (Babson). Steam whistles: Robert Davis interview, Kent County Council Oral History Collection, GRPL. Barricading doors: Wickenden, *The Wayfarers*, p. 53.

24. *Herald*, December 6, 1930 ("whatever is good"); December 12, 1930 (distribution of

Junie and his father, regular *Herald* readers, surely discussed these developments, but no source survives to suggest what they thought. Both were focused on narrower problems: how to keep the family and the business solvent, and how to afford a college education. Jerry Ford was beginning to think of renegotiating payments on the Lake Drive house, if he could, or finding a less expensive home if necessary. (It was during this spring that Junie accidentally burned a hole in the Chandler's spare tire; one can see why his dad was so snappish about the incident.) Junie's eye was undoubtedly caught by a couple of news items in early January: on the one hand, there was talk that the Depression might force eastern colleges to shorten or cancel their football schedules, but a story a few days later insisted that the Big Ten football programs, especially the University of Michigan, unaffected by economic woes, had no plans to cut back.[25]

As admission to Harvard seemed remote, Junie was looking seriously at Michigan as a place to attend and play ball. Admission there was no problem; as a member of the top 10 percent of his class, he was automatically admitted. The school was nearby and partly familiar from his visits with Coach Rose. Moreover, Arthur Krause, principal of South High and a lodge brother of Jerry Ford, was a dedicated Michigan booster, though not an alumnus, and, apparently in the spring, he made the Fords an offer: he would use the school bookstore fund, which he controlled, to create a $100 scholarship for the all-round outstanding student, Jerry Ford Jr., to attend the university. That amount, which would cover a year's tuition, was a powerful nudge in the direction of Michigan.[26]

Tuition was only one of the costs of college attendance, and not the largest. Board — meals for a school year, especially for a large, healthy boy like Junie — cost $200 or more, and a room was only slightly less. Then there were books, $30 or $40; incidental supplies, $25 or so; and travel, $30. Even when one pared down costs like organizations and recreation, usually reckoned at about $50 each, the total cost of a year at Michigan ran over $600. But with tuition taken care of, the outlines of a strategy for affording the cost became visible. Junie's earnings at the paint company — forty cents an hour for "cleaning smelly paint vats, mixing colors and filling thousands of cans" — would amount to $160 or so by summer's end,

wealth); December 17, 1930 (distribution of wealth); January 30, 1930; February 11, 12, and 26, 1930 (Communists); Stiles, "With the Coin We Blew," p. 9; Florence Johnson Moore interview.

25. *Herald*, January 3, 1931; January 9, 1931 (college football programs).

26. Cannon interview, April 24, 1990, GRFL, p. 8

enough to cover the cost of a room. Relatives and friends would contribute money for books and incidentals. That left only the biggest item, the cost of board, and the Fords had a notion of how it could be met.[27]

Besides Mr. Krause and Coach Rose, another booster who had been steering Junie toward Ann Arbor was a business friend of his father's, the best-known athlete in the city. Tall, blond Paul Goebel, a starring end on the Wolverines' teams of 1921 and 1922, had picked up some money after college playing four years on the lightly regarded professional teams of that era and had opened a sporting goods store, Goebel and Brown, in Grand Rapids. Now he refereed Big Ten games and stayed in touch with Coach Harry Kipke, his teammate in 1921. Goebel assured the Fords that the Athletic Department would take care of the board question, by finding suitable campus jobs for an athlete who was willing to work hard.[28]

Kipke himself, sticking to Big Ten guidelines, did almost nothing to ease Junie's path to Michigan. As late as the end of April, when he first contacted Goebel about bringing "one or two good [high school] athletes" from Grand Rapids to Ann Arbor for a visit, he knew Ford's name but very little else about him, referring to "Ford of Ottawa Hills." At Krause's suggestion, he spoke to an assembly at South on June 2 and met young Ford for the first time. Next came a visit, suggested by Krause, at the family home on Lake Drive to sell the parents on the virtues of Michigan. (Art Brown heard that Jerry Ford, ever the salesman, suggested a contract to supply paint for Athletic Department facilities as the price for Junie's at-

---

27. This estimate is based on two reliable accounts from Michigan in this time period: Paul Showers's tabulation of his expenses for (probably) the 1928-1929 school year ("expense sheet," undated, Paul Showers Papers, BHL), and a 1933 estimate by the School of Business Administration, reproduced in Shufro, "The Great Depression's Effect," p. 56. Love, *Hanging On*, p. 77, gives partial data for 1930-1931, which is consistent with the other sources. Summer earnings: Ford, *TTH*, pp. 48-49.

In this and the next few chapters, when college costs are discussed, keep in mind the changing value of American money through the years. As T. H. Watkins explains in *The Hungry Years: A Narrative History of the Great Depression in America* (New York: Henry Holt, 1999), pp. 521-22, one should multiply dollar figures from the early Depression years by twelve to get their worth in current money. The total cost of a year at Michigan in terms of current money — still a bargain — was $7,200.

28. Goebel may have played a more significant role in GRF's decision to attend Michigan than I credit him with here. He was certainly a role model for all serious high school athletes in the city, and well acquainted with the Ford family, though not as close as he later became. But neither GRF nor any other source mentions him as instrumental in the decision.

tendance.) Junie then rode back to Ann Arbor with Kipke and spent the night at his home. The following day was the Michigan-Indiana baseball game; several other prospects were visiting the campus, and Kipke got someone from the athletic staff to show the boys around while he, Goebel, and a couple of friends played a round of golf. Later that day he put Junie on the bus to Grand Rapids, assuring him again that good campus jobs would be found to cover his board costs. Junie, impressed, responded with a warm thank-you note; but Kipke's role had been minimal compared to the recruiting involvement of coaches at other schools — for example, Harry Wismer, a high school back from Port Huron who hitchhiked to Gainesville, Florida, in the summer of 1932 with a strong letter of recommendation from his high school coach, received on the spot from Coach Charlie Bachman a scholarship for "room, board, tuition, books, and odd jobs to keep me in spending money."[29]

For young Jerry Ford, seeing his dream of attending Michigan become reality was the big experience of his spring as a high school senior. For most of the rest of the class of 1931, their big experience was something else, in which Ford apparently had no part.[30] On the morning of April 30, South High students arrived at school to find the building buzzing with rumors and excitement. During the night, someone had painted Communist slogans, in symbolic red, on the sidewalks at several entrances. Not all students saw the painted slogans, evidently, for years later they had diverse memories of their content: some recalled a Soviet hammer and sickle, or "USSR," but the most reliable version had "Stay Out of School May 1st" painted at one entrance and "Free Books" and "Free Lockers" (South High charged students for both) at another. Whatever the words, the intention

29. Kipke to Goebel, April 29; Krause to Kipke, May 11; Kipke to Krause, May 15; Kipke to Goebel, May 5, all 1931, in Board in Control of University Athletics, University of Michigan, BHL; GRF to Kipke, June 3, 1931, GRFL. The narrative in the paragraph, emphasizing Kipke's low level of involvement, differs slightly from my version in *Young Jerry Ford*, pp. 110-11, and is, I believe, truer to fact, when one considers contrasting stories from other colleges like Harry Wismer's: Wismer, *The Public Calls It Sport*, p. 7.

30. The following account is a composite of interviews with Arnold Sisson, Florence Johnson, Marshall Reister, Don Daverman, and Bill Schuiling of the class of 1931, and a letter from Sid Nadolsky to the author, October 23, 1997. As for the actual perpetrator, whose identity was never publicly established, Nadolsky understood that the signs were painted by his friend Abe Sompolinsky, seventeen, a former student who had dropped out of South some years earlier and had been among the Communists arrested at the City Hall demonstration. (This corrects my account in *Young Jerry Ford*, p. 121, where I attributed them to Abe's brother Henry.)

was clear, and it was easy to identify who had done it, in a general way: the little band of Communists from South Division Avenue who had been holding meetings in the public parks ever since warm weather arrived that spring. Florence Johnson, who lived in that area, reported that a band of activists had come over from Detroit earlier to help them plot their strategy. Many students found it frightening that the red hand of "atheistic Communism" had reached out to mark their school.

As the day went on, more exciting details emerged. The Varsity Club had seized the students who did it — or at least a couple of their fellow leftists from the student body — and forced them to scrub the paint off the sidewalk with a paving brick. Then it had doused them in the showers, or, according to one version, thrown them into Plaster Creek, about a mile and a half south of the school. The action, striking a blow against Communism, rated a complimentary mention in the following day's *Herald*.

One of those manhandled by the varsity boys was Sid "Red" Nadolsky, a popular student, an aspiring jazz musician (double bass) who was in demand at several city night spots. He was also a social radical, caricatured in the yearbook sounding off on social issues from a soapbox, whose father had put up bail for some of the arrested Communist demonstrators. Early in the day, a friendly teacher approached Sid to suggest that he go home and avoid trouble, but he chose to stay. When the varsity lads marched him out of gym class, he asked to be taken to the principal's office, but Mr. Krause proved to be away from his desk, and Sid ended up scrubbing the sidewalk at the main entrance. He thought the principal's absence odd, since nothing happened at South without Krause's approval, and it was odd, too, that Junie Ford, usually an eager participant in Varsity Club affairs, was nowhere to be seen. No student recollection, in fact, connected Junie with the events of the day, and the converse is true; Ford never mentioned the May Day incident among his high school memories. The next day he took part in a track meet against Ottawa Hills.[31]

The week after the incident, South's new auditorium, the largest in the city system, which had been under construction during most of the

31. Nadolsky (whose primary instrument was the double bass, not the saxophone as erroneously stated in *Young Jerry Ford*, p. 121) added in his recollection of the incident (letter to author, October 23, 1997) that it had no effect at all on his popularity and social standing among South students. The whole episode was perceived as political theater, like the demonstrations themselves. The hammer and sickle, "USSR," and dunking in Plaster Creek were merely fictional enhancements. Louis Nadolsky posting bail: *Herald*, February 12, 1931; Ottawa Hills track meet, *Herald*, May 3, 1931.

school year, visible from classroom windows to the fascination of bored students and the annoyance of their teachers, was finally opened with a band and choral concert. At the official opening, a speech by Frank Sparks, the city editor of the *Herald*, pointedly praised South High for "keeping its sidewalks clean."[32]

The only recollection of Junie in May came from his track teammate Marsh Reister, who spent Memorial Day with Ford and another trackster, Bob Eckhardt, at a local driving range. After years of avoiding golf, Junie was now getting interested. His idol Coach Rose, who supervised South's golf team, had made him aware that the sport played a big part in the social and business lives of major athletes and coaches, not just the Masons and businessmen of his father's set. But he was still a beginner. Marsh remembered Junie's teeing up: the club twisted in his hand, and he hit a solid 250-yard drive at right angles to the green. Marsh and Bob doubled up in laughter.[33]

For them and the rest of the class of 1931, the beginning of June was a blur of formal activities leading up to graduation on June 19. The warm, steamy Friday evening of the twelfth was Class Day, when Ford and Dorothy Gray received their silver cups "for excellence in scholarship and activities" from Mr. Krause, while their classmates, onstage in summer dresses or white flannel pants and blue serge coats, wondered if they would stick to their folding chairs when they had to exit down the aisles. The auditorium was decked with aeronautical gear borrowed from local businesses, because the theme of the class history presentation was a thrilling ride aboard an imaginary airplane, complete with loop-the-loops, air pockets, and a happy landing. Some of the seniors, aware of the bleak employment picture outside, were doubtful about that last part. Don Daverman's cartoon class history in the *Pioneer* may have come closer to their feelings: its final panel showed a South graduate contemplating a sign that read "No Help Wanted." Next to him loomed a large question mark. Graduation the following week with its caps and gowns, final farewells, and subsequent lake parties temporarily obscured such uncertainties.[34]

A week later Ford had his bags packed for the overnight trip to Washington, leaving from Chicago on the Pennsylvania Railroad's Golden Ar-

32. *Pioneer*, May 7, 1931, p. 20; *Herald*, May 9, 1931; undated essay by Sid Nadolsky, Grand Rapids Junior College, copy in author's collection.

33. Interview with Marshall Reister.

34. Dorothy Gray Guck to author, September 25, 1997; McNitt, "Men of South High School," p. 4; copy of the 1931 Class Day program, author's collection; 1931 *Pioneer*, p. 171.

row with a dozen other boys and seven girls who had won popularity contests, as he had, in other Midwestern cities. The trip was to last six days, with the additional chance of a three-week tour of Europe for the boy or girl who wrote the best essay on "movies and world progress." Amerop, the travel service that handled the tour, was an experienced German outfit that specialized in student tours. The first day out, the students got acquainted over a deluxe luncheon, with roast prime rib, browned potatoes, and apple pie, in the "white-tableclothed splendor," as one student put it, of the dining car.[35]

The next four days were a busy round of activities for the young Midwesterners; they visited the popular government offices, historic sites like Mount Vernon, the new Lincoln Memorial, and the older monuments and museums. They could see new government buildings rising along the Mall as part of the president's public works program. They stood for a souvenir photo with the Capitol in the background, the girls in summer dresses, the boys in coats and ties or high-waisted slacks and short-sleeved shirts, with Junie Ford standing in the middle. The capital was quiet; government was in its usual summer siesta. President Hoover, at the White House, had just announced a moratorium on the repayment of debts European countries owed the United States, in an effort to protect their shaky economies from a collapse that could deepen the American depression, but Congress was in adjournment, not due to reconvene until December. Ford, in later years, said that on this trip he remembered watching a session of the House of Representatives, where he was later to spend most of his career; but that was impossible. He, the other students, and their guide looked down into the vast, empty House chamber with its classical decoration, and perhaps admired the stability of a government that could operate in vacation mode in the midst of a national financial crisis.[36]

Two days later, Junie was back home and ready to go to work to earn his room money for the upcoming year at Ann Arbor. Weeks later, German

35. The original notice of the contest, with a brief description of the tour, is in the *Herald*, February 21, 1931. It called for the trip to be taken during spring vacation in March, but the contest was later extended and the trip rescheduled for after the school year. A copy of the luncheon menu aboard the Golden Arrow is in GRF Scrapbook #1, GRFL. For Amerop's German ownership, see, e.g., Breitman, *U.S. Intelligence and the Nazis*, p. 175. Dining car: Griffith, *The Waist-High Culture*, p. 19.

36. *The Memoirs of Herbert Hoover*, pp. 63-80. The group photo, dated July 1, 1931, is in GRF Scrapbook #1 at GRFL. GRF's recollection: Cannon interview, April 25, 1990, p. 10, GRFL. GRF also recalled that the trip took place in spring, not summer.

banks began to fail, and European currencies lost value, with immediate consequences for American banks. Hoover's idea had been right but too late. The Depression plunged into a new and frightening phase, in which banking and the security of money would take center stage. Edmund Love, years later, would remember it as the "bleak" summer of 1931.[37]

37. Love, *Hanging On*, 83. The European financial crisis and Hoover's attempt to stop it are treated differently in different sources. For a sampling, see McElvaine, *The Great Depression*, pp. 84-85; Smith, *The Shattered Dream*, pp. 60-62; Lyons, *Herbert Hoover*, pp. 270-73; and Roth, *The Great Depression*, pp. 10-11.

1011 SANTA CRUZ DRIVE, EAST GRAND RAPIDS.
JERRY FORD SR., WITH H IS SKILL AS A DEALER,
ACQUIRED THIS HOUSE FOR HIS FAMILY IN THE
DEPTHS OF THE DEPRESSION, IN THE WINTER
OF 1933. THE WING ON RIGHT IS A LATER
ADDITION. (GRPL)

A GLIMPSE OF WORK ON THE FORD PAINT AND
VARNISH FACTORY FLOOR, THE MIXING ROOM,
TAKEN IN 1938. (GRPL)

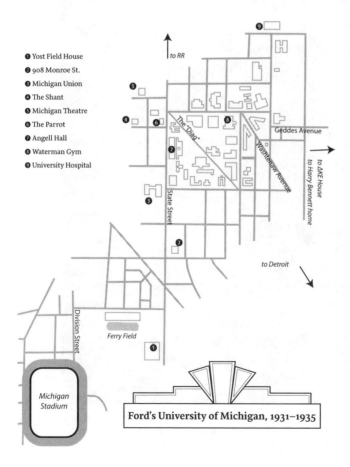

❶ Yost Field House
❷ 908 Monroe St.
❸ Michigan Union
❹ The Shant
❺ Michigan Theatre
❻ The Parrot
❼ Angell Hall
❽ Waterman Gym
❾ University Hospital

to RR

Geddes Avenue

Washtenaw Avenue

to ΔKE House
to Harry Bennett home

to Detroit

The "Diag"

State Street

Division Street

Ferry Field

Michigan
Stadium

Ford's University of Michigan, 1931–1935

FORD'S ANN ARBOR
EXPERIENCE, LIKE THAT
OF MANY COLLEGE
STUDENTS, HAPPENED
MOSTLY NOT ON THE
CAMPUS ITSELF BUT ON
THE PERIPHERY. (LYNNE
PARKER)

FORD CALLED IT THE GREATEST MOMENT OF HIS EARLY LIFE: WINNING THE 1932 MEYER MORTON CHICAGO ALUMNI TROPHY FOR OUTSTANDING FRESHMAN FOOTBALL PLAYER. HERE, AFTER THE CEREMONY, WITH HIS FRIEND HERMAN EVERHARDUS. (GRFL)

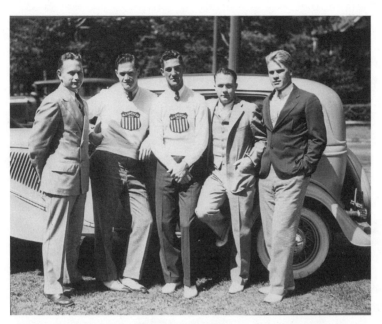

FORD WITH SOME FELLOW WOLVERINES, TWO SEASONS LATER. EVERHARDUS AND
BERNARD ARE WEARING THEIR ALL-AMERICAN SWEATERS. (GRFL)

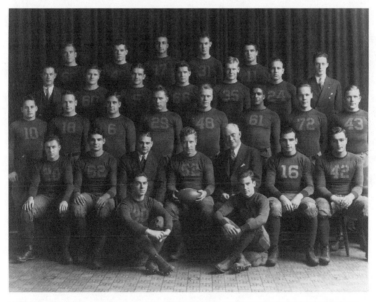

THE TEAM PHOTO FROM 1934, FORD'S SENIOR YEAR: AT CENTER, CAPTAIN TOM AUSTIN,
FLANKED BY KIPKE AND YOST; BEHIND THEM, JERRY FORD, #48, AND WILLIS WARD, #61.
(GRFL)

THE DKE MANSION ON GEDDES AVENUE WAS THE MOST IMPOSING OF ALL ANN ARBOR FRATERNITY
HOUSES. (GRFL)

OMICRON CHAPTER IN 1934-35: FORD AND BECKWITH AT LOWER RIGHT, FRONT ROW; BEHIND THEM,
VAN ZILE AND DUCHARME. PHOTO FROM THE 1935 MICHIGANENSIAN. (GRFL)

CHAPTER 9

Fast Start

The University of Michigan, pride of the state's educational system, seemed in September 1931 to have weathered two years of depression successfully. Its enrollment of 11,000 students, two-thirds male, was down a little from the year before, but the budget was unchanged. It still presented the image of a major university: some thirty large collegiate buildings in various styles, a few of them actually ivy-covered, with the usual complement of lawns and tree-lined walks, at the far eastern end of Ann Arbor, a county seat of 30,000 west of Detroit, and new buildings going up. Several of the existing structures were notable: long Angell Hall, the administration and classroom building with its impressive colonnaded façade; the Michigan Union, a club for male students, with its tower and its recreation rooms; and the "famous" Engineering Arch, so described by one alumnus, through which the Diag, the main walkway, emerged onto the center of the campus. (Ann Arbor itself did not strike most students as especially notable; one recalled it faintly as a "tranquil, subdued" town in a "broad, gentle valley." At night the glow of Detroit was faintly visible to the east.)[1]

Perhaps the most impressive complex of structures lay southwest of the main campus. Three new athletic facilities — Yost Field House, the Intramural Building, and enormous Michigan Stadium, with a capacity of

---

1. Shufro, "The Great Depression's Effect," p. 24; Peckham, *The Making of the University of Michigan*, pp. 172-73; Katzman, "Ann Arbor: Depression City," p. 306; Frantz, "Doctor, Where Were You?" 1-3, 6-7; Stockwell, *Rudderless*, pp. 83, 116-17; Millar, *The Dark Tunnel*, p. 137; Haines, *Blaine of the Backfield*, p. 14.

75,000, a giant bowl nestled in the slope of the terrain — made a powerful statement: Michigan was committed to first-class athletics, including intercollegiate football, with gleaming, modern, state-of-the-art training and playing space. Football had been a $500,000 business in the heart of the university when they were built; now, with less spending money in consumers' pockets, it was worth more like $200,000, but it still operated at a profit and supported an entire department, and the university was still committed to it.[2]

The athletic complex was probably the most welcoming sight to Jerry Ford as he rode into town around the third week of September. Classes and football games would start at the end of the month, but the school year began with two weeks for registering, finding places to room and eat, and organizing classes and fraternities.

Ford already knew where he would be living. He and his neighbor from years earlier on Union Avenue, Donald Nichols, were going to share a room near the campus. Nichols had gone on to Central High and become a good basketball player under Ralph Conger's coaching. Like Ford, he needed to scrimp in order to attend, and it may have been Conger's idea to pair them up so that they could split the cost of a room. The university had no dormitories for men, and male students rented from hard-bitten landladies toughened by years of dealing with college boys. Ford and Nichols occupied one of the cheapest accommodations at 908 Monroe Street, a ten-by-ten room at the back of the top floor with two army cots, a single desk, a single window, and intermittent hot water, for four dollars a week. The water may have been only for shaving and washing; many landladies supplied no bathing facilities and urged their roomers to take baths at the Union.[3]

The two-week period before classes was partly for the newly enrolled freshman class to take aptitude tests en masse — also to get acquainted,

2. The best source on these structures, all conceived by Fielding H. Yost, is Soderstrom, *The Big House*, especially pp. 249 and 353.

3. Ford-Cannon interviews, April 24, 1990, GRFL, p. 8; clipping from *Holland (Mich.) Sentinel*, March 6, 1975, vertical file, GRFL. (The address is in the 1931-1932 student directory; the two sources differ as to whether the room was on the third or fourth floor.) Denham, *Growing Up in Grand Rapids*, p. 125; Paul L. Adams to family, undated, 1926, Paul L. Adams Papers, BHL. The going rate in Ann Arbor, according to *The President's Report for 1931-1932*, p. 31, was around $3.50 for each student in a double room; if Ford and Nichols were splitting the $4.00 rent, they had a really good deal. A fictional sketch of an Ann Arbor landlady is in Douglas, *Disputed Passage*, pp. 21, 26.

develop an identity through meetings and shared activities, and fend off ritual attacks from the sophomores, who had the privilege of "hazing," tormenting the new students with indignities and ridiculous commands. There was a special piece of headgear, called a pot, for freshmen. This whole complex of traditions belonged to a past generation, around 1900, and was gradually dying out. Athletes in particular, who saw themselves as busy with serious activity, found this kind of rivalry childish — "schoolboy sports." It is likely that Ford and Nichols had little or no contact with it.[4]

What they did do was walk to Waterman Gym at the northeast corner of the campus, to undergo the freshman physical exam and have their classes assigned. The physical, carried out by junior medical students, was thorough. Male students waited in line in the "naked mile," holding a paper bag with their clothes inside. "They went over everything I own," a 1933 freshman wrote his brother, "and what they don't know about me now is not worth much." Registration, with its long lines and longer forms, filled with complex instructions, was a new, grueling experience for small-town boys and girls, and even some from bigger towns. A boy who had been working in a car factory to raise the money for college wrote his girlfriend in 1934, "I used to think that the Buick Motor Car Company was bound up with a lot of red tape when it came to getting into the place, but the Buick has to take a back seat after registering in the University of Michigan." "Mass education!" snorted another student.[5]

This is a good place to describe an incident that happened at some time during these two weeks, if not at registration then at one of the class orientation meetings. Ford recognized a face across a large room and went over to introduce himself. Like any Michigan male who followed sports closely, he had heard of Willis Ward, the phenomenal runner who had graduated from Detroit Northwestern High School the previous June, and seen photos of him; in fact, he may actually have seen him at one of the

4. Fred B. Wahr, "Student Traditions and Customs," in Donnelly, *The University of Michigan: An Encyclopedic Survey*, ed. Wilfred B. Shaw, 4 vols. (Ann Arbor: University of Michigan Press, 1951), 4:1766-67; *MD*, September 19, 1931 (see especially the editorial, p. 2); Haines, *Blaine of the Backfield*, pp. 23, 30.

5. Stockwell, *Rudderless*, p. 18; Haines, *Blaine of the Backfield*, p. 31; Frantz, "Doctor, Where Were You?" p. 4; letter of John D. Schultz in "Michigan Today: Memories," March 14, 2009 (michigantoday.umich.edu); Phil Haughey to Will Haughey, September 21, 1933, Haughey Family Papers, BHL; Emerson F. Powrie to Gwendolyn Sutton, September 18, 1934, in Grimm, *Michigan Voices*, p. 155.

bigger high school track meets in the spring. Ward, like Ford, had been chosen to the all-state high school football team. He was easy to spot, he was tall and black, one of only about fifty African American males on the university campus. Ford walked over to him and stuck out his hand — a conventional action between two young men of the same race in 1931, but a surprising one between a black and a white. Like most black men, Ward was used to being avoided by whites out of unfamiliarity or prejudice, so the gesture of this big blond student impressed him with its naturalness. They talked briefly, found they were both going out for football, looked forward to meeting again, and parted with mutually good impressions. It was the beginning of a long-lasting friendship.[6]

The big worry on Jerry Ford's mind all summer had been board; in August he still didn't know how his meals would be paid for, although Paul Goebel had assured him the Athletic Department would take care of it. In September, he checked with one of the coaches and found that he had a three-hour job at University Hospital six days a week. His contact was Dr. Albert Kerlikowske, the assistant administrator — "Kerly," to generations of Michigan athletes, a sports fan and good friend of Kipke. The job — two jobs, actually — paid fifty cents an hour — in other words, he would make nine dollars a week, more than enough for board.

The hospital loomed over the north end of the campus — a massive, modern nine-story structure — and Ford, along with many other athletes, would work in the ground-floor cafeterias, waiting tables in the interns' cafeteria, then busing tables in the nurses' cafeteria, 11:30 A.M. to 2:30 P.M. Like other student waiters, he mastered the technique of carrying multiple plates on one arm and managing towers of dirty dishes. "Jerry worked out there at the hospital," Coach Cliff Keen recalled. "Just like all of them did." (Some had jobs elsewhere on campus; Willis Ward that year became the first black to wash dishes at the Union.) Kitchen work was easy money — Jerry had been doing it since boyhood — and it was standard for athletes; Coach Rose had washed dishes when he was at Ann Arbor. Ford must have felt privileged compared to the scores of students, especially men, that he saw lining up outside University Hall to apply for campus jobs. Like him, they needed money, but they lacked his special status.[7]

6. Fred Delano, "Pigskins and Politics," August 24, 1974, clipping in GRFL vertical file; Sukandasa, "Black Varsity Lettermen," p. 42.

7. Paul Goebel to Harry F. Kipke, August 1, 1931, in Board in Control of University

Classes began September 30. Ford was taking "Elementary French," "English Composition," the first semester of "Western Civilization," and "Mathematics 5, Trigonometry and Solid Geometry." Like other male students, he wore a coat and tie to class. Michigan was a rather dressy campus by Midwestern standards; many men at other colleges dressed like lumberjacks or sourdoughs. All his courses were immense lecture-discussion classes, with hundreds of students meeting in a hall two or three times a week to hear a professor speak, and multiple discussion or "quiz" sections, led by a graduate student, to explain and clarify the lecture and give assignments. With all the other freshmen, Ford had taken the diagnostic English examination during the registration period, to help assign him to the appropriate composition section, but he still found the class a "challenge," and worked on the thousand-word composition, due every Monday, hardest of all his assignments. Most of the composition sections met between 8 and 11 A.M., Monday through Saturday, though, like most football players, he avoided Saturday classes.[8]

Michigan was in the top flight of American colleges, with great scholars in many disciplines, and Ford came in contact with a few of them, especially in his later undergraduate years. But academic learning was not his purpose in attending, and little of the content of his classes impacted him. Apart from his comment about English composition, I have found no reference in his memoirs or later writings to the material he studied as an undergraduate. He made good grades; his final B average was higher than

---

Athletics, University of Michigan, BHL; GRF to Will Perry, February 20, 1974, GRFL; block plans of University Hospital, December 30, 1921, drawer 3, folder 8, Albert Kahn Papers, BHL; Cliff Keen interview with David Pollock, 1983, accession number #2004-NLF-033, GRFL (hereafter "Keen-Pollock interview"); *MD*, September 22, 1931; Dinse, *Mr. C.M.U.*, p. 25; Love, *Hanging On*, p. 108. Albert Kerlikowske's papers, with biographical information, are in BHL. In view of the strong tradition of athletes washing dishes and doing kitchen work, Mary McComb's generalization about Depression-era male college students taking on "the previously undesirable domestic work that had once been the sole domain of women" (*Great Depression and the Middle Class*, p. 55 and note) requires some qualification.

8. GRF's college transcript is in GRFL; the *General Catalogue for 1931-1932* gives information on classes and sections. A fictional freshman in Stockwell's *Rudderless*, pp. 68-69, took a freshman math class with 600 students; Paul Adams in 1926 reported a freshman history lecture with 500 (to his family, October 1, 1926, Adams Papers, BHL). Student dress: Denham, *Growing Up in Grand Rapids*, p. 127; *Michigan Alumnus*, 39:303. The preliminary English examination in Hill Auditorium was given to the entire freshman class (Phil Haughey to mother, September 20, 1933, Haughey Family Papers, BHL). Ford, *TTH*, p. 50.

that of most of his classmates. But the process of making them, though beneficial, was unexciting and routine, like good dental care. Accounts of undergraduate life at Michigan in these years suggest that Ford was not the only student who felt this way.[9]

At the same time as the start of classes, and of much more interest to Ford, freshman football began. All freshmen with an interest in playing for Michigan were asked to report to the field house to be issued uniforms and equipment. They would play on adjacent Ferry Field, which had been the main football field until Michigan Stadium opened in 1927. Over a hundred boys turned out. Many, like Ford, were leading players from Michigan high schools who had received a letter inviting them to come out; some were outstanding players from other states; some had played football in high school or private school and just wanted to measure their abilities against the big boys. They practiced in worn, often ragged uniforms and gear, because the point of freshman practice was to winnow down the hundred-plus aspirants to a core of promising varsity material.[10]

After a day or two of punting and passing, they began playing defense against the junior varsity. Coach Ray Fisher organized them into makeshift teams and sent them out to test their stamina and their football intelligence. This was football as Ford liked it — blocking hard and being blocked, trying to anticipate the other team's strategy. Other college students came down to the periphery of Ferry Field to watch the show — it was real hard-hitting football, in which neophytes without football sense were apt to get hurt, knocked out, or disabled. Spectators scanned the line-

9. In Donal H. Haines's fictionalized account, *Blaine of the Backfield*, p. 60, one student points out to another, "You're doing the stuff not because you want to but because the University won't give you a degree unless you do," and another asserts (pp. 61-62) that undergraduates, in the classic pattern, "work like dogs on the stuff they really want and do just enough to get by in the courses they have to take." Roberts, "Murmuring Michigan," p. 84, quotes an unnamed undergraduate: "Oh, we don't need to study. All we need to do is go to classes and listen to what a prof. says. When we take our exam, we put down what the prof. told us; and if we put it down just the way he said it, we get an A. If we do that often enough, maybe we get Phi Beta Kappa."

10. *MD*, October 1, 1931, reported a turnout of 105; by October 8 it was down to 75. A good account of this phase of practice, somewhat exaggerated for humorous purposes, is in *I'm a Lucky Guy*, pp. 19-28, by Frank B. Gilbreth, who graduated in 1933. According to him, many of the freshmen brought letters from Athletic Director Fielding H. Yost, recognizing their high school performance and inviting them to try out. The description of the uniforms is from the same source.

ups looking for the stars of next year and 1933. Day by day the number at practice dwindled, as boys with sprains and aching muscles made the decision to quit and pursue glory in some other activity. By the middle of the second week they were down to sixty.[11]

Ford himself was out with an injury in the third week, but only for a day. He was already being recognized as a contender for center on the final freshman team. Ward attracted more comment than any other freshman — great things were expected of him, and his performance was very promising. Fisher selected teams and sent them out to play against the varsity — a rough experience that usually gave even the best players a few minutes of "complete demoralization." In the rough camaraderie of the field and the freshman locker room, the players began making acquaintances. Besides Ward, Ford was friendly with Bill "Borgie" Borgmann of Fort Wayne, Indiana, who played guard ("they were like twins," Ward recalled), and with a heavy, expressionless lineman named Jack Beckwith, from the Chicago suburbs.[12]

On the evening of October 20 Ann Arbor turned off its streetlights for fifteen minutes, commemorating the death of Edison, who had done so much to create the wired, illuminated world in which Americans then lived. But quite apart from the inventor's death, the tone of the American business world was darkening as the new phase of the Depression took hold. Affected by the summer's banking and currency crisis in Europe, American banks had begun failing, particularly, it seemed, in the Midwest. Suddenly, families, factories, and school districts were apt to find themselves unpredictably without spendable cash, reinforcing the observation by one historian of the Depression that the four years after 1929 were hardest on the working class, but after 1931 the middle class felt the pain most acutely. At the University of Missouri, a sophomore quit his fraternity, since his hometown bank had closed and his family had lost everything; there were rumors the university itself would close. In Youngstown, Ohio,

11. Gilbreth, *I'm a Lucky Guy*, pp. 20, 26-28; *MD*, October 1, 7, 8, and 10, 1931; Phil Haughey to his mother, September 30, 1933, Haughey Family Papers, BHL; Haines, *Blaine of the Backfield*, pp. 48-49.

12. *MD*, October 8, 10, and 15, 1931; Haines, *Blaine of the Backfield*, pp. 74-77; Willis Ward interview with David S. Pollock, 1983, Acc. Number 2004-NLF-033, GRFL (hereafter "Ward-Pollock interview"), p. 5. William J. ("Jack") Beckwith became one of GRF's closest friends in the DKE fraternity (Philip Buchen interview with Dr. Thomas Soapes, January 18, 1980, GRFL, p. 5); since he went through freshman football with GRF, it seems reasonable to suppose that their friendship began on the playing field.

a young lawyer watched with amazement as established banks across his state failed almost daily.[13]

A letter from a Michigan freshman to her middle-class family near Pittsburgh illustrates the prevalent jitters: "Joe says he doesn't think there's any danger of the banks closing here & besides he has his money in Ann Arbor's Savings Bank too." It was the holdups in Ann Arbor that worried her. A European architecture student wrote his family that he was being cautious about where to put his money. To him it seemed more than jitters; the Depression had terrorized the American consciousness and, as he wrote later in the year, had become "a preaching and spiritual plague." "The sense of imminent disaster," as one historian put it, "the despairing and demoralizing fear of losing one's job, home, and dignity, spread through the middle class as well as the more vulnerable masses."[14]

One at a time, beginning in late fall, students dropped out of the university as economic disaster or the fear of it affected family calculations. One or two were freshman footballers. Ford, Ward, and the rest concentrated even more closely on the game and their classes; actually, their schedules allowed little time for anything else. Ward described his routine: "I would say it [practice] was a good three and a half hours. Time you got there, you walked down from the campus to Ferry Field. And you dressed. Then you went out and went through your deals as a football player. Came back, you showered, and you went back. And I would go back and wash dishes and then eat. Then tired as the devil, I would go back to my room and study." Ford's routine was identical except that his job came at midday.[15]

In October or November he added another job. The offer came from a member of the varsity squad, Herman Everhardus, who let Ford know that his fraternity, Delta Kappa Epsilon, needed an additional dishwasher for its evening meal — thus, two hours' work with the promise of free food, which would enable Ford to save some of his board money for the

13. *MD*, October 20, 1931; Roth, *The Great Depression*, pp. 20, 23, 25-26, and editor's note, 35-37; Wandersee, *Women's Work*, p. 32; Ellis, *A Diary of the Century*, pp. 21-22.

14. Helen M. Loomis to parents, October 24, 1931, Helen M. Loomis Letters, BHL; Wallenberg, *Letters and Dispatches*, pp. 40, 52 (letters of November 7, 1931, and May 15, 1932); Wandersee, *Women's Work*, 28.

15. A back from Florida named Beckwith (not to be confused with Jack Beckwith) and another named Schultz, both good players, dropped out at the end of October. Beckwith was said to be transferring to the University of Illinois; no destination was given for Schultz (*MD*, October 27, 1931). Routine: Ward-Pollock interview, p. 4.

next year. Everhardus washed dishes there himself. Ford accepted. He may not have been experienced enough to recognize this proposal for what it really was, a bid for his membership in Delta Kappa Epsilon, or the "Dekes," as they were called. But it was, in fact, a classic ploy by fraternities to obtain desirable pledges from among freshman athletes. The same thing had happened to Coach Rose, who had been brought into a fraternity to wash dishes and ended as a brother. Kitchen employment offered the athlete indirect financial help, which he often needed. At the same time, it gave the brothers a chance to look him over and decide if they really wanted him. By November 11, when the president of the chapter invited him as a guest to their second open house, it was clear that they did.[16]

Home to the Michigan chapter, officially "Omicron of Delta Kappa Epsilon," was a large, secluded mansion in a residential area half a mile from the campus. In the fall of 1931 the brothers had just reoccupied it, after having been forced to leave by the university administration because of what their secretary called "the unfortunate incident of last February," in which the Ann Arbor police had discovered large quantities of liquor in the house, in violation of both university regulations and federal law. Deke and four other fraternities were shut down until the end of the semester, and deprived indefinitely of social privileges, that is, the right to hold parties. The dean of students, Joseph Bursley, commented privately to a member of the Board of Regents that the Dekes "have more 'skeletons in their closets' than any of the others as far as I am aware, and you and I know that they are damned lucky to get out of this with only a charge of having liquor in the house." At Thanksgiving of 1931 they finally had their social privileges restored.[17]

16. Several versions exist of how GRF became a Delta Kappa Epsilon. The one here is from "Brother Gerald R. Ford, Jr., Omicron '35 Remembered," and gains credibility from the fact that GRF and Everhardus were great friends through freshman year, with the probability that Everhardus gave him a start in student politics (*Big Men on Campus*, pp. 22, 23). Cannon, *Time and Chance*, p. 19, gives another story involving another freshman, Dave Conklin. See also Ford, *TTH*, p. 51; Ford, "In Defense of the Competitive Urge," p. 22; Dinse, *Mr. C.M.U.*, p. 25; *Michigan Alumnus*, 39:3; *MD*, October 4, 1933; Hugh R. Conklin to GRF, November 11, 1931, in GRF Scrapbook #1, GRFL. A good discussion of fraternities' competition to secure leading athletes as members is in Stockwell, *Rudderless*, pp. 140-42.

17. Joseph A. Bursley to Felix A. Jenkins, February 14, 1931; to James O. Murfin, February 25, 1931, University of Michigan, Vice-President for Student Affairs, Records, BHL; *Deke Quarterly* 50, no. 2, (May 1932): 113; Tobin, "The Great Raid."

The Dekes had long had the reputation of a "party house." Their membership fell roughly into two classes, which often overlapped — uninhibited rich boys and leading athletes. Coach Cliff Keen called the Dekes "a pretty snazzy bunch. My recollection and understanding is that the wealthy were in that fraternity." Intelligence and wit were attributes not associated with the chapter, whose academic performance was often nearly the weakest of the sixty fraternities on campus — and the fraternities as a group had a lower average than did undergraduates as a whole. But they were certainly a house that knew how to have a good time — a "brawl," as fraternity parties were revealingly known.[18]

When the teetotaling, nonsmoking, reserved Jerry Ford came out to 1912 Geddes Avenue to wash dishes and socialize with the brothers, he found, surprisingly, that he liked the group. Partly it was the athletic atmosphere. Two varsity football players, Everhardus and sophomore Bethel Kelly, were brothers, and Ford's friend Jack Beckwith was a pledge. Louis Colombo, a junior, was on tap to be manager of the football team the next year. Other sports were well represented too. But the house also appealed to Ford's temperament: he enjoyed hanging out with hell-raisers even though he raised little or no hell himself. The brothers in Omicron probably reminded him of some of his more boisterous friends in the Thirty-Thirties. By the holiday break he was thinking seriously of becoming a Deke.[19]

The first stage of freshman football climaxed November 20 with a game against the best of the physical education freshmen under Coach Wally Weber, before a crowd of several hundred. The opponents were freshmen from the School of Education who planned a career in teaching sports. Some were very good. Ford started at center for Coach Fisher's team, with responsibility for the kicking as well, but he was outclassed by the opposing kicker, a Muskegon boy named John Regeczi, who got off a beautiful 60-yard arc at one point. (Regeczi would end up punting on the varsity during Ford's career.) Wet weather meant a muddy, slippery field and not much impressive play on either side; the final score was 2-0 in favor of Fisher's freshmen. Nevertheless, Ford, Ward, Borgmann, Beckwith,

18. Ford, *TTH*, p. 51; Keen-Pollock interview, GRFL, p. 8. A list of all the fraternities' academic averages in the 1920s and 1930s is in University of Michigan, Vice-President for Student Affairs, records, BHL. "Brawl": Paul L. Adams to family, February 1929, Adams Papers, BHL; Harris, *King Football*, p. 48; GRF to Frederica Pantlind, [September 30, 1933], Ford-Pantlind Letters, GRFL.

19. *Deke Quarterly* 51, no. 1 (January 1933): 38, and no. 4 (December 1933).

and twenty-six others received their "numerals" — in essence, admission to spring freshman football.[20]

Perhaps at Thanksgiving, when students had only one day off, but definitely at Christmas, Ford went home to see his parents and share his college experiences. Few students at Ann Arbor had cars, and most likely he took the Michigan Central. Of course, he had written regularly, mostly in the grand tradition of college freshmen, about how hard he was working; with a ready ear for reassuring clichés, he assured correspondents that he was "too busy for words," "burning the midnight oil," with "a million and one things to do," usually concluding, "I'd better cease my pen pushing for the evening." But letters were no substitute for face-to-face conversation. To the younger brothers, Jerry's return meant games and competition. He would be up early doing push-ups or running laps in good weather, challenging them to shoot pool or shoot baskets. At some point during the college years, he got interested in skiing, a new sport that was just coming into popularity among the rich; it was perhaps introduced to him by one of the Deke brothers. With borrowed or rented equipment he went out to the Kent Country Club and practiced the basics on its snowy slopes. Naturally he got together with old friends — Mary Hondorp, for instance, who was clerking at a store, and Allen Elliott, who was home from Western Michigan College.[21]

From his parents he learned that the paint company was barely surviving, and salaries for all workers from management down had been cut. Business was very slow. His father was spending more time at the Ford-Blake Fuel Company, with its office on Madison Avenue, working with Harold Swain to try to keep that company profitable. The family would have to move again, since the holder of the mortgage on the Lake Drive house was unwilling to work out easier terms of payment. Fortunately, the housing market in East Grand Rapids was in free fall — many Lake Drive homes had no Christmas lights that year, but were dark, empty, and for sale. A clever dealer like his father should be able to pick up something good the family could afford, still in the same area.[22]

20. *MD*, November 20 and December 4, 1931.

21. The academic calendar is on the first page of the University of Michigan *General Catalogue for 1931-1932*. The quoted phrases are from GRF's correspondence with his friend Frederica Pantlind, September 17 and 30, 1933, GRFL. Sports with his brothers are referred to in the Steven and Richard Ford interview at Gerald R. Ford Museum, Grand Rapids, October 15, 2010, and the Richard Ford interview with author, May 31, 2012. Skiing: Harold Bosscher interview.

22. In the 1932 Grand Rapids telephone directory GRF Sr. had a number at the Ford-

With his mother and father he discussed his new contact with the Deke house and his interest in fraternity life. Jerry Sr. knew next to nothing about fraternities, having attended neither high school nor college, and could offer no guidance. For a young man with limited resources, fraternities posed a dilemma. They were expensive and took up a lot of time. Peer pressure within them led young men to increase their expenses on clothes and possessions, to adopt a more costly lifestyle. But they were socially central at Ann Arbor, and there was a good deal of pressure, particularly on athletes, to join. Now here were the Dekes, eager to have Jerry and willing to work out ways to keep his expenses low. Still, it seemed like the wrong decision when family finances were so tight.[23]

Nevertheless, Jerry Ford did in fact join the Dekes and was an active member until graduation in 1935. He incurred the customary expenses on fees, assessments, rent, and the like, and even though some of it was compensated by service to the house, he still spent a good deal. He changed his look to match the brothers' style; that his wardrobe improved is clear from photographs. And yet this indulgence took place in a financially desperate context, in which one year Ford had to beg friends and family for a substantial loan to stay in college. A reader of his autobiography, *A Time to Heal*, which emphasizes his financial difficulty staying in college, might justifiably ask how he managed.

The answer, never mentioned or even hinted at by Ford himself, is elsewhere in his papers: a deposition he made in 1938, when the divorce and child-support suit between his natural parents came up for final settlement. Asked whether his mother gave him financial support during his college years, he replied that every year he was at Michigan he received from his mother (not his parents) sums amounting to $700 or $800. This was a considerable amount in the Depression — for a frugal student, $700 would have paid for all expenses of one semester's enroll-

---

Blake Fuel Company in the 1400 block of Madison Avenue, Southeast; the 1933 city directory listed him as its secretary-treasurer. Art Brown recalled that his family got coal on easy terms through him during the Depression.

23. GRF's initial attitude toward fraternities is hard to establish. He may have wanted to join one from the beginning, despite his lack of funds. One set of recollections from DKE alumni begins with his taking the initiative by visiting the house to get acquainted with the brothers (Henry Berry, "Thanksgiving Eve in Michigan," *Deke Quarterly* 94 [1975]: 95); another, which I have accepted, depicts his contact as beginning indirectly, with the dishwashing job. For what it is worth, Don Nichols, who seems to have been equally pressed for money, pledged Chi Psi in March (*MD*, March 6, 1932).

ment.[24] Some of it doubtless went for books and academic fees, but none for his two largest expenditures, room and board. His meals were paid for by his kitchen work, although the fraternity probably lost money on the exchange — like most football players, Ford had a huge appetite; and as later chapters will show, he paid no room rent for a couple of years. Thus the rest of his mother's support covered fraternity and lifestyle expenditures.

Social success was of high importance to Dorothy Ford. It was she who displayed family heirlooms in the living room; it was she who belonged to the DAR; it was she who maintained the piano as a centerpiece of the living room, although no one played except herself. A woman who stressed the importance of ballroom dancing, courtesy letters, and tea parties would likely have understood the very real social importance of fraternities at Michigan and the avenues to success that they represented for her first-born son.[25]

Moreover, hers was not an atypical viewpoint. Edmund Love, whose career at Ann Arbor was repeatedly interrupted by money problems, kept up his fraternity membership through graduation. So did Ford's friend Jack Stiles, facing the same difficulties. There was evidently a middle-class school of thought that saw fraternities not as frills in a university education but as a basic component — a sort of male finishing school. Unlike many of their counterparts later in the twentieth century, fraternity men of the thirties, even the partying athletes of the Dekes, cultivated "an effortless ease of manner, a poised assurance, a readiness for finding just the right word," and a taste in clothes that enabled them to spot a man who was wearing the wrong tie.[26]

It seems probable, then, that at Christmas of 1931, Dorothy Ford quietly assured her son that if he decided to pledge the Dekes she would see

24. GRF deposition in *King v. King*, June 1, 1939, copy in vertical file, GRFL, pp. 2-3; University of Michigan, *General Catalogue for 1931-1932*, p. 29.

25. A couple of comments in Betty Ford's *The Times of My Life*, pp. 45, 59, spotlight DGF's stress on ancestry and propriety.

26. Love, *Hanging On*, pp. 56-209; Stiles, "With the Coin We Blew," pp. 161-322. Even the university's scientist-president, Alexander Ruthven, conceded "that for a certain type of individual, a fraternity could be an effective means of adjusting to college life" (interview with Peter E. Van de Water, January 30, 1970, Peter Edgar Van de Water Papers, BHL). Cf. Stockwell, *Rudderless*, p. 156: "More and more Tom was coming to appreciate that the books and the classes constituted a very small part of this process of education." On fraternity men's manners, see Haines, *Blaine of the Backfield*, pp. 26, 52.

that the funds he needed were not wanting. This spending, unacknowledged by Ford himself because it undercut his own narrative, which stressed the sacrifice and self-discipline involved in getting through college, lasted four years and played an important part in his education, as succeeding chapters will show.[27]

Immediately after Thanksgiving, freshman basketball began, coached by the same man who coached football, Ray Fisher. About a hundred boys turned out at the field house — Ford, his friend Bill Borgmann, and his roommate Nichols were among them. (Willis Ward did not go out for basketball, probably because he had learned that it was unofficial policy not to play blacks on the varsity — "skin-on-skin" contact was the issue.) As in football, their number dwindled rapidly, as many aspirants found the level too challenging. By early December, they were down to about thirty and ready to play other schools' freshmen. Coach Rose drove over from Grand Rapids to encourage Jerry and to watch. Ford was the same player he had been in high school — aggressive on defense, not very fast, and not too accurate a shooter. By the time they returned after Christmas, a pattern had developed: Nichols played regularly, but Ford and Borgmann spent the game mostly on the bench. Fisher, unimpressed with the freshmen as a whole — "good ball handlers but undistinguished shots," as he called them — had no need of their skills. In recognition of their steady commitment, however, Ford and both friends got their numerals at the season's close in March.[28]

---

27. DGF's aid to her son probably came from the estate of her father Levi Gardner. GRF's understanding was that the estate was not large (Ford-Cannon interviews), but records in the Kent County Probate Court (#26730) show that it amounted to about $30,000, mainly in real property. His grandmother Adele Gardner received $150 a month from rents, and there was at least one distribution of assets. It is not clear how much of this income was available to DGF, but it was enough — perhaps barely enough — to cover the expense of fraternity life. It is not difficult to understand why GRF chose not to mention it. The real story of his undergraduate years was not just financial sacrifice but also the growth of upper-class consumption habits and affiliations.

28. Varsity basketball practice began in October (Report of the Athletic Department, 1934, p. 8, BHL), but freshman basketball can hardly have begun before November 20, since Ray Fisher coached both teams. A January 29 clipping, probably from *MD*, in the Athletic Department Scrapbook #15, gave basic facts about the freshmen and praised Nichols by name for his improvement; GRF and Borgmann were not mentioned. The team photo in the 1932 *Michiganensian*, p. 197, showed all three, GRF with the slightly wild-haired athletic look that he had affected in high school but was about to disappear under fraternity influence. The racial situation is discussed in Sukandasa, "Black Varsity

Ford and Don Nichols associated a lot that winter, on the basketball court, in the locker room, and studying in the room they shared. They seriously attacked the books for semester exams at the end of January. Nichols had plenty of chances to firm up his estimate of the boy he'd known so long, which he shared years later with a reporter. It resembled others' estimates but was of interest because it rested on a longer acquaintance: "I always thought of him as the typical 'All-American image.' He was very clean-cut, a good student, excellent in sports, rather reserved, with high moral standards." He also mentioned Ford's phenomenal concentration, which paid off well that fall: his grades averaged slightly above B, which represented one of the best semesters in his undergraduate career.[29]

Semester grades were sent out in the first weeks of February, on "Black Friday," with the failure slips clearly identifiable by their "particularly offensive shade of greenish yellow." Helen Loomis, a freshman from Pennsylvania, wrote her parents that quite a few girls in her dorm had flunked out, and three others had had nervous breakdowns. But grades were not the only factor; fear of bank closings played a part in the dropouts as well. In the first two months of 1932, a massive number of students dropped out of the university, 771 according to the student newspaper. In the DKE house Ford could see a similar attrition: of the fourteen freshmen who had pledged the fraternity in 1931, only eight remained as sophomores by the time the chapter was photographed for the 1932 annual.[30]

On March 7, pledge day, Ford united with DKE, along with ten other freshmen. After the pledge, administered to him by a brother from Grand Rapids, Edward J. Frey, he had to buy the seventy-five-cent, three-colored enamel button (or "spike pin") denoting his status. He did not move into the house — freshmen were not allowed to room in fraternities — but he

Lettermen," pp. 40-42. Coach Rose: Dinse, *Mr. C.M.U.*, p. 34. Close of season: GRF Scrapbook #1, GRFL.

GRF injured his knee in the fall of 1932, and it was not operated on until spring 1933; with the injury, he clearly made no attempt to go out for basketball as a sophomore (Ford, *TTH*, p. 51).

29. *MD*[?], January 29, 1932, Athletic Department Scrapbook #15, BHL; clipping from *The Almanac*, Thomas Ford Scrapbook, GRFL, p. 27. GRF's University of Michigan transcript, 1935, GRFL. A plausible guess would be that GRF's heavy participation in fraternity and football affairs from March 1932 on reduced his study time and affected his grades in later semesters.

30. Helen Loomis to her parents, February 17, 1932, Helen M. Loomis Letters, BHL; *MD*, March 29, 1933. 1931 *Michiganensian*, p. 183; 1932 *Michiganensian*, p. 351; Haines, *Blaine of the Backfield*, p. 175. Cf. Love, *Hanging On*, p. 106.

did relax his rigorous schedule a bit, enjoying life like a fraternity man with the assurance of his mother's backing. He took in an occasional movie in the college town across State Street from the campus, unapologetically explaining, "between work and football I must have my diversion." Initiation and full-scale membership would come afterward, at "Hell Week" in May.[31]

Two days later came the most important day of the semester, in Ford's personal calendar: Head Coach Harry Kipke announced the beginning of spring football practice, during which the next fall's varsity football team would be selected. All returning varsity players, plus the best of the freshmen, were invited to turn out to the field house, where the sessions would be held three evenings a week until the weather warmed up enough for outside work. They would be practicing under the immediate supervision of the top two coaches, Kipke and Athletic Director Yost.[32]

Not a big man — at 5 feet 9 inches, he was smaller than Ford or Ward, with slicked-down black hair — Kipke was young to be a head coach of a major athletic power, only thirty-three, but he had the energy and emotional intensity for the role. He had been one of the greatest punters ever to play for Michigan, on Yost's undefeated teams of the early 1920s. In fact, he, like the field house, the great stadium, and the athletic program as a whole, was a creation of Fielding Yost, the tall, white-haired, patient man who stood on the sidelines of each practice, watching and occasionally commenting. Yost was in sober fact a living legend in college football, along with Amos Alonzo Stagg and Walter Camp. He had been coaching since the beginning of the century, when he had been known as "Hurry Up" for his urgent style of play and his "Point-a-Minute" teams; later Michigan alumni knew him as the determined, resourceful academic infighter who mobilized support and money for his grand vision of a field house, a stadium, and an intramural program; now journalists wrote of him as Michigan's Grand Old Man. In theory, he was retired from coaching, but in fact, he was almost always present; football was his life.[33]

---

31. *Deke Quarterly* 50, no. 2 (May 1932): 113; *MD*, March 6, 1932; Shufro, "The Great Depression's Effect," p. 50. The price of a pledge button is from the list of "Fraternity Supplies" on the back cover of *Deke Quarterly*. "Spike pin": Haines, *Blaine of the Backfield*, p. 73. GRF to Frederica Pantlind, October 8, 1933, Ford-Pantlind Letters, GRFL.

32. Clippings in Athletic Department Scrapbook #15, March 7, 1932; GRF Scrapbook #1, GRFL.

33. Soderstrom, *The Big House*, pp. 2-3, 356-57; Denham, *Growing Up in Grand Rapids*, p. 128.

Candidates for the 1932 varsity were aware that they had a tradition to uphold. The 1931 season had been another success for the Wolverines: they had won eight games, with one tie and a loss to longtime rival Ohio State. It ended anticlimactically, in a three-way tie for the Big Ten championship. Those who were lucky enough to make the next season's team aimed to match, and if possible surpass, that record. Divided into Yellow and Blue teams, named for the two team colors, aspirants battled in regular scrimmages. Ford found himself on the Blue team, playing alongside varsity stars like quarterback Harry Newman, the immensely talented runner and passer who was going into his senior year; halfback Stan Fay, who had scored two touchdowns in the 1931 Princeton game; end Ivan Williamson, whom Kipke called "the smartest player I ever coached or hope to coach"; and tackle Whitey Wistert, in addition to Everhardus.[34]

Center does not seem like a position that would lead to the kind of notability enjoyed by Newman and Fay, but Ford found that in the Michigan system — Yost's system — the center had an unusually vital role. Yost's strategy, which had been mocked for years by opponents as "a punt, a pass, and a prayer," was basically defensive; Michigan teams punted the ball often, sometimes on second or third down, to get better field position, and then tried to force the other team's offense into mistakes, on which they seized for quick scores. The defensive center, who effectively captained the defensive team and could change the formation on his own at any time, was a crucial man in that scheme. The Wolverines had a tradition of outstanding centers: Maynard Morrison, the all-American who had just graduated, had begun as a back but was retrained as a center by Kipke and Yost. An article by Kipke expressed his mentor's viewpoint: "Most big coaches open the season with a hunt for two tackles, but Michigan looks for a center. We regard the center as the most valuable single defensive unit on the team." Ford knew that if he did well, he could go far.[35]

He did spectacularly well. Late in March the weather eased and the team moved outside, drawing progressively larger crowds of students to watch practices. There was a lot of comment about Ward and fullback Russell Oliver, and about varsity players like Newman and center Chuck Bernard, but the blond center from Grand Rapids caught observers' at-

34. Perry, *The Wolverines*, pp. 137-41, 147.

35. Kipke and Fitzgerald, "A Punt, a Pass, and a Prayer," pp. 12-13, 58; Kipke and Fitzgerald, "Take Your Eye Off That Ball," pp. 16, 82; McGregor, "A Tale of Two Centers," p. 27. By "defensive center" here, I simply mean the center in his defensive role; this was before the advent of the two-platoon system.

tention with his steady aggressiveness, and his name came up again and again. Practice closed on May 7 with a final Yellow-Blue game in the big stadium. Over 300 high school coaches, in Ann Arbor for a coaching clinic with Kipke, watched, along with a scattering of university students, in the warm spring sun. The Blues won decisively, 33-7, and the coaches retired to discuss prospects for the fall and to name the outstanding freshman player, who would receive the highly coveted Chicago Alumni trophy.[36]

Immediately after the end of spring practice, Hell Week — the initiation period for pledges — began in the fraternities. In many houses, it was no longer a full week, but more like a weekend. The content and the purpose were the same, however — traditional rituals of humiliation and subordination, the object of which was to bind the pledges more closely to the group they were joining. An earlier practice of sending the pledges out into the community to carry out ridiculous or hazardous assignments had gotten out of hand in the twenties and was largely discontinued; most of the action took place in the house.

At least two accounts exist of Hell Week in Michigan fraternities of this era. The Dekes were not the subjects of either one, but their ritual was doubtless similar enough to this 1930 description to give readers an idea of what Ford and the rest went through:

> The pledges had been compelled to go around the house with nothing on but a celluloid wing collar around their necks and a wooden paddle of their own making in their hands. Whenever any member requested them to do so they handed him the paddle, stooped down in a certain undignified posture, and received very stimulating admonitions upon their flanks. There were endless variations to this game; and especially around meal time, when all the fellows were assembled in the house, this process happened many times during the hour. The only relief in such periods came from the fact that after many successive blows a certain blessed numbness was certain to follow.

Or, as Edmund Love put it succinctly, "The two basic ingredients of Hell Week were sleeplessness and paddling."[37]

36. Athletic Department Scrapbook #15, clippings from March 19, April 2, May 2; GRF Scrapbook #1; *MD*, May 7, 8, and 12, 1931.
37. Stockwell, *Rudderless*, pp. 106-7; Love, *Hanging On*, p. 72; Morris, *American in Search of a Way*, p. 40.

Ford saved some of his instructions, so we know that "Neophyte Ford" had to sleep in the room of Louis Colombo, the football manager, and shine his shoes every morning; that he was not allowed to speak unless spoken to nor leave the dinner table without permission; and that at midnight every night during the period, in a ritual peculiar to DKE, he had to kiss the bottom step of "the goddess's shrine" in a curious little building off State Street, called the Shant. This was where, on May 7, with his probation completed, after the welcome dinner at the house, he got up and recited his prepared piece:

> I'm the great Jerry Ford of football fame,
> In many large cities they know me by name.
> Grand Rapids, Muskegon, all call me their own,
> For my playing is great — many games have I won.
> The people all say that I have lots of "it"
> So why should I put up with this sort of shit,
> Give me my pin! ---- I'm sick of this crap,
> What the hell guys do you think I'm a sap.[38]

And he received the five-dollar, lozenge-shaped black-and-gold pin with its Greek letters.

The following week, on May 12, all football players were required to attend the final dinner at the Union. Dressed in suits, singly and in pairs, they walked to the towering student center — students were not allowed to drive cars — where the Chicago Alumni trophy, a full-sized silver football on a pedestal, sat on a table at the front of the room. Later in the evening Meyer Morton, for whom the trophy was named, made the presentation, for "improvement, attitude, regular attendance, and promise," amid enthusiastic applause from the whole room. It went to Jerry Ford — the first center to win the trophy in its eight-year history. Almost ten years later, Ford still considered this the greatest accomplishment of his life — a substantial honor in front of his peers — an assist for his chapter in its battle for prestige with other fraternities — and, more than that, a promise for the rest of his years at Michigan. It guaranteed that he would be on the

38. The poem and the instructions are in GRF Scrapbook #1, GRFL. The authorship of the poem is unclear, but GRF seems at least to have made final changes in the wording. "It" in line 5 presumably refers to "It" as a synonym for "sex appeal" during the 1920s (e.g., Clara Bow, "The 'It' Girl"), and I have put the word into quotation marks for clarity. For more on the Shant, see the next chapter.

varsity, wearing the maize and blue uniform. He would play ball with the best from then on. Ford, in other words, could do what he most enjoyed, while putting together the credentials for adulthood.[39]

39. A photo of GRF, holding the trophy, standing with Herman Everhardus, who had been the recipient in 1931, is in *Grand Rapids*, October 1974, p. 29. Both are wearing suits for some formal occasion — probably not the award dinner itself, which was in the evening. It is described in *Michigan Alumnus*, 38:593, *Detroit Free Press*, May 13, 1932, and in a clipping from the *Herald* in GRF Scrapbook #1. GRF's elation at winning is in Ray Barnes's cartoon profile, "Razzing the Rapids," *Herald*, November 16, 1941.

The Chicago Alumni trophy was called the Meyer Morton trophy in honor of an outstanding alumnus from the class of 1912, who had become a Big Ten official. GRF in *TTH*, p. 51, refers to it by that title.

The ban on student automobiles began in 1927 and lasted through World War II; despite some student opposition, it was largely accepted at the time and fondly remembered afterward: Frantz, "Doctor, Where Were You?" p. 24; *MD*, September 22, 1931; *Michigan Alumnus*, 40:163; F. Bruce Kimball letter to *Michigan Today*, January 22, 2008 (online); Denham, *Growing Up in Grand Rapids*, pp. 128-29. A late-night collision on Packard Avenue during spring vacation 1932, in which Hugh Conklin, the president of the DKE chapter, was involved, illustrated the dangers of driving in the 1930s; the other driver, also a student, died of a skull fracture (*Michigan Alumnus*, 38:307).

CHAPTER 10

Transformations

One month later, Ford was back in the little non-air-conditioned concrete-block factory on Crosby Street, in the heat of a Grand Rapids summer, mixing and pouring paint at a wage that had been cut to twenty-five cents an hour, with Elliott and two or three other young men. They worked from 7:30 A.M. to 4:30 P.M. Younger brother Tom, now on the payroll pasting labels on paint cans, observed Jerry with amusement — "the sloppiest guy in the place," he called him. All the factory floor workers got paint on their hands, which they wiped off on their pants legs — but Jerry, shirtless and sweaty, wore cutoffs and wiped the paint directly on his legs. He got more on himself than anyone else on the floor; the family joke was that he bathed every Friday to wash it off. "It was a real muscle-building job," said his co-worker "Yutz" Kaler. "You'd never have known he was the boss's son."[1]

Business was slack and supplies were short. Tom used varnish instead of glue to paste the labels on the cans, and slid a page from an old business

1. Tom Ford's reminiscences are in Vestal, *Jerry Ford, Up Close*, pp. 51-52, and a clipping from the *Lansing State Journal*, May 6, 1965, in the Ford Paint and Varnish Scrapbook, GRFL. I also used the reminiscences of George ("Yutz") Kaler in Fran Glennon and Evelyn Hofer, "Jerry Ford's Grand Rapids," and Richard Ford's interview, May 31, 2012. Besides Kaler, one other worker, George Zylstra, was identifiable in the 1930 census; both were about GRF's age. The firm's financial condition is suggested by the fact that it had suspended payments to Simpson for its machinery early that year; Grand Rapids Wood Finishing Company Records, Ledger 11, account 84, Grand Rapids Public Museum. In the bank crisis of 1933, when GRF Sr. lost access to the company bank account, he reduced wages to $5 a week paid out of pocket from current receipts (the same wage he paid himself) and pledged to make up the difference when times improved. He kept the promise (Vestal, p. 51).

directory under the can in case of spills. Local contractors stopped by to purchase their supplies, fewer than the previous year but enough to keep the business barely alive.[2]

Young Ford did not work at the plant the entire summer in any of the years he was in college, but in 1932 he had a particularly pressing reason not to — a severe problem with hemorrhoids ("I was having a hell of a time"). Luckily, Grand Rapids had a small private clinic that specialized in colon and rectal surgery — locals called it the "butt hospital." Its prices were high, but Jerry Sr. once again showed his skill in the art of the deal: Jerry Jr.'s problem was taken care of in exchange for enough Ford paint to redo the whole clinic. (This solution may have been the beginning of a new sales approach; in the next few years, the company sold its products to hospitals, clinics, and sanatoriums all over Lower Michigan.) For the rest of the summer, young Ford convalesced — part of it, probably, at the Congers' Ottawa Beach cottage.[3]

It was a presidential election year, and the Fords, with their civic interest, must have spent some time discussing President Hoover's reelection prospects against the popular governor of New York, Franklin Roosevelt, a cousin of the great Teddy. No direct evidence exists, but it seems likely that the loyally Republican Fords felt the election was Hoover's to lose. Hoover had been trying hard, and he felt successfully, to manage the Depression. There was no reason to believe that Roosevelt would do any better. A rising sophomore at the university felt in October that Hoover would win reelection, though he would "have to work for it." So did most of her classmates; Hoover won the straw vote held at the university in November by almost two to one. An architecture student from Sweden with a less provincial view of American politics, Raoul Wallenberg, however, understood as early as September that Roosevelt was far in the lead, even in Michigan. In Michigan, as elsewhere, voters needed someone to blame for the rising unemployment, the failing banks, and the generally miserable conditions. Without embracing the claims of the young socialist campus orators that business or the capitalist system had brought on the crisis, most Michigan voters saw the dour, righteous president as a convenient scapegoat. Moreover, Roosevelt's election meant the end of Prohibition, which had become

2. Vestal, *Jerry Ford, Up Close*, pp. 51-52.

3. Ford-Cannon interviews, April 25, 1990, p. 3, GRFL. The history of the Ferguson Droste Ferguson (FDF) Clinic — GRF called it "Dosty Ferguson" — is told in its "Patient Handbook," 1967, in the GRPL vertical file. The Ford Paint and Varnish Scrapbook in GRFL contains several testimonials from clinics and medical establishments in the 1930s.

bitterly unpopular in hard economic times. In November Roosevelt would carry the state.[4]

There was not much else to talk about that summer of 1932. That the paint company was still open was amazing, when one looked at other families and other businesses. In Flint Edmund Love's father's coal company had lost all its employees; as Love put it, "We still had no money and could look forward to absolutely nothing." (Harold Swain's coal company, too, was on its last legs.) The Fords, at least, could talk about their search for a new house in East Grand Rapids, which was still ongoing when Jerry returned to Ann Arbor in September.[5]

Ford was eager for a year of football and fraternity life. He would room at the Deke house, his meals paid by continuing to wash dishes every night of the school year. He moved his few possessions into a room he shared with Jack Beckwith. Before long he would have stationery printed for himself with 1912 Geddes as the address.[6]

His surroundings on Geddes Avenue differed radically from the modesty of his family's house. The Deke house was the largest fraternity house on campus, a forty-room Tudor revival mansion built in 1912 and purchased by the chapter in 1922 from banker-politician George Millen. It occupied its own three-and-one-half-acre domain across from the University Arboretum, and had such features as a porte cochere, an elevator, a tennis court, a six-car garage, and a third-floor ballroom. Ten years of occupancy by the Dekes had left it rather battered in spots — it is not clear, for instance, whether the elevator still worked — but the paneled, baronial living room and dining room conveyed an image of luxury.[7]

4. *MD*, October 26, 1932; Helen M. Loomis to her parents, November 6, 1932, Helen M. Loomis Letters, BHL; Raoul Wallenberg to Gustav O. Wallenberg, October 22, 1932, in Wallenberg, *Letters and Dispatches*, p. 80. In the campus straw vote November 2, Hoover beat Roosevelt about 2 to 1 among students and by a slightly smaller proportion among the faculty (*MD*, November 3, 1932). Socialist orators on the Michigan campus are mentioned almost daily in *MD* during September and October, and in *Michigan Alumnus*, 39:27. *MD*, October 29, 1932, mentioned fears of the "rising socialist vote" on campus. In the November straw poll Norman Thomas received 420 votes — about 15 percent of the total student vote, and considerably better than his share of the Michigan state returns, only 2.35 percent. Roosevelt's share of the state vote was 55 percent.

5. Love, *Hanging On*, p. 95.

6. Ford, *TTH*, p. 51. His letters to Freddy Pantlind in the fall of 1933, at GRFL, were written on letterhead stationery with the Geddes Avenue address.

7. Basic information about the house, with a postcard view from c. 1930, is in an entry at the Ann Arbor District Library blog submitted by Wystan Stevens, www.aadl.org/

Twenty-six brothers, from sophomores to seniors, lived in the house, with the more senior brothers on the upper floors. The sophomores, including Ford, were in an extension built over the servants' quarters, with two-man rooms lined up off a long hall and a group bath and shower for them all. This part of the house was relatively spartan — but even here, the brothers enjoyed the services of the house caretaker, butler, and factotum "Moose" Muirhead, a lean, smilingly dignified African American, originally from Tennessee, who had been with Omicron for years. In white coat, Moose presided at the punch bowl when the big parties were held; in the morning, he roused the brothers from sleep with standard lines about "beans and greens" or "the girls will be choosing husbands today." He had a wife, who cooked sometimes for the Dekes and sometimes at other houses; as in Fitzgerald's Princeton, Ann Arbor fraternities considered it almost obligatory to have a black servant or two.[8]

The Dekes, moreover, had something no other fraternity could boast: its own downtown "chapel," the Shant, built in 1878 before the chapter even had a house of its own. The small Gothic brick building behind a high stone wall was used only for meetings and initiations, only at night. It had, on one hand, a ceremonial feel, like a strange riff on Victorian Christianity — gas fixtures, stained glass, ecclesiastical-looking mahogany furniture including the "Beta Throne" — but it was also a bit of a playroom, with features like a hand-operated elevator and a subterranean chamber where the brothers sang songs that echoed spookily in the upper floors. Pledges were brought in blindfolded to a dark, windowless room and left to find their way upstairs to the "shrine." Ford, in adulthood, recalled scaling the ten-foot wall outside for some reason. Here, every Saturday night during the academic year at eleven o'clock or midnight, chapter meetings took place, often with a certain amount of drinking. In the small hours, the

---

node/9306. The description, with interior and exterior photos, comes from Omicron of DKE Yearbook, 1924, and *Delta Kappa Epsilon* booklet, c. 1965, in Howard M. Ehrmann Papers, both BHL, as well as *Ann Arbor News*, October 16, 1968. According to *MD*, March 20, 1934, it had the highest assessed value of any fraternity house on the campus.

8. *Delta Kappa Epsilon* booklet. Details in this paragraph are from Omicron alumni Jim Grady of Bloomfield Hills, on the layout of the house, and Lin Hanson of Chicago, on Moose Muirhead. I want to express my appreciation to both. Clarence B. Muirhead, caretaker, and his wife Mary were listed at the Geddes Avenue address in the 1933 and 1935 city directories; in 1941, however, according to the same source, Mary was cooking at another fraternity. Another example of an African American fraternity retainer is in Gilbreth, *I'm a Lucky Guy*, p. 85.

brothers emerged from their chapel and marched in double file past the president's residence, with locked arms, loudly singing Deke songs, up South University and back to the Geddes Avenue house:

> "When we came to college, we were all on studies bent —
> Hazing, smoking, et id om were far from our intent,
> We'd not the faintest thought what college really meant,
> Delta Kappa Epsilon forever."[9]

As a full-fledged brother, Ford's first job was rushing — helping to interview all prospects for the year's new class of pledges. University enrollment was down in fall 1932, and a number of potential applicants were too financially strapped to consider joining a fraternity; but there were still plenty from families unaffected by the Depression, and they had to be invited to meals and politely grilled about their interests, "where they lived, where they were from," while brothers scrutinized their dress and tried to judge if they would fit well into the chapter. It was a pain, dressing for dinner every night, standing around and being "inanely polite," but it was preparation for adulthood. The constant questioning, and attempting to remember all the answers, was enough to make a fellow "crazy, or at least a little bit *queer*," Ford complained in a letter to a friend.[10]

But rushing had only a small part of his attention anyway, for it took place in the two weeks just before the fall semester, in which practice for the varsity football team began. Ford reported to the field house Wednesday, September 15, to pick up his varsity uniform: cleated shoes, tan lace-up pants, and a navy blue jersey with his number, 48, in large maize numerals. The number was on both front and back, an innovation that had begun just two seasons earlier. Although the era of plastic and synthetic fibers had not yet dawned, the clothing incorporated some protections: shoulder pads, for instance, and hip protectors "of Belgian fiber rubber" with an air cushion. The black leather helmet was nothing but

9. "Brother Gerald R. Ford, Jr., Omicron '35 Remembered"; *Michigan Deke*, July 1981, pp. 4-5, copy in GRFL; *MD*, November 9, 1952; June 23, 1971; Frantz, "Doctor, Where Were You?" pp. 36-37; Stiles, "With the Coin We Blew," pp. 162-63; lyrics of some DKE songs are in the Howard M. Ehrmann Papers, BHL ("et id om" is undergraduate Latin for "and all that").

10. Rushing is described in Stockwell, *Rudderless*, pp. 27-28, 34; Edwards, *Undergraduates*, pp. 54-56; Haines, *Blaine of the Backfield*, p. 247; and GRF to Frederica Pantlind, September 30, 1933, GRFL.

leather, but it was high-domed to forestall concussions; the pants were duck or canvas to resist the impact of cleats. Improvements in protective gear, like knee braces, ankle taping, and so forth, were an ongoing part of college football in the thirties, spurred by public and press concern about injuries and deaths on the field. As recently as February, the coaches had met and made rules changes in six major areas, protective gear being one, to make the game safer.[11]

Suited up at last, Ford would become one of only forty-one boys who carried the university's reputation into contests with other schools. They were the nearest thing to nobility on campus. It was good to rejoin his teammates and hear their stories of the summer. Newman, Fay, and Everhardus, the backs, the glory boys of the team, were back and ready for action, as was Johnny Regeczi, the champion punter. Ivan Williamson had hurt his leg over the summer and was on the sick list, but was expected to be okay by the first game. Beckwith had dropped out of football, but Borgmann was still playing guard. Ford himself was in good shape; despite his time at the Droste Ferguson clinic, he had put on some extra pounds and now weighed in at 187, heavier than he had ever been.[12]

Willis Ward had been building muscles in factory work, like Ford, and told him all about it. Some players from the Detroit area, like Ward and Stan Fay, had begun benefiting in the early 1930s from Coach Kipke's close relationship with the Ford Motor Company. The contact was Harry Bennett, chief of security at Ford Motors, who lived farther out Geddes Road east of town and had become Kipke's fast friend. Through him Kipke had access to as many factory jobs as his players needed. A few years later it was charged that many of these Ford jobs were bogus, excuses to subsidize players while they honed their football skills on secluded parts of the River Rouge property, and that charge was a factor in Kipke's firing in 1937. It is hard to state how far such employment arrangements had progressed by 1932, but Ward was certainly a beneficiary — the classic example of a talented player who needed a summer salary.[13]

11. Clipping probably from the *Herald*, September 18, 1932, in GRF Scrapbook #1, GRFL; the 1932 uniform is described at blog.heritagesportsart.com/2010/08/university-of -michigan-football-uniform.html and www.mvictors.com/?pag_id=63647. For protective design changes in and before the 1930s, see "Griffon," "Softening Football's Thuds," p. 84, and *Detroit Free Press*, February 16, 1932, "Coaches Plan to Make Game Safe but Hard."

12. *Herald*, September 16, 1932; 1932 team roster in GRF Scrapbook #1, GRFL.

13. Four players for the Wolverines during GRF's three years on the varsity — Newman, Fay, Bernard, and Ward — found full-time jobs with Ford Motor shortly after

Kipke started the boys off with conditioning exercises and progressed to scrimmages after a few days, trying to decide on the best starting eleven for the Michigan State College game on October 1. Four players were potential centers to succeed all-American Maynard Morrison, who had graduated; Ford was one. The leading candidate, however, was Chuck Bernard, who had been on the varsity the year before. He was bigger than Ford and a first-rate defensive player. After a couple of days' practice, it was clear that Bernard was in top shape and deserved the starting post. Kipke was impressed by Ford and wanted to use him as well, but as in the past, Jerry lacked the speed to play tackle or guard. "He has a wonderful competitive spirit," Kipke told one of the ever-present reporters. "He has his place cinched as second string center, as I don't think he can displace as great a player as Chuck Bernard."[14]

The problem with being second-string center in 1932 was that it meant almost no playing time. Under the restrictive rules of substitution, a player who went out of the game could not come back on the field during the same quarter. (Prior to the 1932 rules change, he could not return until the next half.) Kipke did not want to risk taking any first-string player out for a large part of a half, especially one playing the important position of center, when he was faced with what looked like a series of tough games to open the season. The Wolverines' first game, as always, was with Michigan State College; the game with the little agricultural school had historically served as a warm-up contest for the conference games, but this year State happened to be strong, and eager to embarrass Michigan.

---

graduation in 1934 or 1935, as Kipke himself did after his firing in 1937. A wire story by Watson Spoelstra, carried in the *St. Petersburg Times*, July 12, 1943, under the head "Ford Industrial Empire Boasts Sports Notables," mentions the first three; Ward worked for Ford 1935-1939 and then left to attend law school (Greg Dooley, "Remembering Willis Ward," www.mgoblue.com/sports/m-footbl/spec-rel/101912aaa.html). Ward, Fay, and Newman were all Detroiters. It seems reasonable to suggest that they all benefited from the Kipke-Bennett relationship, which is mentioned in Kipke Scrapbook 1937, Box 2, Kipke Papers, BHL, and in numerous posts on the mvictors.com Web site. Ward certainly did: Kipke and Bennett, he said, "had been very nice to me in giving me jobs in the summertime on occasion" (Willis Ward interview with David S. Pollock, 1983, GRFL, p. 10). For background on Bennett, a colorful character, see Culver, "Harry Bennett: Hatchet Man, Architect, Artist, and Animal Lover," in the March 2000 issue of *Impressions*, the Washtenaw County Historical Society newsletter, pp. 1-5. His friendship with Kipke went back at least to 1934, and probably a few years before.

14. Clippings, probably from the *Herald*, on p. 40 of GRF Scrapbook #1, GRFL; *MD*, September 20, 1932.

Then came Northwestern, another normally weak team with a group of unusually good players, and then Ohio State, Michigan's bitter rival. Ford could expect to sit on the bench most of these games, with little chance to play before November.[15]

As it worked out, Ford did get some playing time in the game against State, which proved easier than Kipke had expected. By the end of the third quarter, with a twenty-point lead, the coach felt comfortable taking out his whole first string and putting in their replacements, so that Ford had his first thrilling experience of playing in Michigan Stadium before a crowd of 60,000 — heart pounding with excitement like any sophomore, worried about doing something stupid in front of that crowd. Like other athletes, he found that once he was actually on the field, he lost all awareness of the stands, the cheers, and the music, and focused entirely on the game; but when he first entered the stadium to the sound of "Hail to the Victors," there was a real, breathtaking feeling of attainment. He hoped his parents shared it; they had driven over from Grand Rapids, as they would do for every home game for the next three years, with the little brothers in tow. Tickets were a hefty $3.50 apiece in 1932.[16]

Apparently Ford did not play the following week against Northwestern, but he did on October 15 at Ohio State. The train ride to Columbus for his first out-of-town game was especially appealing to a boy who had traveled little in his school years. Ford always felt he learned a lot from his visits with the team to other Midwestern universities, and travel by rail was fun in itself. It was like the journey to Washington after graduation, with the difference being that he was with congenial, rowdy teammates. The atmosphere was a combination of luxury and horseplay, like a fraternity party: they swiped Pullman towels, ran plays up and down the aisles, and competed for the biggest steaks at dinner. The team left Thursday,

15. "How Are the New Football Rules Working?" *Literary Digest*, November 12, 1932. GRF, "In Defense of the Competitive Urge," p. 22, recalled the rules change but inaccurately placed it in 1934, not 1932. Arthur Miller commented, "In my day [1935] State was an agricultural college, and Michigan was 'The Harvard of the West'" ("University of Michigan," p. 132).

16. Russ Oliver, in his installment of "This I Remember," #37 (1966), mentioned his nervousness playing as a sophomore in the Ohio State game that year. GRF described himself as totally oblivious of events in the stands ("Gerald Ford," *MD* clipping, GRFL vertical file); the same attitude is expressed in Wood, *What Price Football?* pp. 30-31. *MD*, October 1 and 2, 1932, describes the game and the crowd; ticket stubs in the University of Michigan Club of Detroit correspondence, BHL, give ticket prices. Ford-Cannon interviews, April 26, 1990, p. 3, BHL, mentions his parents' attendance.

with an entourage of thirteen and trunkloads of equipment, to have time to practice and get the feel of the opponent's field, ignoring Friday classes; they stayed in a first-class hotel, with first-class meals up to game day. Game time was Saturday afternoon.[17]

The Ohio State game threw a wrench into the rest of Ford's sophomore season. Michigan won, but it was a hard-fought, very physical game, as encounters with Ohio State were apt to be. Ford was substituted in late in the fourth quarter, just long enough to injure his left knee in the same way he had hurt the right one in high school. His was by no means the only injury that afternoon — Stan Fay broke a rib, and halfback Jack Heston an ankle. The train trip back to Ann Arbor was even quieter than usual. For Ford, the knee turned into a chronic problem. Kipke used him in a couple of later games wearing a knee brace, but before long concluded that surgery was the only answer. Ford would continue to practice with the team — two hours a day, squad meetings two nights a week — but his season was essentially over. Fortunately, his services as backup center were not needed anyway. Chuck Bernard stayed unhurt and was in top form.[18]

Three solid victories over feared opponents, without a single point scored against them, awakened Kipke and the national sports press to the possibility that this team might be something special. In fact, the 1932 Wolverines went on to one of their best seasons in history, unbeaten and untied. The key was quarterback Newman; a remarkably accurate passer who had been off his form in 1931 but had now regained it, he was by consensus the best quarterback in college football that year. But he had great support. Bernard's consistent performance at center earned him a nomination as all-American. Johnny Regeczi's kicking was nearly as spectacular as Newman's passing, and in the next games two more outstanding players stepped into the spotlight, Ted Petoskey and Willis Ward.[19]

17. Potter, "Legacy of Leadership," p. 30. A good account, from 1926, of the team's train ride to an out-of-town game is in Soderstrom, *The Big House*, pp. 291-93; a photo of some of the baggage for an out-of-town trip is in the 1935 *Michiganensian*, p. 37. For the entourage, see Art Carstens's column in *MD*, November 3, 1934. See also Wood, *What Price Football?* p. 25

18. Harry G. Kipke to GRF Sr., October 25, 1932, Thomas G. Ford Papers, GRFL: "Jerry was very unfortunate in hurting his knee last week and of course was unable to play in the Illinois game. He is coming along fine and ought to see service next Saturday." See also *MD*, October 16 and 20, 1932, and *Michigan Alumnus*, 39:61-62. The knee brace is described in "Griffon," "Softening Football's Thuds," p. 84. Practice routine: "Gerald Ford," *MD* clipping, GRFL vertical file.

19. For a good, brief summary of the season, see Perry, *The Wolverines*, pp. 142-46.

The Ohio State slugfest affected Ward's playing career in the opposite way from Ford's. Fay's broken rib necessitated a reshuffling of backs and ends; two Saturdays later, against Princeton, Ward started at right end. Princeton was supposed to be a respite from the demanding Big Ten schedule, but fifteen minutes into the game the score stood Princeton 7, Michigan 0, and Kipke and his players were trying to figure out what was wrong. Kipke thought Ward might be part of the problem, and asked Ford and another sophomore, Russ Oliver, to keep an eye on him. At that moment Regeczi got off a beautiful, high, 50-yard punt and Ward broke down the field to cover it. "I hesitated the first 20 yards," Ward recalled, "in order to get the defensive left halfback to commit himself. I theorized that the minute he committed himself to a position where he thought he could throw a block at me at the 'crossroads,' I would turn on maximum speed and be by him, leaving him flat footed." Ford and Oliver, not grasping Ward's plan, hollered from the bench, "Ward is loafing"; but at that very moment, he put on full steam, shot past his blocker down the field, and neared the end zone at the same time Regeczi's punt descended. The Princeton player who was receiving fumbled the ball, which rolled into the end zone. As he tried to scoop up the ball and run it out, Ward let go with a flying tackle Yost later called the best he had ever seen, nailing the Princeton player for a safety. Only two points, but it changed the momentum of the game.

Two minutes later, with Michigan in possession, Harry Newman noticed that the whole Princeton backfield was covering Petoskey, the usual receiver for his passes, and that Ward was open in the end zone. He fired an unerring pass, and Ward hung on to it for the touchdown. In minutes, Ward had made eight points to turn the game around. From then on his starting position was assured.[20]

Ford played very little but continued with the varsity. Probably Kipke had already come to appreciate his total commitment to the team and his ability to stimulate teammates to do their best. He shared the amenities of varsity life: on the Friday of home-game weekends he and the other players left campus after classes for an evening of isolated leisure at Barton Hills Country Club, outside town on the river. Safe from the temptations of the campus and the visiting alumni, they ate well-cooked meals and

20. Willis Ward, "This I Remember," #29 (1965), pp. 13, 41. After the touchdown, tackle Whitey Wistert picked up Ward in the end zone and kissed him on the cheek, provoking comment from Ward's father, a straitlaced Baptist deacon who was attending his first football game: "Son, why did that boy pick you up and kiss you?"

relaxed in the kind of affluent display that impressed a college athlete from a lower-middle-class background: "Chairs as soft as mounded jello invited the loller, and were in brilliant colorings: wine, red, burgundy, blue, purple, green. The thick green-blue carpeting was like unmown grass in the fall." To be sure, this enforced seclusion on weekends destroyed any chance of a social life, but Ford, less keen on dating and dancing than the average fraternity man, did not see it as a deprivation.[21]

November 17, the Thursday before Thanksgiving, Ford was one of twenty-six players who boarded the train for the Minnesota game, the last one on the schedule. This was the match that would decide whether the Wolverines kept their unbeaten, untied record, and received recognition as the (hypothetical) national college champs. Kipke started him at practice the next day, but replaced him with Bernard halfway through, and he ended up not playing. The game turned out to be an endurance contest almost as challenging as South versus Union two years before. November in Minneapolis meant extreme cold — that was understood — but at game time Saturday afternoon the thermometer was at five degrees and falling. "I can still see the Michigan bench," Russ Oliver recalled, "with each substitute 'buried' in blankets, jackets, gloves, and hay knee deep attempting to keep warm." The bands could not coax a note from their instruments, Newman could not hold the ball well enough to pass, and Minnesota fumbled eight times in the first half. It was Bernard's recovery of one of those fumbles, and Newman's subsequent field goal, that gave Michigan three points in the first half — the only points scored in the game. For the rest of the game the defense held off Minnesota to clinch the victory. When it was over, Coach Yost, a little boy at heart despite his sixty-one years, charged into the showers in his trademark hat and overcoat and hugged all the team members.[22]

21. Carol Inglis, "University Team Vanishes and on Eve of Battle, Too," GRF Scrapbook #1, GRFL; Mayhew, *Par Excellence*, pp. 30-31, 33; Manfred, *The Primitive*, p. 207. GRF recalled that the purpose of the isolation was "to keep us away from the alumni" ("Gerald Ford," *MD* clipping, GRFL vertical file).

22. *MD* coverage of the whole sequence, game, journey, and pregame practice, is in November 17, 18, 19, and 20, 1932. Newman's account of the game is in "This I Remember," #26 (1965), pp. 13, 41; see also Ivan Williamson, "This I Remember," #30 (1965), p. 13, and Russell D. Oliver, "This I Remember," #37 (1966), p. 13. Kipke's version is in Kipke and Fitzgerald, "A Punt, a Pass, and a Prayer," p. 59. (Notice the varying figures given for Saturday's temperatures.) The game was also notable for an episode in the long saga of the Little Brown Jug, emblem of the Minnesota-Michigan rivalry over the years. I have ignored it here because GRF did not mention the rivalry in any speech I have read;

Ford took full part in the postgame celebration at the 800-room Curtis Hotel, the largest in the Upper Midwest. The players passed around copies of the dining-room menu (on which the table d'hôte menu, at the bottom of the Depression, cost one dollar) to autograph for each other, as well as the game ball. When they arrived at the Ann Arbor station on Sunday, the band, with a sizable contingent of students and a hundred autos, was there to meet them and hail the end of a triumphant season.[23]

With the season over, it was time, as one player said jokingly, for the players to get back to campus and find their classes. Not Ford — he "was very faithful about participating in class," recalled Lewis Vander Velde, who taught him in "U.S. Constitutional History" that semester. "His activities didn't interfere at all." As he had done in high school, he sat in class with a group of other athletes, but he was interested and took good notes. One of the very few anecdotes about him in the classroom involves a lecture Vander Velde was giving on Daniel Webster that fall. The young professor called Webster the greatest American orator; a noisy shout of disagreement came from the jocks' group, stopping the class momentarily. After class, one of them came up to the professor's desk and identified Ford as the disrupter. Vander Velde was skeptical; he knew that Ford's grades were consistently good, and being from Grand Rapids himself, he knew a little about Ford and his family. Sure enough, a few days later, Jerry came by his office to say that the whole thing had been a joke by his buddies, which he hoped the professor had not taken seriously. Vander Velde set his mind at ease.[24]

Jerry must have studied fairly seriously that semester, for he ended with three B's and two C's. One C came in French, and marked his last struggle with that language. He may also have spent some time helping his roommate: Beckwith was an undisciplined student, regularly on academic probation and, to judge from his transcript, constantly on the lookout for "pipes," courses a student could pass without much effort or regular attendance. "Ancient Greek Life," which he took that fall, may have been such

readers who wish to follow it can do so in Greg Dooley, "When the Little Brown Jug Vanished (1931-33)," posted September 26, 2011, on www.mgoblue.com/sports/m-footbl/spec-rel/092611aab.html.

23. Both the game ball and the menu are in the GRFL museum in Grand Rapids. For the Curtis, see "The Lost Hotels of Minneapolis," www.lileks.com/mpls/hotels/index.html. *Michigan Alumnus*, 39:163.

24. Capos, "My Years at Michigan," p. 6. Vander Velde's letter to his family, October 26, 1930, in the Vander Velde Papers, BHL, shows that he knew Ralph Conger.

a course; it or similar courses are mentioned in the recollections of other Michigan students. Beckwith, whose scholastic performance was fairly typical for a Deke of his time, was on probation when the year began; he got off it in February, perhaps with Ford's help.[25]

From Thanksgiving 1932 until the following March, there is little material about Ford and his family — a pity, since this was one of the most eventful periods of modern American history. It was the very bottom of the Great Depression. Roosevelt took office, the Nazis came to power in Germany, Prohibition ended, half the wage earners in Detroit were out of work, and, closest to an Ann Arbor student, in February the governor closed all the banks in Michigan, to forestall a panic of bank failures across the state. Cash became unavailable. Rumor had it that the university itself would close — its budget had already taken a substantial cut. It was a typically vicious Ann Arbor winter: temperatures reached twenty below in February, streetlights came on at three in the dimness of winter afternoons, and farm families in sleighs drove their horses into town and mocked those in autos struggling to get around in the brown slush. Students had to get by on whatever pocket money they had, scrip issued by local merchants, and any amount of credit they could get.[26]

In Grand Rapids, the credit of Jerry Ford Sr. was good. He received a telegram from DuPont, one of his main suppliers, to the effect that he should go on ordering what he needed, that they would trust him until normal business relations resumed. About a week after Roosevelt's inauguration that resumption took place, as all the banks in the country that were closed by the new president in order to check their financial soundness were reopened with the government's approval.[27]

In January, moreover, the Fords finally succeeded in finding a new

25. GRF's transcript is in GRFL; Beckwith's is in his "Necrology" file in BHL. Pipes: Grimm, *Michigan Voices*, p. 155; Stockwell, *Rudderless*, pp. 47, 184-85; Frantz, "Doctor, Where Were You?" p. 30; Gilbreth, *I'm a Lucky Guy*, p. 82. For academic standings, see *MD*, September 25, 1932.

26. For the general background, see Kennedy, *Freedom from Fear*, especially pp. 87-89; Warren, *Herbert Hoover and the Great Depression*, pp. 280-92, has a good account of the nationwide banking crisis that came to focus on Michigan. For the crisis as it affected the university, see Peckham, *The Making of the University of Michigan*, p. 173; *Michigan Alumnus*, 39:376; *MD*, March 7, 1933; and Helen M. Loomis to family, February 17 and 20, 1933; March 1, 1933. For Ann Arbor winter weather, see Douglas, *Disputed Passage*, p. 25; *Michigan Alumnus*, 39:147; Helen M. Loomis to family, February 10, 1933, Helen M. Loomis Letters, BHL.

27. Vestal, *Jerry Ford, Up Close*, pp. 50-51.

home. Jerry Sr. assumed the mortgage on a newly built house that was nicer in some ways than the one on Lake Drive — a two-story colonial revival, built with several shades of tan-colored brick, with four bedrooms. It was located only a few blocks distant, on Santa Cruz Drive, a street laid out two years earlier that still had only three houses on it. They settled the deal in December but waited until after the holidays to move in. Ford's parents would live in the new house until after World War II.[28]

The surviving story from this period involving young Jerry Ford is related to the end of Prohibition. Right after Roosevelt's inauguration in March, spring football practice began, and Ford had to schedule the much-deferred operation on his trick knee. For some reason, the prospect of it may have been on his mind, for the night before the operation he let himself be talked by his roommate Beckwith into having his first drink, at the Spanish Room in Ann Arbor. Ford had been raised in a dry household and had not experimented with smoking or drinking in high school; but that evening found him sipping tequila and smoking long cigars in convivial company. Technically, Prohibition was still in force, but since Hoover's defeat the law had become a dead letter, since Repeal was so obviously on its way. Beckwith was a serious drinker who had had liquor in his desk even during Prohibition and who, the following year when the state liquor store opened, would get up early to be the first in line to make a purchase. Under his guidance, Ford drank enough tequila to acquire the worst hangover of his life. Next morning, the operating team took one look at him and told him to come back some time later — which he did.[29]

From then on, moderate social drinking was part of Ford's repertoire — a useful skill for both the legal and athletic worlds. He and Beckwith may have become drinking buddies; later references suggest that when together, they sometimes got pleasantly loaded. He started smoking, too,

28. The description of 1011 Santa Cruz Drive is from photos and real estate cards at GRPL. The street itself appears for the first time in the 1931 city directory. Details of the move remain obscure. The 1933 city directory, compiled toward the end of the year, gives the Santa Cruz address; but the Bell Telephone directory for January has the family still living on Lake Drive. By July the telephone listing was on Santa Cruz. GRF Sr. did not begin paying city tax on the property until 1935, according to East Grand Rapids tax records, and my guess is that he acquired it through assuming a mortgage.

29. The story is told in *TTH*, p. 51. GRF recalled the place as the "Spanish Club"; no doubt it was the same as the Spanish Room from the 1933 city directory, in the student area of Ann Arbor. For the climate of opinion in Michigan after Roosevelt's election and before Repeal, see Love, *Hanging On*, p. 112. Beckwith: Denham, *Growing Up in Grand Rapids*, p. 130.

infrequently — a pipe, fashionable among college men. The knee healed as planned, though it took months.[30]

Second semester drew toward an end, and a flurry of government activity, later to be called the "Hundred Days," was reported out of Washington. Jerry Ford found his own money getting short. His meals at the DKE house balanced out against his dishwashing at lunch and dinner, and his mother's contributions helped with tuition, books, and clothing — but that left lodging unaccounted for, and upperclassmen's rooms at the fraternity house cost probably thirty dollars or more a month. Since he no longer waited tables at the hospital, he had only his mother's money to finance an increasingly active social life.[31]

He had found one ingenious way to pick up spending money, used by many undergraduates, male and female: selling blood to the hospital. It required steady nerves. The surgical wing required blood transfusions for its operations, and since techniques for storing blood were still undeveloped, they needed a live donor on the spot — of the same sex as the patient, so that decency was observed. Donors were called on the basis of blood type; they could donate every two months. When the hospital called, the student sat in the operating room with a tube in his or her arm, blood flowing directly into the body of the patient, who was of course under anesthesia. The tension of the operation and the disgusting smells and strange sounds of the operating room made the experience hard to forget. For the donor's contribution the hospital paid $25 — using the twelve-to-one multiplier, that would be the equivalent of $300 in contemporary money. Some students found the process stressful, but it certainly put money in one's pocket.[32]

30. For GRF and Beckwith, see Philip Buchen interview, Grand Rapids Oral History Collection, GRFL, p. 5; GRF to Frederica Pantlind, November 2, 1933, Pantlind Letters, GRFL; and "Brother Gerald Ford, Omicron '35, Remembered," p. 3. That a student publication in his senior year could describe him as a nonsmoker and nondrinker (1935 *Michiganensian*, p. 364) suggests that he indulged moderately. Schapsmeier and Schapsmeier, *Date with Destiny*, p. 11, stated he began smoking a pipe in college; a story in the *Detroit Free Press*, May 12, 1934, maintained that it was later, during World War II. Several "big men" on the Ann Arbor campus were described as pipe smokers in 1934 (*Big Men on Campus*, pp. 14, 20).

31. Love, *Hanging On*, pp. 106-18, narrates a similar semester of scarcity punctuated by windfalls. University of Michigan, Interfraternity Council, *University of Michigan Fraternities*, 1932, p. 6, gives average costs for room — $20-30 a month; for board — $25-35 a month; and for initiation fees — $50-125 — at a fraternity house.

32. Ford-Cannon interviews, April 25, 1990, GRFL, pp. 3-4; Eugene S. Brewer, "The

Some impoverished students, typically those not in fraternities or sororities, adopted the older American method of cutting expenses to the bone: in the fall of 1932 the *Michigan Alumnus* published a story about malnourished students who were trying to stay in school by spending as little as eighteen cents a day on food. One of them, it said, "was reluctant to ask for a loan, fearing the spectre of debt."[33]

Within the world of the Greek letter societies, however, students learned to rely on debt. The gentlemanly ethos of fraternity life required that brothers should trust one another; it was unmannerly to make demands for payment. The consequence was that most brothers, Ford included, owed a large amount of money, and some got by without paying it at all. The *Michigan Daily*, in March of 1934, was blunt: "There is no dodging the fact that a large allowance for bad debts must be carried by any Ann Arbor merchant doing business with fraternities and that seniors regularly leave the campus owing bills to their houses to such an extent that a special committee of the Interfraternity Council was once appointed to consider withholding of credits of men who are thus delinquent."[34]

Omicron chapter, with a depleted treasury, was itself trying to get by on credit from local merchants for coal, food, and basic necessities. The Dekes were far from alone in this situation. Almost every fraternity in Ann Arbor had a sizable number of brothers whose parents had been hit hard by the bank shutdowns, and every chapter had to make do with inadequate funds. In fact, DKE could consider itself lucky — seven fraternities, mostly newer and smaller ones, had closed their doors in 1932-1933. Economics 51-52, "Principles of Economics," which Ford passed that year with a B, might have started him thinking about the inevitable contraction of credit

---

Oyster," Hopwood Awards, 1935: Minor Fiction, passim; Bulletin No. 2, "The Handling of Blood Donors," May 15, 1934, Box 26, University Hospital Records, BHL.

33. *Michigan Alumnus*, 39:155.

34. *MD*, March 29, 1934. The comment of the *Michigan Alumnus*, December 9, 1933, that "sound business practice and curtailed credit are frequently subordinated to the brotherly spirit behind fraternity life," expressed the same idea less directly. GRF's situation in this paragraph derives from the sources discussed in the following chapter, pp. 175-76 and note. All versions of his story seem to imply that, while he thought his finances were stable, he was accumulating a sizable debt. The sources of the debt differ slightly from one version to another: "the fraternity, the room where I lived," in Hersey, *The President*, p. 89; "clothes, lodging, books, and supplies" in *TTH*, p. 51; and "school . . . my fraternity" in Ford-Cannon interviews, p. 12. The central element on all these lists is the lodging bill to DKE. This story continues into the next chapter of this book.

that was coming, but apparently it didn't. He was in for an unpleasant surprise the following year.[35]

From the student viewpoint, the indisputable climax of the year came off campus on May 11. A *Michigan Daily* headline described it succinctly: "Michigan Welcomes Return of Legal Beer: Thousands Throng Downtown Gardens." "Downtown" meant the courthouse and business area a mile west of the campus; under a local ordinance, beer could not be sold near the university. West of Division Street, however, the Stroh's, Budweiser, Kingsbury, Edelweiss, and Prima flowed freely, and thirsty collegians exhausted the stock of some restaurants. And Jerry Ford, with his new college-man sophistication, was very likely in the throng.[36]

35. Peckham, *The Making of the University of Michigan*, pp. 187-88, briefly discusses the fraternity crisis of 1933-1935; for general coverage of its beginnings, see *MD*, March 5, 6, 7, 8, and 16, 1933. A complete list of Greek letter societies that ceased to exist in these years is in "University of Michigan, Fraternity and Sorority Scholarship Record," 1932-1935, in University of Michigan, Vice-President for Student Affairs, Records, Box 1. GRF's grade is from his college transcript at GRFL.

36. *MD*, May 12, 1933.

CHAPTER 11

Big Man

Santa Cruz Drive, on which the new Ford home in East Grand Rapids was built, at the very fringe of suburban development, had no side-walks. A dairy farm still functioned at the end of the street. And only a few other families, all of them from the Hill District, had moved to the area. Jerry, home for the summer, made new friends from the upper level of Grand Rapids society: Fred Bigelow, the president of Consolidated Chemical, and his family, whose backyard on Argentina Drive abutted the Fords' driveway, and next to the Bigelows, the widow of Fred Pantlind, who had owned and managed the grand hotel downtown, and her daughter Frederica (Freddy), a high school senior. Jerry, thanks to his two years at Ann Arbor, had the credentials for acceptance, as a letter written years afterward shows. The writer was eighteen-year-old Peggy Turner, a cousin who was visiting the Bigelows for the summer from the Twin Cities. There was much visiting between them and the Fords. "I was, of course, quite 'smitten' with the big blond football hero, as was Freddie Pantlind," she recalled. "But you spent most of your time playing golf."[1]

Ford and Freddy Pantlind went out together enough to become fast friends — nothing romantic, just pals. When he returned to college in fall 1933, he wrote her a series of letters that together give a picture of his

---

1. "Save Ford Home? Choice Is Wide," *Press*, August 15, 1974; Mary M. Nueske to GRF, August 21, 1976, GRFL. The Ford house was at the corner of Argentina Drive, the Bigelow house was on Argentina, and the Pantlind house was at the corner of Argentina and San Lucia Drive. GRF also worked at Ford Paint and Varnish for part of the summer.

campus social life. From them it appears that the serious athlete (or as he modestly called himself, "would-be athlete") spent a lot of time arranging a social life — dancing at Chubb's, a nightclub; attending movies with friends; having occasional dates; and enjoying the crowds and craziness of the big social weekends like the midwinter J-Hop. During football season, as a varsity player, he was either out of town or sequestered at Barton Hills part of every weekend; but he still found time to party, and now and then to sip a beer or two ("quite refreshing"). On big weekends the Deke house, large as it was, was overcrowded — one Sunday night Ford slept on a convenient sofa; the previous night everything was full and he didn't explain where he slept.[2]

Freddy had visited Ann Arbor and the Deke house at some point — she had a male cousin at the university — so Jerry felt free to enliven his letters with accounts of Beckwith and his exploits. (He and Beckwith were not rooming together that year; Ford shared a room with Eddie Landwehr, scion of a rich Holland, Michigan, family, whose brother had been killed in a speedboat accident when Ford was a Sea Scout, and who also became a good friend.) Beckwith was caught driving his girlfriend's car and faced disciplinary action, but somehow got off ("it might mean getting kicked out . . . but they don't do that so much any more"). He and Jack, early in the semester, tried unsuccessfully to get romances going with a couple of coeds to bolster their romantic credentials — it would be "too disgraceful for a couple of 'Dekes'" to be without girlfriends.[3]

Ford and his friends had frequent dates with female students, "coeds" in the parlance of the thirties — arrangements to get together for a dance, movie, or social activity (as in, "I'll stake you to a hamburger and a glass of beer if you feel like walking down to the Pretzel Bell"). What he and Beckwith were pursuing was a more or less regular series of dates with the same coed (one for each) over a period of time, a "romance" that might last a year or more. Helen Loomis dated the same engineering student for most of four years, and in a relationship like that marriage was clearly contemplated; but a shorter series of regular dates with the same person, a "romance," might or might not involve emotional commitment. Either

---

2. GRF to Pantlind, October 24 and November 12, 1933, Ford-Pantlind Letters, GRFL.
3. GRF to Pantlind, September 30 and October 8, 1933, Ford-Pantlind Letters, GRFL; Philip Buchen interview, Grand Rapids Oral History Collection, p. 5, GRFL; Denham, *Growing Up in Grand Rapids*, pp. 129-30. Pantlind clearly had met Beckwith, because she made some sort of "crack" about him in a letter in October (GRF to Pantlind, October 23, 1933).

way, it added a bit to the boy's reputation, and hence was a good thing for a Deke, or any male, to have.[4]

Whether social or serious, such a romance generally followed the rules of serious courtship, with the girl insisting on sexual restraint — kissing, some physical contact, but no intercourse. Girls who failed to follow this pattern on dates found themselves defined as "fast" and excluded from some social occasions. Even the Dekes at one point passed a resolution "that all girls except respectable girls be kept from the house." Coeds, after all, were the future marriage partners of most university males, and they had an interest in eventually acquiring wives who could control their own sexual behavior. Many aspired to the same self-control in their own case. Romances, then, were pleasant but generally lacked the spice of sex.[5]

In fraternities, on big dance weekends, there was often another kind of date. A boy who had no serious romantic attachment might arrange a date not with a coed but with a "fast" girl from Ann Arbor or Detroit, put her up at a local hotel, and devote some of the weekend to sex. As one undergraduate sourly put it: "Tonight is the famous J-Hop when out-of-town girls come to dance with their in-town sweethearts and the Dekes and the Sigma Nus import whores, both amateurs and professionals, from their home-towns or (that course failing) Detroit." Probably it was this sort of date that was meant in the comment, in Ford's senior year, that he had never had a date until then. He came from a religious, moral background; Stan Fay of Detroit, the captain of the 1933 football team, described him in two words: "upright" and "reserved." It was big news in fraternity circles one weekend in senior year when he asserted his Deke identity and registered a woman at the hotel as "Mrs. Anderson" (taking "a lot of razzing" in the process, according to fellow Deke Jack Stiles). This would seem to have been a date of the second kind.[6]

4. GRF to Pantlind, October 24, 1933 (dates); Loomis Papers, passim; Love, *Hanging On*, pp. 169-71, narrates the history of one such romance that displayed the classic dilemma: it was serious to one partner, social to the other.

5. Edwards, Arthman, and Fisher, *Undergraduates*, pp. 190-91; Stockwell, *Rudderless*, p. 92; Omicron chapter meeting minutes, March 2, 1929, records of Omicron chapter of DKE, BHL. The auto ban at Michigan diminished opportunities for sex, although there was still the university-owned Nichols Arboretum, on Geddes near the DKE house, where the winding paths offered opportunities for contact and students reported finding condoms on the bushes (Walter Morris, "From Day to Day," p. 87 ["Portfolio II," Hopwood Prize Awards, 1934]).

6. Paul Showers to parents, February 8, 1929, Paul Showers Papers, BHL. The 1935 *Michiganensian*, p. 364, noted that GRF "broke forth the middle of his senior year with a

In junior year, however, the big event was a stag party at Beckwith's home in the Chicago suburbs, the weekend of the Michigan-Chicago game, to which Ford and Herm Everhardus were invited. They passed up a chance to visit the Century of Progress Exhibition for Beckwith's shindig — "what a brawl it's going to be, win or lose." Since there were no dates, booze was presumably the main attraction — though Jack, like the generous host he was, may have provided films or some sort of entertainment. Ford did not describe it in his next letter to Freddy. He did tell her of two high school students from Grand Rapids, Bob Gamble and Ron Thwits, who were "seeing college life in the raw, I really couldn't say how raw, that can be left to your imagination."[7]

In his letters to Freddy, Ford probably colored his accounts of Ann Arbor society to impress his high-school-age friend. From other sources, notably his DKE brother Fred Stiles, it is clear that he also spent considerable time at the nonalcoholic Parrot, across from the campus, with Fred or dates or both. They also bowled a lot, Stiles recalled — which sounds like a natural Ford activity, competitive and physical.[8]

In the same way, although Ford claimed in his letters that he almost never studied — January found him studying for exams "after loafing all semester" — and that he was averse to hard study, planning to take "a bunch of 'pipes' next semester . . . no use studying too hard," he actually took an overload, all economics, history, and social science, and maintained his B average. He understood that in the football/fraternity world, study, like personal hygiene, was something one did behind closed doors and didn't talk about.[9]

One activity totally unmentioned in the letters and very little elsewhere was student politics. Michigan, like most colleges, had an elaborate,

---

date." This noteworthy date is probably identical with the one mentioned by Jack Stiles in Sheridan, "Portrait of the Next President," p. 24, and explained more carefully, also by Stiles, in a footnote to Ter Horst, *Gerald R. Ford*, p. 45. (Stiles also said he didn't know more than five girls whom GRF dated.) Capos, "My Years at Michigan," p. 5, gives Fay's estimate.

7. GRF to Pantlind, November 2 and 12, 1933; February 17, 1934, Ford-Pantlind Letters, GRFL. GRF did not miss the World's Fair entirely; he stayed, by his account, twenty-five minutes.

8. A novel of student life at Ann Arbor in the late twenties pointed out that for many students, the sophisticated, dissipated attitude was a pose, just like piety at home. Students were "simply being good fellows. They are keeping in the swim" (Stockwell, *Rudderless*, p. 49). Fred Stiles: Capos, "My Years at Michigan," p. 34.

9. GRF to Pantlind, December 11, 1933; January 25, 1934, Ford-Pantlind Letters, GRFL.

insignificant student government, whose offices were symbolic prizes for fraternity men inclined to compete. Two parties or factions, Washtenaw and State Street, contested the elections. Sometimes the *Michigan Daily* reported the results, sometimes it ignored them, but the intrigue, horse trading, and shifting interfraternity alliances of the campaigns were vital matters to the candidates and their managers. Ford told an interviewer in later life that he had taken some part in college politics and wished he had had time to do more; he enjoyed the "confrontation" and "challenge." A student publication in his junior year described him as "a successful politician in the last three years." His good friend Herm Everhardus held some conspicuous offices, like sophomore class president, and Ford may have learned the ropes from him. Apparently he held no office. It is not even recorded which faction he belonged to. But it does show, at the very least, that he had learned to enjoy the game of politics.[10]

The college year of 1933-1934 was less thrilling than its predecessor — no national election, no banking crisis, no fears of revolution. Enrollment continued to decline, to just under 8,000. The university had sustained a considerable budget cut and eliminated sixty-six positions, but the football program was undisturbed and beer was legal, which made the sluggish economy easier to bear. Social life for men got slightly easier toward year's end, with the advent of the zipper fly. There were even signs that business might be improving. As part of Roosevelt's New Deal, new government programs with strange names were visible on campus, mostly issuing announcements. At Michigan, as across the country, the relief people felt at the end of three years of worry and fear was almost palpable. As Edmund Love put it, "There were two Depressions. There was the Depression of Herbert Hoover and there was the Depression of Franklin D. Roosevelt. . . . At last we had a man who was *doing* something."[11]

10. GRF interview, *Business Today*, Winter 1992, p. 28; *Big Men on Campus*, pp. 22-23.
11. Peckham, *The Making of the University of Michigan*, p. 173; *MD*, September 26, 1933; October 3, 1933; *Michigan Alumnus*, 40:30; University of Michigan, *President's Report for 1933-1934*, p. 1; Love, *Hanging On*, p. 133. On zipper flies, see the full-page ad in *MD*, "On the Fly," June 3, 1934. On the importance of legal beer in changing the national mood, the comment of GRF's friend Jack Stiles is pertinent: "Back in 1932, being a son of prohibition, I couldn't understand why millions of Americans predicted relief from gloom and depression if the slogan 'Light Wines and Beer' became law. The first glass of foaming beer, however, sipped gingerly taught me beyond doubt both truth and consequence. Beer encouraged theory, and theory bred hope" ("With the Coin We Blew," p. 192).

At some point during his junior year — one version of the story says it was in the fall, but circumstantial evidence seems to favor spring semester — Ford was suddenly made aware of the $600 that he owed — mainly to the chapter, mainly for his lodging — when the chapter began pressing for immediate payment. Paradoxically, this demand was a product of the modest improvement in the economy. Ann Arbor merchants, now that business seemed to be stabilizing, had started trying to collect a backlog of debts from the Greek letter societies. Getting no response, they turned to the administration. A national committee of financial experts, called in by several national fraternity headquarters to assess the situation, reported without naming names that roughly half of the fraternities still open had badly mismanaged their treasuries and needed to shape up or close their doors. Sternly proclaiming that "no student should be permitted to be a member of a social group which was financially irresponsible," the university threatened the fraternities with extinction and appointed a faculty committee to scrutinize their financial practices. The Deke chapter, which had been skating around the administration's requirements, saw trouble ahead. As an upperclassman and a big man in Omicron, Ford saw it with special clarity; understandably, he seems to have panicked as he realized its effect on him. Everyone was probably a little panicky.[12]

Unable to turn to his parents, who were already stretched to their limit, he decided to make a bold move and write for help to Leslie King, the grinning stranger he had seen on that morning in 1930, his "real" father, who still owned thousands of acres in Wyoming and elsewhere in the West, so Ford understood. Not only the relationship but also his status as a member of the national championship college team and his honorable career plans entitled him to aid from the man responsible for his existence,

12. R. P. Briggs to H. E. Stone, August 2, 1935, University of Michigan, Vice-President for Student Affairs, Box 3, source for the quote in the paragraph, places the climax of the crisis, which led to the appointment of a faculty committee on fraternity finances, at the end of the 1933-1934 school year. As early as May of 1933, the Interfraternity Council required fraternities to make monthly financial statements, which, according to Vice President Bursley, brought "certain fraternities to a better realization of their financial condition than they have had before" (University of Michigan, *President's Report for 1933-1934*, p. 51). But the Dekes seem to have evaded this requirement; over a year later, they admitted to Bursley that "in the past no budget has been prepared" (Chester Thalman to Joseph A. Bursley, February 12, 1935, in University of Michigan, Office of the Vice-President for Student Affairs, Records, Box 3).

he felt. He had the address; he wrote the letter, but there was no answer, and Ford realized his hopes had been naive.[13]

When relief finally came, it was not from the West, but from Grand Rapids. "Uncle Ralph" and "Aunt Julia" Conger had been intimate with the Fords since Jerry was a small boy. The two families got together for athletic events and social occasions, and swam together at Ottawa Beach. Both Congers found Jerry not just likable but also admirable, a youngster full of promise for a life of real worth. Ralph Conger, a few years later, was to state on a government form that Ford was the only young man he rated higher than his own son. Julia had just come into an inheritance, and Jerry, knowing that fact, wrote them to ask if they could help him stay in college. She promptly sent him a check for the amount he needed. It was an act of generosity that reflected her faith in his capacity to become a good, perhaps a great, adult member of society.[14]

Other Michigan students — for instance, Ford's fraternity brothers Fred and Jack Stiles of Grand Rapids — had a simpler solution to lack of funds: drop out for a semester or a year, go to work at Ford Motor or one of the other auto plants that were gradually recovering and rehiring, earn the money required to pay their debts, and return to school — or even take a night-shift job at Ford during the college year. Ford's loyalty to the football team may have made this alternative unacceptable to him. Instead, his reaction to the scare perfectly illustrated his mother and stepfather's

13. This story, which GRF told primarily to illustrate the disinterest of his biological father as contrasted with the generosity of Grand Rapids friends, is a major source of information about his college finances. He told it to three interviewers over a seventeen-year period, and the three versions differ significantly among themselves. In Hersey, *The President*, pp. 89-90, the Congers are not mentioned, the focus is on Leslie King, and the events are dated as happening during his junior year at Michigan. In *TTH*, p. 51, junior year is also the time frame, specifically the fall, and Julia Conger is credited with sending a check for $600. In the Ford-Cannon interviews, April 24, 1990, these events are placed in his senior year and the amount of the check is $1,000. I believe that the squeeze on GRF was a part of the general fraternity crisis, which climaxed in his junior year as discussed in the preceding note. As for the amount of the check, either version seems plausible. Julia Henning Conger's immediate family in Ann Arbor was working-class, but she had rich relatives in a previous generation, one of whom had subsidized her education at Wellesley.

14. Ralph Conger's statement is part of an Office of Naval Intelligence investigative report on GRF, January 10, 1942, in GRFL. Note that although Cannon states in *Time and Chance*, p. 20, that the check came from Ralph Conger, GRF in his interview cited above said that it was from Julia Conger. The GRF photograph files contain several photographs of the Conger and Ford families together at Ottawa Beach.

Progressive-era preference for solving problems by working through institutions. He decided that he would work within the chapter and straighten out their cash-flow problems. The next chapter will show how he went about it and what he accomplished.[15]

All this activity — social, academic, and even financial — was secondary in Ford's mind to his real mission at Ann Arbor: excelling in football. Although he had worked in the paint plant for part of the summer as usual, he wrote Freddy that the opening of practice on September 15 found him in "wretched condition" — and having to give up beer for the milk-only regimen at the training table only added to the discomfort. (Again, he may have been exaggerating for effect.) Like all the team, he was keyed up and eager to see if the 1933 Wolverines could match their performance of the previous season. They had lost Newman's phenomenal passing and Williamson's sure-handed receiving, but they still had Everhardus and Fay, Regeczi's kicking skills, Ward's running, and of course, Kipke's coaching. Kipke was now being touted in the press as a new football sage, like Rockne or Stagg; he had a deal with the *Saturday Evening Post* to publish articles, which he turned out with the help of a professional writer, regaling the country with the real inside truths of college football. Backing up all these assets was the serious institutional commitment, ahead of its time in college football, recalled by Newman: "It was all very organized at Michigan. We had spring practice, summer workouts, that kind of thing. It was a very important thing there, the football team."[16]

As in 1932, it took three games to reveal what sort of team the Wolverines were in 1933. The Michigan State game, the opener, featured one quarter of good football, the first, in which Michigan took a twenty-point lead. After that, Kipke sent in all the second-string players to show what they could do, and the result was three quarters of very sloppy football, in a chilly rain, with the final score 20-6. But the Cornell game October 14 clarified things. Everhardus made three touchdowns, the Michigan line was impregnable, and the result was Michigan 40, Cornell 0. Again, Kipke made a lot of substitutions in the second half, this time with happier results: the second string, Ford among them, performed at a high level. Cornell, however, was a team from the effete East. Ohio State, the next

15. For the Stiles brothers, see Stiles, "With the Coin We Blew," pp. 152, 196-97, 216, 223. Edmund Love's college career followed a similar pattern.

16. GRF to Pantlind, September 17, 1933, Ford-Pantlind Letters, GRFL; Whittingham, *What a Game They Played*, p. 108.

opponent, was always physical and always fought hard; the Wolverines' first conference game would be the real test.[17]

Well before October 21, newspapers reported high excitement in Ann Arbor, with exceptional ticket sales. Ohio State and Michigan were understood to be the main contenders for the conference championship; many fans were coming from Ohio. Equally important, the game was the first conference match in Ann Arbor since the return of legal liquor. The Athletic Association ordered additional seats built, and by game day sales exceeded 93,000. (The State game had attracted fewer than 20,000 spectators.) In terms of mass participation, the day lived up to its billing: university authorities reported nine auto accidents and twenty-three arrests for drunk and disorderly behavior. Four children and one woman went missing. Two men dropped dead in Michigan Stadium.[18]

In the Michigan locker room before game time, the atmosphere was tense. As a rule, Whitey Wistert recalled, the coaching staff avoided pep talks, but that afternoon they decided they needed one, and gave the responsibility to assistant coach Frank Cappon. "He called us down to the end of the dressing room nearest the door," Wistert remembered.

> We sat on benches with our helmets on the floor at our feet. In three short minutes he managed to raise us to an emotional pitch that was unbelievable. I glanced at Chuck Bernard next to me. His tears were falling into his helmet. I dared not look around any farther. . . . When Cappie finished and shouted, "Let's go," we almost tore off the dressing room door. The impact of bodies on the opening kickoff was unbelievable.[19]

A solid victory followed that impact, 13-0, but opinions varied on the game. The *Michigan Alumnus* called it "one of the greatest," but Jerry Ford, from his vantage point (mostly) on the bench, was less enthusiastic: "Too many people," he wrote Freddy. "I think everyone was afraid of their [sic] own shadow." In other words, the huge, boisterous crowd spooked even some players. There was certainly some exciting football that afternoon, notably Ward's interception and 50-yard return of an OSU pass. In the last

17. *Michigan Alumnus*, 40:45-46, 57, 63; Phil Haughey to his mother, [October 8], 1933; to Will Haughey, [October 13], 1933, Haughey Family Papers, BHL.

18. *Chicago Daily News*, October 20, 1933; *New York Times*, October 22, 1933; *MD*, October 24, 1933. According to *Michigan Alumnus*, 40:77, the final count of attendance at the Ohio State game was 82,000.

19. Perry, *The Wolverines*, pp. 146, 148.

quarter another interception by Chuck Bernard set up Michigan's second touchdown. But too many opportunities were missed, by both teams.[20]

Nevertheless, the victory generated a feeling that Michigan once again had a championship team — a feeling that grew stronger with an unbroken string of victories, even if some were excruciatingly close ("Michigan was lucky to get away with their pants," wrote a skeptical undergraduate after the 7-6 Illinois game). Regeczi was certainly the best punter in college football that year; Bernard looked to many observers like an all-American as well. Ted Petoskey was a splendid end, and the formidable Michigan line, including Wistert, gave up only eighteen points all season. Quarterback was the weak spot, but Bill Renner, struggling to fill Newman's shoes, improved in the course of the season, which ended again without a single defeat. A strong Minnesota team held Michigan to a scoreless tie, and there was that frighteningly close call with Illinois; otherwise, the string of victories ended in another conference championship.[21]

For Willis Ward it was an excellent year. He started in all eight games and was hailed after the Ohio State game as the "savior" of the team. In later games his running skills and his interceptions made a crucial difference. His ability on the field sometimes attracted verbal abuse and racial slurs — in both Chicago and Ann Arbor he heard "nigger" shouted from the stands — but he "paid no attention, attending strictly to business." In track he was Michigan's greatest asset — one sportswriter called him a "one-man track team." A bona fide star, he attracted crowds to his performances in the high jump and the 60-yard dash. Like a celebrity, he gave interviews on Detroit radio stations. At the beginning of the school year, when the car carrying him, several friends, and their trunks to college had a breakdown en route and had to be pushed from Ypsilanti to Ann Arbor, it was in the Detroit newspapers. On the road, he and Ford generally roomed together.[22]

20. *Michigan Alumnus*, 40:73; GRF to Pantlind, October 23, 1933, Ford-Pantlind Letters, GRFL.

21. Perry, *The Wolverines*, summarizes the rest of the 1933 season on pp. 146, 148. Bernard and Wistert were named that year by a majority of the organizations that published their selections for all-American status; there was no single official list. For details, see the Wikipedia entry for "1933 College Football All-America Team," en.wikipedia.org/wiki/1933_College_Football_All-America_Team.

22. *Michigan Alumnus*, 40:73, 161-62; John Behee, "In Quest of a Dream: The Story of Michigan's Black Lettermen," typescript, Box 8, Ward Papers, Detroit Public Library, pp. 13-14; Dude, "Crisis in '34"; *Detroit Free Press*, January 27, 1934; *Detroit Times*, October 2,

For Ford, 1933 was a season much like the preceding one. He sat on the bench behind Chuck Bernard, playing in five of the eight games, sometimes only briefly. His play in the Cornell game drew praise from the student newspaper: "Jerry Ford, subbing for Bernard, was a replica of the big 'Buster.' He stopped everything which came his way." (Such praise, however, raised the question: Why settle for a replica when the real thing was available?) He also drew critical comment from a Detroit reporter for a flash of lurking hot temper that surfaced after he missed an interception and shot the ball back to the referee a little harder than necessary: "Tut, tut, Mr. Ford; everybody drops a pass now and then even though it is right in his hands. Control yourself."[23]

Kipke still wanted to have Ford on the starting eleven, and experimented with using him at guard, but again the idea was abandoned; speed presumably was the problem. The whole coaching staff was aware that when Bernard graduated Ford was in line to become starting center, the most important position in the lineup after quarterback. The center was "the key man," as Bennie Oosterbaan put it. "If the center screwed up, you were helpless." Jack Blott, the line coach, took Ford in hand to polish his centering skills. He had no doubt that Ford could do it; like all the staff, he had high regard for the boy's dedication. (This did not mean they thought of him as any kind of prodigy. Oosterbaan, who found Ford "quiet" and "sincere," added in an interview years later, "If one would have told me at that time that he sometime was going to be president of the United States, I would have said, Don't give me that crap.")[24]

The comment of *Big Men on Campus*, the student publication that appeared in the spring of 1934, made the same point. "Jerry has been on the squad for two years, and has the size and ability to become a star." In terms of football, that is, Ford was still a work in progress. His standing as

---

1933. Standard practice for out-of-town teams with a black player was to put him up for the night with an obliging family of his own race. Kipke, however, always insisted that Ward stay in the hotel where the rest of the team was (Willis Ward interview with David S. Pollock, 1983, GRFL, pp. 6-7), and the fact that GRF was rooming with him would ensure his not being shunted by the management to some closet or converted storage room.

23. *Michigan Alumnus*, 40:57. The 1933 team roster from the official program, in GRF Scrapbook #1, GRFL, gives his position as "C-G." MacGregor, "A Tale of Two Centers," p. 28.

24. *MD*, September 28, 1933; *Cincinnati Post and Times-Star*, October 18, 1974, clipping in GRF Scrapbook #1, GRFL; Oosterbaan interview with David Pollock, 1983, Acc. #2004-NLF-033, GRFL, p. 7.

a BMOC reflected not his football prowess, but something quite different. Kipke put it this way: "Jerry Ford," he told the *Grand Rapids Herald* in May,

> is one of the finest boys I have ever met. I'm not now talking of football ability, but of character. . . . He never allows himself to get "down." Two years he has been forced to sit on the bench wishing every minute he could go in and fight for Michigan. But he has never complained, never crabbed, never felt that he wasn't getting a square deal, always has been boosting for Bernard, who was keeping him on the bench. He's always in condition. . . . Give me eleven boys with the disposition of Jerry Ford and even if none of the eleven were of world championship caliber, it would take a mighty good team to defeat them.[25]

Many other people on campus had similar views. Ford, though a second-stringer, was voted a member of Sphinx, the junior honor society; and when the time came to choose the football captain for senior year, a number of the players wanted to elect Ford, who had never started a single game. (Others favored tackle Tom Austin. "That doesn't bother me," Ford told his friends. "I would like to be captain. But Tom has played regularly, and I didn't. He has earned it.") Without putting himself forward, he had become the moral center of the team. As Oosterbaan said, he said little, but he led by example. Stan Fay envied his good grades and his uprightness.[26]

By the spring of 1934, then, as a result of scores of small interactions, most of them unchronicled, Jerry Ford had built a reputation among his fellow students, his coaches, and part of the college community as an unusually reliable young man of good moral values. At the same time, he had learned to enjoy himself and taken on the fraternity-man persona. Without striving for it, he was now, on the threshold of his senior year, a "big man" in the class of 1935.

25. *Big Men on Campus*, p. 23; *Herald*, May 17, 1934.
26. *Big Men on Campus*, p. 23; Cannon, *Time and Chance*, p. 19. It is interesting that both leading candidates for captain were linemen, since the post typically went to a back. This fact tends to reinforce the idea that there was a lack of leadership in the backfield, which was to become marked in the next few seasons.

CHAPTER 12

Surprise Ending

It was the summer of 1934 when things began turning around. Back in 1932, Grand Rapids Wood Finishing had stopped collecting $150 a month on the Crosby Street plant from Ford Paint and Varnish because the smaller company was unable to pay; now the money began flowing again. In December of that year Ford Paint and Varnish also resumed the monthly payment of $200 toward purchase of the plant machinery, valued at $10,000. Resumption of payments meant that Ford's paint business had turned some kind of corner, in the mini-recovery that was buoying Michigan's economy. It looked likely to survive the Great Depression and become an established part of the Grand Rapids manufacturing scene. Tough challenges remained, but Ford could congratulate himself on a real accomplishment. In 1935, he began paying taxes on the Santa Cruz Drive house. When Dorothy Ford, the same year, became a member of the Women's City Club, a group of upper-class women with an interest in public affairs, it was a seal of approval — the Fords had arrived.[1]

This sense of success for the family was shared by Jerry Jr., who was working again in the Crosby Street factory. Its direct consequences for him, however, were small, since he was about to leave the nest. His parents had other sons to educate: Tom, a rising junior in East Grand Rapids High that year, expected to go to Michigan, and behind him came Dick and Jim.

---

1. Ledger 11, Grand Rapids Wood Finishing Co. Collection, Public Museum of Grand Rapids; email to author from Carol Dodge, Women's City Club, June 13, 2012. Ford-Blake Coal Company, on the other hand, which GRF Sr. was trying to rescue for his nephew Harold Swain, disappeared from the city directory between 1933 and 1934.

Jerry was looking to his final year at Ann Arbor as a first step in his own adult career. By July of 1935, when he would be twenty-two, he would have played as starting center on another winning Kipke team and racked up a winning record in the annals of Michigan and the Big Ten; he would have graduated as a star or something like it, with the promise of a job on Kipke's coaching staff. That, with his summer earnings, would finance his first year at law school in Ann Arbor.

So he thought.

To Harry Kipke 1934 looked like a rebuilding season. The team had lost twelve members, including eight starting players, to graduation. With Wistert and Bernard gone, the line was going to be weaker, perhaps a lot weaker. Jerry Ford, starting at center, was an asset — he was aggressive, though not fast. Possibly he could fill Bernard's shoes. (Yost thought so; he wrote to a correspondent in 1934, "You will see a much more aggressive center on the Michigan team this year than Bernard ever thought of being.") Johnny Regeczi, although a sensational punter, was not skilled at passing and slow as a runner. Bill Renner had finally pulled himself together in the last game of 1933 and completed five passes, but who knew how he would be in September 1934? Willis Ward was the only known quantity on the squad — a splendid runner, a fine pass receiver if there was someone to throw to him, absolutely consistent; but he couldn't carry the team by himself. In his preseason statement to the press, Kipke made a flat prediction: the Wolverines would lose three games in 1934. He refrained from mentioning his biggest worry: besides Regeczi and Renner, with their limitations, there was no one in the backfield. Fay and Everhardus had graduated, and not a boy on the team seemed ready to step into their places. Actually, Kipke may have had his fingers crossed when he said three games.[2]

Practice began as usual September 15, in the glare of public attention. Because of Michigan's consecutive championship seasons, reporters from the Associated Press, the *Chicago Tribune*, the *Detroit Free Press*, and lesser papers hung around Kipke and the team commenting on every move, while the Board in Control of Athletics discussed selling broadcasting rights for all home games. During the spring an MGM film crew had

2. Kipke and Fitzgerald, "Watch That Lateral Pass," p. 56; Fielding Yost to James O. Murfin, September 27, 1934, GRFL; Perry, *The Wolverines*, p. 150. The student sports columnist of the *Michigan Daily* expressed the same worry indirectly: "On Renner, we feel, depends the fate of the team" (*MD*, September 18, 1934).

filmed the 1933 team's plays, presumably for consumption as entertainment. If college athletics was becoming a business, as critics charged, this was Michigan's moment in the showroom.[3]

The second week of practice on Ferry Field, Renner broke his ankle. The doctors judged at first that he would be out for three weeks; it ended up being the entire season. With three weeks until the Michigan State game, Kipke juggled various possibilities for quarterback — Russ Oliver, a sophomore named Ferris Jennings, Willis Ward. He was still undecided when the referee tossed the coin to start the game with State. The first half was a scoreless tie; in the second half, the Wolverine line grew tired under State's restless attacks and breakthroughs started coming — one touchdown, then another. To the astonishment of 25,000 spectators, the Spartans beat the Wolverines for the first time in almost twenty years, 16-0. The following week against Chicago, usually an easy victory for Michigan, Kipke's team was again unable to advance the ball and again the line grew tired. Regeczi's punting lost its accuracy. Chicago won, 27-0. In the first two games, the victors had scored more points, combined, than all of Michigan's opponents had in the previous season. The signs pointed to a miserable year — and, in fact, 1934 turned out to be the worst season in the team's history — one victory and seven defeats, some by wide margins.[4]

Kipke's interviews with the press as the season went on sounded increasingly like Herbert Hoover's — full of plans for improving or mitigating the situation, evasive on the question of what had happened since 1933. But that question was precisely what fascinated sportswriters and the public: how the national championship team of 1933 became the defenseless victims of 1934. Ford, when asked about it in later years, had a quick, snappy answer, borrowed from sportswriters of 1934: "In those days Harry Kipke's offense was called a punt, a pass, and a prayer. Well, we lost our punter. We lost our passer. All we had was a prayer, and that was not enough." In fact, the problem was that when they lost Renner and Regeczi, there were no backups. "They were short of backs that year," Ford's

3. *Detroit Free Press*, September 16-27, 1934; *MD*, April 25, 1934. Cf. Haines, *Blaine of the Backfield*, p. 253. The *Michigan Daily* did not explain how the footage of the 1933 team was to be used.

4. *MD*, September 25, 1934; October 7, 13, and 20, 1934. The Chicago team also had an all-American halfback, Jay Berwanger, who later told a reporter, "Ford has a little scar on his cheek, and he says he got that from the heel of my football shoe when he tried to tackle me in that 1934 game. I'm sure I ran over him more than once" (William S. Wells, comp., "Ten Men Who Knocked Gerald Ford on His Ass," *Esquire*, October 1975, p. 168).

roommate Earl Townsend explained. They were short of linemen too. In an account he wrote of the 1934 defeat by Minnesota, 34-0, Ford wrote matter-of-factly that "the score might have been reduced if Michigan's line replacements had been stronger and in greater numbers." (The limited substitution rules aggravated the problem — coaches were unwilling to take starters out early in the game.) The vaunted Michigan football machine was short on talent not just in 1934, but for several years following. "I think those four big seasons [1930 through 1933] made us a bit fat-headed," Bennie Oosterbaan said, looking back. "We hadn't obtained manpower to fill the places of the great talent which had made those four years so great." The oversight cost Kipke his job.[5]

As this catastrophe unfolded around him, Jerry Ford behaved like the Boy Scout he was: on and off the field, week after week, he exhorted his teammates to stick together and do their best. His eloquence, before and during the game, was passionate; his sincerity and consistency said more than words. In the Georgia Tech game, he "proved himself an aggressive leader," according to the student newspaper, after Austin went out with an injury, and from then on Michigan's opponents began to view him as the key man who held the team together, the "sparkplug," a formidable 198-pound player who had to be neutralized to facilitate victory. They "seemed to pick him out" in every game. "I saw him get some terrible beatings," recalled Townsend, a starting basketball player. A fraternity brother recalled hearing Ford, in the heat of one collision, yell "Daaamn you!" in a clear voice that carried to the heights of Michigan Stadium. Townsend remembered the Northwestern game, the season's last, which Michigan lost, 13-6: "I took Jerry home after the game. His legs were gone. He could hardly get into the house. . . . We got him inside. He could hardly talk. For hours afterward, he just sat in his room."[6]

5. Cannon, *Time and Chance*, p. 19; "Brother Gerald R. Ford, Jr., Omicron '35 Remembered"; Al Cotton, "100 Years of Michigan Football," p. 23, in "This I Remember," September 22, 1979. GRF's account is in "This I Remember," October 9, 1965, p. 41. Whether Kipke fully understood his problem is a good question. He wrote that in his pregame talk before the Ohio State game he told the team, "This Michigan squad is strong at every position. We have excellent replacements. You all know that. We can jerk five men at once and we'll be just as strong" (Kipke and Fitzgerald, "Dying for Dear Old Rutgers," p. 11). Perhaps a coach says what he has to say in a given situation.

6. *MD*, September 22, 1935. On the mature GRF's eloquence in a football context, see Don Penny, interview with Richard Norton Smith, December 13, 2009, GRFL, p. 4: "It was passionate, and it was eloquent and it was moving and the kids were blown away." Targeting GRF: recollection of Joe Henshaw, clipping from *Cincinnati Post and Times-*

Ford himself remembered best the Minnesota game in midseason. The Gophers were a formidable team that year, and in fact went on to become national champions. But Michigan had dominated Minnesota over the years, and the Wolverines hoped the long-standing spell would last one more year. "We showed little outward apprehension of Minnesota's reputation as a bone-crushing steamroller," Ford said in his written account for a 1960s program. "Respect, yes. Fear, no. . . . There were pregame predictions that our fullback Cedric Sweet and I at center would have a busy afternoon backing up the Michigan line. How true. . . . I don't know about Sweet, but I didn't sleep too well the night before the game." For the whole first half, Ford, Sweet, and the rest of the line did wonders against a crushing offense. Then, in a replay of the Michigan State game, they tired under the pressure, and Minnesota touchdowns started coming. Despite the accurate kicking of Regeczi, who was off and on all season, and Ward's defensive skill, the Gophers crushed Michigan, 34-0. Ford and tackle John Viergever walked off the field "with our arms around each other's shoulders, tears running down our faces, completely worn out," in Viergever's recollection.

Ford ended his story differently: when the team train pulled in next day to the Ann Arbor station, they found the usual cheering crowd of student supporters. There was a "rousing and supportive parade to the Union building headed by the Michigan Band . . . a meaningful tribute to the fight the Wolverines had put up." In Ford's version, the whole weekend taught the value of loyalty and team play — "never stop trying, and don't be afraid of tackling a job with the odds against you." To be sure, he wrote up his memories for a Michigan football program, where an upbeat conclusion was called for; he made no claim to be giving an account of his feelings at the time. Yet that was who he was, even as a college student — he saw defeat as a learning experience. The learning was more important than the details of the experience. You wept, and you learned.[7]

There is evidence that he had developed into the outstanding center predicted by Yost and Kipke. A journalist of the 1970s interviewed ten

---

Star, October 18, 1974, in GRF Scrapbook #1, GRFL; "Brother Gerald R. Ford, Jr., Omicron '35 Remembered". Townsend connected his recollection with the Ohio State game, and the physical brutality sounds like Ohio State, but that game was played in Columbus in 1934. GRF was taken out of the Northwestern game at the beginning of the second half (*Michigan Alumnus,* 41:147).

7. "This I Remember," October 9, 1965, pp. 39-41; Nelson, "1934 Michigan," p. 13; MacGregor, "A Tale of Two Centers," p. 29.

players, mostly linemen, who had squared off against him in 1934, and published it under the title, characteristic of the time, "Ten Men Who Knocked Gerald Ford on His Ass." A majority of them remembered Ford as a "tough" opponent, who "played for keeps," more apt to knock them down than the reverse, though the fortunes of the game featured the usual give-and-take. All-American guard Rip Whalen of Northwestern called him the best blocking center he had ever faced. After the Illinois game, a hard-fought, close struggle in rainy weather, with the field a "quagmire" and Michigan frequently backed up against its own goal line and forced to punt a slippery ball, Old Man Yost, unlit cigar in mouth, came up to him in the locker room and said, "Ford, that was one of the finest exhibitions of centering I have ever seen." Many students of Michigan football agree that, had Ford played on a championship team, he might well have been named an all-American; as it was, he had to settle for the endorsement of his teammates. They voted him most valuable player.[8]

Of the eight games of the 1934 season in which Ford started, the one that has gotten the most attention is the October 20 clash with Georgia Tech. Not because it was an exhibition of great football — on the contrary, Bobby Dodd, who was then an assistant to Tech head coach William Alexander, described it accurately as "a poorly played game between two weak teams." Georgia Tech was one of the few teams that year in college football with a record as bad as Michigan's — the Yellow Jackets won only a single game, and lost more than the Wolverines because they played a longer season. The focus of the 1934 game between them was not football at all, but race relations in New Deal America.[9]

Willis Ward and Ford were good friends, but Ward did not share with Ford the bad news he learned during the summer: the university administration was planning to bench him during the Tech game because Georgians refused to play against blacks. It was bad news as well for Harry Kipke, who stood to lose not only his best player but also his credibility; he had recruited Ward by promising him fair treatment and equal rights with white players, and up till then he had kept his word. The decision had been Old Man Yost's. Yost had scheduled Georgia Tech and had embraced the strategy of muting the racial issue until the eve of the game and then announcing that Ward would not play. Unfortunately, members of the Detroit African American community, suspicious that that might be the

8. Ford, *TTH*, p. 53; Wells, "Ten Men," pp. 168-69.
9. Dude, "Crisis in '34."

plan, contacted members of the Board of Regents and tried, without success, to ensure that Ward would be given a chance. Their effort, although widely covered in Detroit's black newspapers, was at first ignored by the white media. At some point Ward wrote Kipke expressing his disappointment and threatening to quit the team; Kipke's reaction was to arrange a meeting with Harry Bennett, who promised good postgraduation jobs at Ford Motor for Ward and any friends he might care to name if he stayed on; Ward acceded.[10]

Ford and the rest of the team apparently knew nothing of this until the Tuesday before the game, when Kipke held Ward out of practice. By that time, the issue had reached the campus through the efforts of some white socialist students whose friends in Detroit had alerted them to this instance of discrimination. Protest letters were circulating, signed by professors and local clergy as well as students. Several players, Ford included, outraged at losing an important teammate out of deference to a bizarre Southern custom, asked Ward what he felt they should do. He could hardly tell them to quit, since he had just declined to do so himself; presumably he told them to stay together and whip Tech. Then he disappeared for the rest of the week; he had hoped to sit on the bench and cheer the boys on, but Yost decided he might become a focus for a protest from the stands, and suggested he go on a bogus out-of-town "scouting" assignment to check out some forthcoming opponent. Ward turned down that offer and listened to the game on the radio in the black fraternity house on Huron Avenue.[11]

Ford, outraged at the way Ward was being treated — he was not even permitted to support the team from the sidelines — considered boycotting the game in protest. He spoke with Kipke, who urged him to think it over, and he called his stepfather for advice. Jerry Sr. told him this was a decision he had to make for himself. He also recalled speaking with Ward; but Ward recalled nothing of the sort, and it is hard to reconstruct how a

10. Willis Ward interview with David S. Pollock, 1983, GRFL, pp. 9-10 (hereafter "Ward-Pollock interview"). Some white media, e.g., the *Detroit Free Press*, said nothing about the racial issue before or after the game. Two reasons why Ward himself did not wage a campaign against his exclusion suggest themselves: first, he was not temperamentally an activist; second, he hoped against hope until the last minute that the protests of Kipke and black leaders in Detroit would bring a reversal of the decision.

11. *Detroit Free Press*, October 17, 1934; Ward-Pollock interview, p. 10; Behee, "In Quest of a Dream," pp. 21-23. Behee's well-researched work is a splendid, underutilized source on this whole episode.

conversation might have taken place, with Ford at the country club and Ward in an undisclosed location. Perhaps he was thinking of Ward's earlier talk with the players, when he urged them to stay with the team. That, in any case, was the anguished choice Ford finally made.[12]

Two important meetings took place the night before the game, one public and one private. The public rally held by Ward supporters in Hill Auditorium turned into one of the "wildest and strangest" pregame assemblies in Michigan history. It was invaded by a group of fraternity men (possibly including some of Ford's Deke brothers) who presented the administration, pro-Tech viewpoint and shouted down anyone who tried to debate them. Angry Ward supporters, including faculty members, fired back. Finally, a resolution was passed blaming the administration for scheduling the contest in the first place. While this was going on, Kipke and his staff held a meeting with Tech's coaches, with Kipke arguing passionately that it was unsportsmanlike to use the race question to deprive Michigan of its best player. Coach Alexander agreed to make a comparable sacrifice and bench his starting right end, Emmett "Hoot" Gibson.[13]

12. The sequence of events in this paragraph rests on firsthand testimony. (1) Ward had his talk with Kipke and Bennett sometime prior to the week before the game (Ward-Pollock interview). (2) The rest of the team (including GRF) learned about it Tuesday or Wednesday and expressed their outrage to Ward, who told them, in substance, to stay in and lick Tech, and that he would be cheering them from the bench (interview). (3) Thursday or Friday, Ward found out that Yost wanted him out of town, or at least out of the stadium (interview). I infer that this additional discrimination against his friend was what set GRF off, although in *TTH*, p. 52, he recalled that he felt it "morally wrong" to bench both Ward and Gibson (see next paragraph) and called home for advice. He recalled GRF Sr.'s telling him to do whatever the coaches said to do; but he also told two early biographers (Vestal, *Jerry Ford, Up Close*, p. 60, and Ter Horst, *Gerald R. Ford*, p. 42) that his stepfather told him to decide for himself, and this is the version I have preferred. Then, he says, he spoke to Ward, who advised him to play. Ward asserted there was no conversation at that stage, on the eve of the game (interview), and I assume that GRF scrambled the sequence in his memory, and thought of his earlier conversation in which Ward urged the team to go on with the game.

The nature of GRF's struggle with his conscience has been romanticized and sensationalized in some recent accounts. He believed in racial fairness, but he was not an activist. The whole affair has been carefully analyzed by Douglas Smith in "Presidential Myth: The Real Story of Gerald Ford, Willis Ward, and the 1934 Michigan/Georgia Tech Game," at www.washtenawwatchdogs.com, January 2014.

13. *MD*, October 20, 1934; apparently the fraternity counterprotest had been surreptitiously encouraged by Yost (Behee, "In Quest of a Dream," p. 21 n. 10). Coaches' meeting: Dude, "Crisis in '34"; Martin, *Benching Jim Crow*, p. 31. Martin calls the compromise "bizarre," but the biblical-sounding principle of "an end for an end" may have salvaged the

Next day in a chilly rain the Yellow Jackets took the field amid "endless booing" from the Michigan crowd, many of whom were as angry at their own administration as at Tech. Tech's starting center Charles Preston had the bright idea of taunting the Michigan line about it — "Where's your nigger?" he mocked. Next play he was hit so hard by a combination of three Michigan players — Ford, Borgmann, and Sweet — that he broke three ribs and was out the rest of the game. Ford had finally used his bottled-up rage in a good cause, although Preston always maintained that it was Borgmann who actually broke his ribs. Then, after Austin hurt his hand and had to go out, Ford assumed the coordination of the entire team and guided them to a 9-2 victory, concluded with sportsmanlike congratulations and handshakes. The score hints at the sloppiness of the contest. Michigan did not make a single first down in the second half. Tech fumbled the wet ball seven times and ended with negative yardage. It was that kind of game. But the team had won one for Ward, as they proudly told him the following week.[14]

Ward, however, felt that whole incident cost the team its essential morale and feeling of unity. If the 1934 Wolverines ever had a chance to recover from their bad start, it was gone after the Georgia Tech fiasco. He himself lost his zest for sports and failed to develop into the major track star many expected. A breach opened between Kipke and Yost that eventually contributed to Kipke's dismissal. The university's reputation suffered; President Ruthven bitterly regretted that he had left decisions in the hands of the Athletic Department. Gibson was bitter at being taken out for no reason. By comparison, Ford muddled through honorably.[15]

The bruising Northwestern game was the last of the season and, for

---

game for Kipke and Michigan. He also attributes it to unnamed "administrators," but the account of Bobby Dodd, who was there, in the Dude article is more convincing.

14. The "endless booing," game-ending courtesies, and other details are in a reminiscent exchange of letters between Dave Wilcox, Tech guard (April 13, 1976), and GRF (April 19, 1976), both in GRFL. Preston's injury: Vestal, *Jerry Ford, Up Close*, p. 61; Ter Horst, *Gerald R. Ford*, p. 42; and *Detroit Free Press*, October 21, 1934, which attributed Preston's injury to end Matt Patanelli. Preston himself said it was the guard, that is, Borgmann (Wells, "Ten Men," p. 169), but his recollection that he stayed in the game is contradicted by the *Detroit Free Press* account; maybe he was more shaken up than he remembered. The *Georgia Tech Alumnus*, November-December 1935, p. 26, called him "rather badly injured." Nelson, "1934 Michigan," summarizes the game as a whole; Dude, "Crisis in '34," mentions the team's pride in winning.

15. Ward-Pollock interview, pp. 10-11; M'Manis, "Tragic Note Marks End of Ward's Career as Michigan Athlete."

most of the team, the last of their college football careers. But before his injury took him out of the game, Ford had a very good day against Northwestern's all-American guard Rip Whalen ("I just blocked the shit out of him," Ford recalled), who mentioned his performance to his coach Dave Hanley. Hanley that year was one of the two coaches for the East team in the postseason Shrine Bowl. This was before the postseason had developed into the extravaganza of the late twentieth century; the Shrine Bowl was mainly a fund-raiser for crippled children and a trip to California for good college athletes, and also to some degree a chance for players who wanted to sign with the pros to show off their abilities. On the strength of Whalen's recommendation, Hanley named Ford to the East team — the only Michigan player so honored — and wired him December 8 asking for his "head gear jersey trouser and shoe sizes."[16]

In a letter to the team, Hanley urged players to be in top physical shape and treat the experience seriously, not as just a joyride to the West Coast. No doubt most, like Ford, were elated to be named and eager to do their best, but he was among those who had to accept the trip mainly as a joyride: he was the backup center for George Akerstrom of Colgate and might not play much, if at all. After reporting in Chicago a week before Christmas, he went through the drills, enjoyed the luxury of the Union Pacific passenger service, met the other players, and took in the dramatic Western scenery, already somewhat familiar from Hollywood cowboy movies. In Reno he won a "couple of bucks" playing the slot machines, according to Indiana halfback Don Veller, an East teammate. He signed up for an extra trip to Hollywood after the game. Scouts for several pro teams were on board, but they were courting the big names like Pug Lund of Minnesota and Les Borden of Fordham, not small fish like him. They arrived at San Francisco's Palace Hotel December 23.

The game was at Kezar Stadium in Golden Gate Park, on New Year's Day. Oddly, the close of his football-playing career replicated what had happened in his sophomore season at South High School, when he first played on a varsity squad. He started as a backup; within two minutes, the starting center, Akerstrom, got hurt and had to leave the game. Ford played fifty-eight minutes and had "a very good day." Although the East

16. GRF's trip to the West Coast to play in the Shrine Bowl, the subject for the next four paragraphs, is mentioned in most of his biographies. This account relies especially on Cannon, *Time and Chance*, p. 20; Ford-Cannon interviews, April 24, 1990, pp. 10-11; and GRF, "In Defense of the Competitive Urge," p. 22. Hanley's December 8 telegram is in GRF Scrapbook #1, GRFL.

team lost, 19-13, his individual performance was noticed and commented on. On the train to Hollywood after the game, suddenly the pro scouts knew his name and were all over him with contract offers. Curly Lambeau of the Packers, he recalled, sat next to him all the way to Los Angeles. The contrast amused him, but that was all; professional football played no part in his plans, and he went on to have a wonderful time in Hollywood, enjoying the palm trees and glamour, having his picture taken at Warner Brothers studios with the comedian Joe E. Brown. One account has him going on to Hawaii with a selected group of players for a game against the territorial university.[17]

Absent from classes for at least three weeks during the postholiday, preexam period, Ford nevertheless did well enough when he got back to make straight B's for the semester. He may have asked his professors, all in business administration or economics, to give him assignments for the period of his absence, for the Indiana back who was with him at Reno also described him as "studious," an uncommon adjective for a football player on vacation.[18]

One of the courses he passed with a B was Professor Clark Dickinson's "Programs of Social-Economic Reform." No record survives of his reaction to the ideas of Professor Dickinson, a progressive who numbered Keynes, Paul Douglas, and Gunnar Myrdal among his correspondents, but he can hardly have failed to notice its relevance to the campus around him. Since the advent of the New Deal, the university campus had teemed with reformist meetings and organizations. As early as 1931, socialist students had been active in small numbers, but with the Roosevelt administration things changed. New Dealers were receptive to their views as previous

17. Additional sources for these paragraphs are partly from GRF Scrapbook #1, GRFL (Dave Hanley's December 10 letter; Union Pacific Railroad menus) and partly from the vertical files at GRFL (photo of the Warner Brothers studio visit; a photo aboard the westbound train; a clipping from the *Tallahassee Democrat* recounting Don Veller's recollections), and another mentioning the Hawaii trip. Evidence for the latter is a bit shaky. GRF did not mention it, and the records of arriving passengers in Honolulu in 1935 do not include his name ("Honolulu, Hawaii, Passenger and Crew Lists, 1900-1959," Provo, Utah, Ancestry.com Operations, Inc., 2009). Commercial air service to the islands did not yet exist in January; it would begin later that year. The Shrine Bowl was not, strictly speaking, the end of GRF's playing career, as he also played in summer 1935 with the College All-Stars against the Chicago Bears in a game gotten up by *Chicago Tribune* sportswriter Arch Ward (*TTH*, pp. 54-55; Peterson, *Pigskin*, p. 127).

18. University of Michigan transcript; *Tallahassee Democrat* clipping, vertical file, both GRFL.

administrations had not been, and their programs like the Federal Emergency Relief Administration were popular on campus, emboldening socialists and other leftists to organize and demand more reforms. Their feisty spirit had been visible in the massive protest against Ward's exclusion from the Georgia Tech game. Fraternity men as a rule stayed aloof from protest and reform movements — Arthur Miller, a wide-eyed freshman reformer from Brooklyn, derided the brothers almost as beings from another time, sitting on their front porches on Washtenaw Avenue doing nothing, singing nostalgic songs just as they did in the movies. Ford was no social reformer, but one leftist-sponsored movement did apparently get his attention: the student antiwar protest.[19]

The nationwide campus antiwar movement, strongest between 1933 and 1936, was largely organized by leftist students but appealed to a much wider variety of people — Christian pacifists; readers and moviegoers impressed by *All Quiet on the Western Front*, either the 1927 novel or the 1930 film; and Americans for whom George Washington's warning against entangling foreign alliances seemed basic, including Midwestern Republican politicians. To many Midwestern minds it seemed obvious that when the United States was at peace and unthreatened by any other country, it had no business getting into another foreign war, especially after the disaster of the Great War. If the Fords felt this way, they were in line with many of their neighbors. Only a few years later, when Jerry Ford was an applicant first for a job with the FBI and then for a U.S. Navy commission, the government's investigation of his college years found evidence to identify him with the antiwar movement.

This action is interesting as Ford's first recorded involvement with a social or national political group striving for change, and one wishes there was more specific evidence about what he did. He may have gone, as many students did, to hear Republican Senator Gerald Nye, in the fall of his senior year, denounce American participation in the Great War and urge noninvolvement in future European conflicts. He may have been among the 450 who signed the Oxford Peace Pledge in the spring of 1935, especially since the FBI informant reported that he called war a "futile and unacceptable way of settling international disputes," which was a quote from the pledge. He could have been, but probably was not, among the

19. Z. Clark Dickinson's papers are in BHL. For a good overview of this period, see Peckham, *The Making of the University of Michigan*, pp. 189-91. Miller, "University of Michigan," p. 143.

few who walked out of classes April 12 as a protest for peace. Looking back on whatever it was, he called himself a "real isolationist."[20]

But his real involvement that senior year, once football was over, was with Delta Kappa Epsilon. Part of it was merely social, but enjoyable and meaningful at the time. Witness the blissful reminiscence of the J-Hop, the traditional midwinter dance, in 1935, from a coed who was at the Intramural Building that icy February night:

Fraternity booths lined the sides of the gym with their identifying Greek letters emblazoned in silver on blue panels. On gilded daises, opposite one another, Hal Kemp and Henry Busse had assembled their bands, resplendent in full dress. Their gleaming brasses flashed in the light of five enormous chandeliers. Two of the "greats" in an era of great bands. . . . It was exciting. It was glamorous. It was a night filled with splendor. It was, in fact, everyone agreed, "the nuts!" The bands played old favorites like "The Tiger Rag" and Henry Busse's famous "Hot Lips." They played the slow and dreamy "Blue Moon" and Skinny Ennis sang "Stars Fell on Alabama." The floor was always crowded, the bandstands constantly besieged. We danced nearly every dance, stopping only occasionally for a drink at the punch table. . . . We improvised on the foxtrot. Most of us did the break-away. The dip was popular and some were suave enough to get through the hesitation waltz. . . .

It was after one when they played the last sad-sweet strains of "Good Night, Sweetheart." . . . The stars were out. The moon was bright on the snow. Our feet were sore from dancing but no one ordered a cab. We hobbled up State Street to the Union where breakfast was being served.[21]

Ford's main goal, however, was nothing less than rebuilding the finances of Omicron chapter. He said nothing about it in telling his own story, and only fragments of the events survive to indicate what a substantial change it was. At the end of junior year, after the scare with his

20. Department of Justice, FBI Special Agent Application, 1941, GRFL. For general background on the movement, see Eagan, *Class, Culture, and the Classroom*, especially pp. 115-26. The text of the peace pledge, quoted practically verbatim by the FBI informant, is on p. 60. Miller signed the pledge in 1935 (Bigsby, *Arthur Miller, 1915-1962*, pp. 84-85), which might make it unique as a document signed by both him and GRF. A 1934 meeting to endorse it also took place, reported in *MD*, May 6, 1934; and see the editorial "Less Profit, Less War," in the March 11, 1934, issue.

21. "The J-Hop Revisited!" *Michigan Alumnus*, January 1975, pp. 6-7.

finances, he requested the post of house manager for the next year. It meant considerable work, overseeing the kitchen and general housekeeping, but the salary would also take care of his bills for room and board. The house manager lived on the top floor like other seniors and had a desk in a little balcony on the second floor, where he collected money for meals and heard complaints. Ford was remembered as a good manager, hardnosed but fair. He put up with the inevitable kidding from the brothers about how the quality of the meals was going down while the quality of his wardrobe was going up. His management style stressed cooperation and teamwork, but in the boisterous atmosphere of the Deke house, more forceful methods were sometimes necessary. At one point in the year all the freshman pledges, a rowdy bunch, rushed Ford's office en masse to complain about one of his strict rulings. According to fellow senior Cal Markham, Ford said he'd settle the problem if they wanted to take him on one at a time; and the place "needed some housekeeping" when that settlement was over. The freshmen retired to the first floor and made no more trouble.[22]

His biggest contribution, however, came as chapter treasurer, to which he was elected at the same time he became house manager. The chapter for years had been run very casually, and financial records were inadequate — money for maintenance never seemed available, and the mansion had become shabby and rundown. This lack of leadership had doubtless contributed to the panic in Ford's junior year when the chapter tried to call in all its outstanding debts. But in his year as treasurer, as the auto industry began pulling out of its slump, Omicron alumni who lived in Detroit were brought in as rescuers: the house was repainted and the furniture spruced up. Senior members of the chapter met in Detroit every month with the alumni board and developed good working relationships, while the sophomore pledges dedicated themselves to cleaning and redecorating the Shant, which had hardly been touched since its construction in 1878.[23]

22. Capos, "My Years at Michigan," p. 6; "Brother Gerald Ford, Omicron '35, Remembered," p. 4; clippings from *Detroit Free Press*, October 14, 1973, and *Ann Arbor News*, September 22, 1974, vertical file, GRFL. GRF's reticence about his role in rescuing Omicron's finances may stem from his politician's sense that most people would not be inspired by a tale of heroic efforts to benefit a group of rich elitist college boys.

23. The two sources for the reforms of 1934-1935 are Chester Thalman to Joseph A. Bursley, February 12, 1935, in University of Michigan, Office of the Vice-President for Student Affairs, Records, Box 3, and the chapter reports in *DKE Quarterly* 53, no. 1 (February

Ford got considerable credit for this dramatic change: the 1935 year-book praised him as the man who "put the D.K.E. house back on a paying basis," and the chapter's own report called him "one of the best chapter treasurers in years." But he cannot have done it alone. The effort entailed a lot of meeting and negotiation, especially during football season; ir-responsible, liquor-loving Jack Beckwith, apparently a very persuasive salesman, may have been the key. Beckwith was the spokesman at the crucial Thanksgiving meeting when the chapter members as a body met the alumni at the Detroit Club. Another probable leader was an "intensely competitive" student-politician from the class behind Ford and Beckwith, Phil Van Zile, whose father, a Detroit judge, was, not coincidentally, presi-dent of the Detroit alumni organization. Charles DuCharme, a sophomore brother from a prominent Grosse Pointe family also with a father active in alumni affairs, seems to have been involved as well. When the chapter had its picture taken for the yearbook, these four — Ford, Beckwith, Van Zile, and DuCharme — formed a conspicuous phalanx in the lower right. It would be interesting to know more about the share of leadership and enterprise each brought to the plan.[24]

Ford must have visited Detroit repeatedly during his senior year. University-related sources suggest that although train service was avail-able, students preferred to go there by car, braving the congested, noto-riously freewheeling traffic. Despite the auto ban, it was always possible to scare up a vehicle. One headed east to Ypsilanti and picked up U.S. 112, Michigan Avenue, through a mixture of industrial and working-class neighborhoods, with the awesome Detroit skyline in the distance — half a dozen modern skyscrapers, over thirty stories each, all built in 1928 or 1929. The tallest, the forty-seven-story Penobscot Building, had a great light on its peak, visible out on the lakes, to signal airplanes after dark. With the worst of the Depression over, fewer beggars and lines of the job-

---

1935): 36, and no. 2 (May 1935): 92. At the beginning of 1935 Raoul Wallenberg commented to his grandfather, "Times seem to be getting better and better at least in the Detroit area where automobile production is leading all industries in a small boom" (January 26, 1935, in Wallenberg, *Letters and Dispatches*, p. 130).

24. 1935 *Michiganensian*, pp. 281, 364; clipping from Delta Kappa Epsilon publication, GRF Scrapbook #1, GRFL; *DKE Quarterly* 53, no. 1 (February 1935): 36; Denham, *Grow-ing Up in Grand Rapids*, p. 139; "Who's Who in the Alumni," *Michigan Alumnus*, 39:73; obituary of DuCharme's grandfather, *Michigan Alumnus*, 47:51. "Brother Gerald Ford, Omicron '35, Remembered," p. 3, shows that GRF and Van Zile remained friends at least until the late 1940s.

less were on the streets, but the jarring mixture of misery and modern affluence was still very much present. ("Raw desolation hangs over Detroit like a cold grey cloud," a Michigan student wrote after a visit in 1934.) The Dekes' destination was typically the exclusive Detroit Club, with its paneled dining rooms of various sizes, luxurious business-class food, and formal manners.[25]

One piece of the seniors' initiative was unusual for Omicron: each member of the chapter chipped in to an eighty-dollar award fund: fifty for the brother whose grade point average improved the most, semester to semester, and thirty for the runner-up. All the seniors collectively endorsed the plan to see that the Dekes were no longer at the bottom of the comparative fraternity grades year after year, but the stress on academics sounds like something Ford would have fought for.[26]

A letter in May, when Ford wrote his mother to say that he was not coming home for Mother's Day because he had to keep his grades up and "must not slip up now," showed that he was still full of ideas for improving the chapter, and maintaining the house. Next year, he thought, it might be possible to have a mothers' weekend on the pattern of the successful fathers' weekend every spring. The fathers were treated by the fraternity to an athletic event and a "smoker," an all-male social affair; entertainment for the ladies "might be more difficult" but could be arranged, and the mothers might want to "do little things to fix up the house." "You perhaps wouldn't be affected right now," he pointed out, "but maybe so in a couple of years."[27]

These last words referred indirectly to the last and most important happening of Ford's senior year at Michigan. Ford had come to accept the fact that he was not going to be at Ann Arbor the following fall. (Thus Mrs. Ford would not be affected by the new program until Tom entered the university, "in a couple of years," and, presumably, became a Deke.) His first inkling of this bad news for his career had come in February, as

25. Beasley and Stark, *Made in Detroit*, pp. 304-5; Morris, "From Day to Day," pp. 75-76, 113; Eckert, *Buildings of Michigan*, pp. 67-69.

26. Chester Thalman to Joseph R. Bursley, February 12, 1935, Box 3, Records, University of Michigan Vice President for Student Affairs, BHL.

27. "Junior" to "Dear Mother," Friday, May 14, [1935], typescript, vertical file, GRFL. Whoever copied this letter (the original is not in GRFL or any known repository) conjecturally dated it 1932; but May 14 fell on Friday only in 1935 during GRF's college years. Other references in the body of the letter, for instance, to Frederick Stiles, make it clear that it was written after 1932. Fred Stiles Jr. joined DKE only in 1934 (*DKE Quarterly* 52, no. 2: 69).

the state budget process came together. Kipke had earlier assured Ford of a place on his coaching staff, but the reduced budget gave him only a couple of hundred dollars for the position. Ford, even if he continued as house manager for the fraternity, needed much more, for living expenses, fees, and his debt to Aunt Julia. To keep his promise, Kipke said he'd start looking elsewhere for suitable college coaching jobs for him.[28]

An obvious source of funds was available in the form of the offers from Lambeau of the Packers and Potsy Clark of the Lions. Both had offered to pay him $200 per game for the next season. One season consisted of fourteen games, so that meant $2,800. But not a shred of evidence suggests that Ford gave their proposals any consideration. Strange as that decision may seem to a twenty-first-century reader, it reflected the standing of professional football in the years before television. Confined to a few Northern industrial cities, pro football was unknown to most Americans, and even in its home markets it was covered only sporadically. To be a pro football star was a lot like being anonymous. A historian of the sport describes it in this era as "the raggedy stepchild of the glamorous college game." The professional game, Ford said in 1975, "did not have the allure it does now."[29]

Some excellent Michigan players, to be sure, had gone on to the pros. Chuck Bernard played for Detroit in 1934-1935 — though only for one year. Harry Newman, having played with the New York Giants, sat that season out because of a contract dispute, which points up another way in which the money of the pros was often less of a sure thing than it seemed. But in becoming professional players, such men laid their own characters open to question in the eyes of many: they were athletes who had given up on their higher mission, that of building character through sport, in favor of the lower one of becoming professional entertainers — and had become, as Nick Skorich would put it in his reminiscences, "athletic bums who couldn't get any other kind of work." "The pros were not looked on favorably," Bennie Oosterbaan recalled, and assistant coach Cliff Keen told his players, "Don't bother with pro football."[30]

28. The basic story is told in Ford, *TTH*, pp. 53-54.

29. Ford, *TTH*, p. 53; Rader, *American Sports*, p. 252; Whittingham, *What a Game They Played*, pp. 77, 134; Peterson, *Pigskin*, p. 109. GRF, "In Defense of the Competitive Urge," p. 22. An excellent contemporary assessment of the career options open to college football players is Savage, *American College Athletics*, pp. 107-9.

30. MacGregor, "A Tale of Two Centers," p. 29; Whittingham, *What a Game They Played*, p. 113. Inabinett, *Grantland Rice and His Heroes*, p. 103, pointed out that a player by turning pro "seemed to shatter in the image of the gentleman-scholar," and Michigan's

True to his word, Kipke notified Ford in March when football coach Raymond (Ducky) Pond of Yale came to Ann Arbor in search of an assistant to handle the line. Pond already had one Wolverine, Ivan Williamson, on his coaching staff, and evidently was so satisfied with him that he wanted another. Kipke mentioned Ford's name. Ford's memory of what happened next was clear and comprehensive:

> Over lunch at the Michigan Union, Pond offered me the chance to visit the campus in New Haven to see if I liked it there and if the Elis approved of me. Although I had gone to Washington, D.C. . . . I had never been to New York or New England. As soon as the check for my ticket arrived in the mail, I was on my way to New Haven, with a brief, wide-eyed look at Grand Central station when I changed trains.
>
> The Yale campus, an attractive place today, was even more beautiful then. Everywhere I went, I discerned an atmosphere of scholarship, dignity, and tradition. At the end of my second day, Pond offered me $2,400 a year if I would join him as an assistant and also coach the freshman boxing team. I knew nothing about boxing, but I promised to take instruction at the Grand Rapids YMCA before returning.

Husky, dark-haired Pond, about the same age as Kipke, was perhaps the first New Englander Ford had met, a Connecticut man and a Yale graduate. Curious to see if he could set up at Yale the arrangement he had in mind for Michigan, Ford asked him if he could take some courses at Yale Law School during the year. Dubiously, Pond agreed to ask the law school. Their answer, which came back after Ford returned to Michigan, was negative, not too surprisingly; they were unfamiliar with Ford's propensity for taking on multiple responsibilities at the same time. But he had already devised his future strategy: he would save his money, do as good a job coaching as he could, and ask again in a year or two. He and Yale finalized the position in April. By May, then, he knew he would be out of the DKE house for a couple of years at least.[31]

1920s star Benny Friedman, who did turn pro, published a magazine article in 1933 in which he urged college players to forget the professionals and not throw their intelligence away on sport (Greenberg, *Passing Game*, p. 432). Oosterbaan and Keen's comments are from their interviews with David Pollock in GRFL, p. 14 (Oosterbaan) and p. 2 (Keen).

31. Ford, *TTH*, p. 54. The final telephone call that nailed down the Yale position came from Ivan Williamson, according to a high school friend of GRF who was present when it came through (Marshall Reister interview). GRF told one biographer (Schapsmeier and

With the job and his money problem unexpectedly settled, Ford was free to enjoy the end of his senior year, with its blend of satisfaction and separation: the last spring football banquet May 8, the big weekends and parties with the brothers of Omicron. As a member of the senior honor society, Michigamua, he attended their meetings in the Union tower, conducted and recorded in a mock-Indian jargon, childish even in 1935 and now actually offensive (as a center, he was given the "Indian" name "Flippum Back"). Michigamua was a meeting place for big men of the student body and the faculty — Yost was a dedicated member — and reflected the values of nineteenth-century male fraternal societies, with ridiculous rituals and distinctive ceremonial garb. It made the Dekes seem almost conservative. Ford seems to have valued the honor, but had little to do with the meetings.[32]

On May 25, with Roundy Raab, the letter carrier who delivered mail to the Deke house, Ford sat atop the concrete bleachers at Ferry Field to take in an athletic doubleheader — a baseball game on one side and the Big Ten track championships on the other. He had been friends for a couple of years with Raab, a devoted Wolverines fan who never missed a game. The track meet might have been a spectacular showdown between Willis Ward and Ohio State's sophomore sensation Jesse Owens, but Ward was on the injured list, badly off form, and took part in only a few events. It was Owens's day: by the end of the meet, he had set four world records before the stunned spectators. He would be going to the Berlin Olympics the next year to challenge the racism of the Nazi regime. Had things gone differently in the fall, Ward might have been on the Olympic squad as well. Instead, he had the promise of a good desk job at Ford Motor. Jerry Ford surely went down after the meet to speak with his old friend and wish him luck.[33]

Weeks later, the big morning came, Monday, June 17. Jerry and Dor-

---

Schapsmeier, *Date with Destiny,* p. 12) that his father had opposed his taking the job, but did not explain why. The next few years, however, were to show that GRF Sr. opposed his son's pursuing any career in sports, whether the unsavory role of entertainer or the dignified one of coach — he seems to have felt that the whole field lacked the respectability appropriate for a serious man's career. In this he agreed with Bud Wilkinson's father that "coaching was not a proper occupation for someone of [his] skills — that he was simply frittering away his time" (Wilkinson, *Bud Wilkinson,* p. 14).

32. *Michigan Alumnus* 41 (June 8, 1935): 421, 423. Gilbreth has a satirical description of Michigamua in *I'm a Lucky Guy,* p. 79. The records of the organization are in BHL.

33. Behee, "In Quest of a Dream," p. 15; Treml, "Football Booster."

othy Ford, with the younger brothers, sat among a crowd of 9,000 packed into Yost Field House because of the weather. The droplets of a summer shower pounded at the high, arched windows. Technicians fiddled with the loudspeaker as Secretary of State Cordell Hull gave the commencement address, and finally got it working — sound amplification was still a new technology, subject to problems even at an up-to-date place like the university. In their black gowns, the graduates of '35 lined up to receive their sheepskins from President Ruthven. As young Jerry crossed the stage, his blond hair visible under the flat hat, he could be sure that many spectators knew who he was, that the president recognized him: he was graduating with social if not academic distinction. He was a far more poised, sophisticated young man than the South High athlete who had arrived in Ann Arbor four years earlier.

But the meaning of the occasion differed from what he had expected. There was a strangeness in the fact that he would not be coming back in the fall to help the Wolverines to a winning season and make the Dekes an outstanding house on the campus scene. Instead, he was already thinking about boxing and the Y, the smoky, dynamic grandeur of New York City and the Gothic serenity of New Haven, as scenes in a new part of the world where he would be entirely on his own. But he was up to the challenge; his eagerness to learn and his capacity for hard work would do the job, as they always had. His education was not over yet.[34]

34. *Michigan Alumnus* 41 (July 13, 1935): 441.

Afterword

Fourteen years after he began coaching football linemen at Yale, Jerry Ford was elected to the United States House of Representatives — a surprising transition, even in times of social upheaval like the Great Depression and World War II. Two paragraphs will suffice to explain how it took place.

At New Haven Ford discovered the career in the world for which he was best qualified: coaching football. He was a natural coach, and would surely have been a great one if he had stuck with it. His personal warmth, his phenomenal memory for plays, his intuitive understanding of motivation, his commitment to teamwork, honesty, and fair competition combined to make him superior, as any number of Yalies attested — including fairly distinguished ones like U.S. senators-to-be William Proxmire of Wisconsin (Democrat) and Robert Taft of Ohio (Republican). There are indications, in fact, that Ford considered it as a career, but his father repeatedly reminded him of his commitment to law. He returned to Ann Arbor in the summer of 1937 to try his hand at a couple of law courses, and did well. The next year the Yale administration allowed him to take law courses there, and he found that he could earn above-average grades even in the competitive Ivy League. He went on to earn an LL.B. from Yale in 1940.

At the same time, his conversations at Yale enlarged his understanding of the world and the menace of Fascism. He became convinced that the United States had a crucial international role to play, and that young men like himself could help to make that happen. Thus when Pearl Harbor plunged the country into war, he eagerly enlisted and served in the Pacific with distinction. Having helped to slay the dragons of Fascism and aggression overseas, he was, in 1945 at war's end, ready to return to Michigan and polish off the lesser dragons of corruption and narrow-mindedness in the Grand Rapids Republican Party. He entered politics as a reformer, determined to defeat the power-hungry, unscrupulous boss Frank McKay and to strengthen U.S. influence for good in the world. In 1948 he unseated a conservative Republican and began a twenty-five-year career in the U.S. Congress.

But Ford's political career is beyond the scope of this book, which considers only the preliminary achievements that laid the ground for it. The other thing I would like to do here is to suggest answers to the questions posed in the preface, about the origin of his abilities and the reason they impressed his contemporaries so strongly.

Genetic endowment was a mixed blessing where Gerald Ford was concerned: along with strength, good health, and a solid basic intelligence, he inherited a tendency to sudden, violent rage. Then the agonizing circumstances of his parents' separation and divorce, arguably, left a trauma that showed itself in childhood stuttering and reluctance to speak. His mother, Dorothy Ford, devoted years of patient effort to overcoming these tendencies, with remarkable success. Ford's boyhood is a real testimony to the power of steady, loving parental discipline: his mother gave him study habits that carried him to Yale, and emotional control that almost always kept his rage under wraps, and a mastery of basic middle-class social routines that enabled him to relate with others despite his reticence. Jerry Ford Sr. was just as important in the model he gave his stepson of persistent effort under difficulties, steady focus on a set of goals, and a consistent set of rules.

Religion was not as important an influence as it might have been, because of Dorothy and her son's exclusion from full church participation on minor doctrinal grounds. Not surprisingly, Ford in adulthood saw religion as a very personal matter, not an institutional activity. He followed, again, his mother's example of adopting the church's values, without a strong church identification. This was essentially the Boy Scout position too: a generalized belief in service and good will, without a definite doctrine behind it.

The community values of Grand Rapids, on the other hand, were a strong influence on Ford's development; as an observer acutely put it, "Jerry Ford was fortunate to grow up in a town that rewarded virtue." The civic rituals, the organizations, and the communication media combined to reinforce the value system of lawfulness, respect for religion, and mutual help, expressed in the Boy Scouts, the YMCA, the welfare program, and the schools. Ford felt uniquely comfortable in Grand Rapids because of the good fit between his values and the community's.

The third big influence on Ford's development was football — not just the development of a set of motor skills, but the internalization of its core values of competitiveness, teamwork, and satisfaction through physical release. The football world provided a social base from which to reach out into other areas; at Ann Arbor, this role was shared by the football team and his fraternity.

Bibliography

Manuscripts

Adams, Paul L. Papers. BHL.

Baldwin, Ralph B. Papers. GRPL.

Behee, John. "In Quest of a Dream: The Story of Michigan's Black Lettermen." Typescript, Box 8, Ward Papers, Detroit Public Library.

Boy Scouts of America. Records. GRFL.

Boy Scouts of America, Troop 215, Grand Rapids, MI. Records.

Brewer, Eugene S. "The Oyster." Hopwood Awards, Minor Fiction, 1935. Special Collections, Harlan Hatcher Library.

Butler, Leslie H. Papers. BHL.

City of East Grand Rapids. Property tax records, 1932-1935.

Composite Grand Rapids Accessions. GRFL.

Cornelius, L. A. Scrapbook. GRPL.

Daughters of the American Revolution. Sophie de Marsac Chapter, Grand Rapids, MI. Record book. GRPL.

Delta Kappa Epsilon. Omicron chapter, University of Michigan. Records. BHL.

Department of Justice, FBI Special Agent Application of Gerald R. Ford, 1941. GRFL.

Dewitt Clinton Consistory. Records. Michigan Masonic Museum.

Dodge, Carol. (Grand Rapids Women's City Club.) Email to author, June 13, 2012.

Ford, Gerald R. Academic transcript, University of Michigan. Copy in GRFL.

————. Letter to mother, May 14, [1935]. Vertical file. GRFL.

————. Letters to Frederica Pantlind, 1933-1934. GRFL.

————. Scrapbooks 1a, 39, and 40. GRFL.

Ford, Thomas G. Scrapbook. GRFL.

Frantz, Charles H. "Doctor, Where Were You?" BHL.

Glennon, Fran, and Evelyn Hofer. "Jerry Ford's Grand Rapids." GRFL.

Grace Episcopal Church, Grand Rapids, MI. Register of Communicants.

Grand Rapids, School District of. High School Scholarship Record of Gerald R. Ford. GRFL.

Grand Rapids real estate files. GRPL.

Grand Rapids Wood Finishing Company. Records. Public Museum of Grand Rapids.

Guck, Dorothy Gray. Letter to author, September 25, 1997.

Hanchett, Benjamin S. Papers. BHL.

Haughey Family. Papers. BHL.

Judd, Dorothy L. "A Lifetime in Grand Rapids." Bound typescript. Judd Papers. GRPL.

Kahn, Albert. Papers. BHL.

Kent County Marriages, 1845-1929. Vol. 18. GRPL.

Kent County Probate Court. Record of Levi Gardner estate, 1915-1939.

King v. King. District Court records, Douglas County, NE. Copy in GRFL.

Loomis, Helen M. Letters. BHL.

McIntosh, Joseph F. Scrapbook. GRFL.

McLachlan, Veronica. "Hometown for a President." McLachlan Papers. GRPL.

Membership records, Michigan Masonic Museum, Grand Rapids, MI.

Michigamua (student honorary society). Records. BHL.

Michigan, Department of State. Public Acts of the Legislature for 1931.

Michigan Masonic Museum. Grand Rapids. Membership files.

Michigan State Telephone Company. Grand Rapids Exchange Directory, 1930-1934.

Morris, Walter. "From Day to Day." "Portfolio II," Hopwood Prize Awards, 1934. Special Collections, Hatcher Library.

Nadolsky, Sid. Letter to author, September 27, 1997.

"Necrology" file of Michigan alumni. BHL.

Newaygo County, Michigan. Deed records.

Nueske, Mary M. Letter to GRF, August 21, 1976. GRFL.

Office of Naval Intelligence. Investigative file on Gerald R. Ford. GRFL.

Oosterbaan, Bennie. Papers. BHL.

Palmer, Alfred James. Scrapbook. BHL.

Russell, Mrs. Huntley. Engagement book. GRPL.

St. Mark's Church, Grand Rapids, MI. Register of Communicants.

Showers, Paul. Papers. BHL.

South High School. Scrapbook. GRPL.

South High School. *Star-Tler*, 1931. GRFL.

Stiles, John R. "With the Coin We Blew (An American Goes to College)." Hopwood Manuscript, Major Essay, 1940. Special Collections, Hatcher Library.

Todd, Stanton M. Papers. BHL.

United States Census, 1920, 1930, manuscript census return. Kent County, MI (microfilm, GRPL).

University of Michigan. Athletic Department. Report, 1931.

———. Scrapbooks.

University of Michigan. Board in Control of University Athletics. Papers. BHL.

University of Michigan. University Hospital records. BHL.

University of Michigan. Vice-President for Student Affairs. Records. BHL.

University of Michigan Club of Detroit. Records. BHL.

Van de Water, Peter Edgar. Papers. BHL.

Vander Velde, Lewis. Papers. BHL.

Vertical files. GRFL.

White House Central Files, Presidential Personal. GRFL.

Periodicals

Ann Arbor News
Deke Quarterly (before 1957, *Delta Kappa Epsilon Quarterly*)
Detroit Free Press
Georgia Tech Alumnus
Grand Rapids Press
Grand Rapids Herald
Grand Rapids Mirror
Grand Rapids Spectator
Harvard (Ill.) Herald
Literary Digest
Manistee (Mich.) News-Advocate
Michigan Alumnus

Michigan Daily

Michiganensian (1932-1935)

Michigan Tradesman

New Pioneer (alumni newsletter of the class of 1931, South High School)

Pioneer (South High School student literary magazine)

Pioneer (South High School yearbook; designated by year)

Trolley Topics (Grand Rapids Railway Company monthly). GRPL

Unionite (student literary magazine)

Books and Articles: Printed Primary Sources

Bass, Jack, and Marilyn W. Thompson. *Ol' Strom*. Atlanta: Longstreet Press, 1998.

Benevolent Protective Order of Elks, Grand Rapids Lodge No. 48. *Golden Jubilee: Fiftieth Anniversary, 1886-1936*. Grand Rapids: Knickerbocker Press, 1936.

Berry, Henry. "Thanksgiving Eve on Campus." *Deke Quarterly* 94.

Big Men on Campus (student publication). Ann Arbor: N.p., 1934.

Bissell, Irving J. *A Sow's Ear*. New York: Julian Messmer, 1937.

Bissell, Richard. *My Life on the Mississippi*. Boston: Little, Brown, 1973.

Blanco, Gail. *Then Sings My Soul*. Nashua, N.H.: Privately printed, 1974.

Boorman, W. Ryland. *Personality in Its Teens*. New York: Macmillan, 1932.

Boy Scouts of America. *The Official Handbook for Boys*. Garden City, N.Y.: Doubleday, Page, and Co., 1911.

—————. *The Revised Handbook for Boys*. New York: Boy Scouts of America, 1927.

Brown, Paul. *PB: The Paul Brown Story*. New York: Atheneum, 1979.

Butler, Linda Lather. *Live, Live, Live*. Tucson: Pepper Publishing, 1992.

Capos, Claudia. "My Years at Michigan Made Me a Better Person. . . ." *Michigan Alumnus*, February 1974.

Chapin, F. Stuart. "Socio-Economic Status: Some Preliminary Results of Measurement." *American Journal of Sociology* 37 (January 1932): 581-87.

Chicago City Directory. Chicago: Chicago Directory Co., 1916.

College Entrance Examination Board. *Annual Handbook, 1941*. Boston: Ginn and Co., 1941.

—————. *Thirty-First Annual Report of the Secretary, 1931*. New York: Published by the Board, 1931.

DeJong, David. *With a Dutch Accent*. London: Victor Gollancz, 1944.

Denham, Robert H. *Growing Up in Grand Rapids*. South Bend, IN: Privately printed, 1997.

Douglas, Lloyd. *Disputed Passage*. Boston: Houghton Mifflin, 1938.

Edwards, R. H., J. M. Arthman, and Galen M. Fisher. *Undergraduates: A Study of Morale in Twenty-Three American Colleges and Universities*. Garden City, N.Y.: Doubleday, Doran, and Co., 1928.

Ellis, Edward Robb. *A Diary of the Century*. New York: Kodanska Press, 1995.

Ferguson Droste Ferguson Clinic, Grand Rapids, MI. *Patient Handbook*. 1967.

Ford, Betty. *The Times of My Life*. New York: Harper and Row, 1978.

Ford, Gerald R. *A Time to Heal*. New York: Harper and Row, 1979.

———. "In Defense of the Competitive Urge." *Sports Illustrated*, July 8, 1974.

———. Interview. *Business Today*, Winter 1992.

Fuller, Florence. *Map and Guide of Mackinac Island*. N.p., 1926.

Gilbreth, Frank T., Jr. *I'm a Lucky Guy*. New York: Thomas Y. Crowell, 1951.

Gingrich, Arnold. *Cast Down the Laurel*. New York: Knopf, 1935.

Gleason, Richard D. "Reflections of Grand Rapids Camps." *Grand Rapids Mirror*, August-September 1934.

Grand Rapids, Board of Education. *Official Proceedings*, May 1, 1929, to May 1, 1930.

Griffith, Thomas. *The Waist-High Culture*. New York: Grosset and Dunlap, 1959.

"Griffon." "Softening Football's Thuds." *Saturday Evening Post*, November 29, 1931.

Grimm, Joe, ed. and comp. *Michigan Voices*. Detroit: Wayne State University Press, 1987.

Haines, Donal Hamilton. *Blaine of the Backfield*. New York: Farrar and Rinehart, 1937.

Harvard Alumni Directory: A Catalogue of Former Students Now Living; Including Graduates and Non-Graduates, and the Holders of Honorary Degrees. Boston: Harvard Alumni Association, 1919.

Hersey, John. *The President*. New York: Knopf, 1975.

Hoover, Herbert. *The Memoirs of Herbert Hoover: The Great Depression, 1929-1941*. New York: Macmillan, 1952.

Houghton, Percy D. *Football and How to Watch It*. Boston: Marshall Jones Co., 1922.

"How Are the New Football Rules Working?" *Literary Digest*, November 12, 1932.

Hynes, Samuel. *The Growing Season*. New York: Viking Penguin, 2003.

Kipke, Harry G., and Harold A. Fitzgerald. "A Punt, a Pass, and a Prayer." *Saturday Evening Post*, September 30, 1933.

———. "Dying for Dear Old Rutgers." *Saturday Evening Post*, November 17, 1934.

———. "Take Your Eye Off That Ball." *Saturday Evening Post*, November 11, 1933.

———. "Watch That Lateral Pass." *Saturday Evening Post*, September 29, 1934.

Lewis, Sinclair. *Babbitt*. New York: Random House, 2002; first published 1922.

Love, Edmund G. *Hanging On; or, How to Get through a Depression and Enjoy Life*. Detroit: Wayne State University Press, 1987; first published 1972.

Luckman, Sid. *Luckman at Quarterback*. Chicago: Ziff-Davis, 1949.

Lynd, Robert S., and Helen Merrill Lynd. *Middletown: A Study in Modern American Culture*. New York: Harcourt Brace Jovanovitch, 1957; first published 1929.

———. *Middletown in Transition: A Study in Cultural Conflicts*. New York: Harcourt, Brace and World, 1937.

Mackinac Island. Chicago: Mackinac Island Civic Association, 1927.

McKay, John. *McKay: A Coach's Story*. New York: Atheneum, 1974.

McKenzie, Roderick Duncan. "The Neighborhood: A Study of Local Life in the City of Columbus, Ohio." *American Journal of Sociology* 27, no. 2 (September 1921).

Manfred, Frederick [Feike Feikema, pseud.]. *The Primitive*. Garden City, N.Y.: Doubleday, 1949.

Meanwell, W. E., and K. E. Rockne. *Training, Conditioning, and the Care of Injuries*. Madison, Wis.: W. E. Meanwell, 1931.

Mercer, E. Leroy. "Special Values in Football and Other Body-Contact Games." In *Aims and Methods in School Athletics*, edited by E. Dean Calkins. New York: Wingate Memorial Foundation, 1932.

Michigan Department of State. Registration of Motor Vehicles, Titles, Operators, Chauffeurs, Etc. Lansing: Michigan Department of State, 1920, 1925, 1930.

Michigan High School Athletic Association. Yearbook for 1927-1928, 1928-1929, 1929-1930. Lansing: Michigan High School Athletic Association, 1928, 1929, 1930.

Millar, Kenneth [Ross Macdonald, pseud.]. *The Dark Tunnel*. Boston: Gregg Press, 1980; first published 1944.

Miracle, Andrew W., and C. Roger Rees. *Lessons of the Locker Room: The Myth of School Sports*. Amherst, N.Y.: Prometheus Books, 1994.

Mitchell, Alice Miller. *Children and Movies*. Chicago: University of Chicago Press, 1929.

Mitchell, Elmer D. "The Growth of Physical Education and Allied Movements in the State of Michigan: A Study of Institutional Acceptance and Integration." Ph.D. diss., University of Michigan, 1938.

M'Manis, John E. "Tragic Note Marks End of Ward's Career as Michigan Athlete." *Detroit News*, June 2, 1935.

Morris, Walter. *American in Search of a Way*. New York: Macmillan, 1940.

National Paint, Oil, and Varnish Association. *Proceedings of the 43rd Convention, October 14-17, 1930*.

Parker, Wilford E. "A Comparison of the Work Done at the University of Michigan by the Members of the High School National Honor Society with That of Other Students." M.A. thesis, University of Michigan, 1933.

Polk's City Directory for Ann Arbor, Washtenaw County, etc. 1925-1935.

Polk's City Directory for Grand Rapids, Michigan. 1922-1935.

Roberts, Kenneth. "Murmuring Michigan." *Saturday Evening Post*, March 21, 1934.

Roberts, Stewart A. "Comparison of Medical and Hospital Costs for Individuals in Moderate Circumstances." *Bulletin of the American College of Surgeons* 13, no. 4 (December 1929): 24-25.

Roth, Benjamin. *The Great Depression: A Diary*. New York: Public Affairs, 2010.

Seager, Allan. *Amos Berry*. New York: Simon and Schuster, 1953.

"Shawandossee Camps for Boys." *[South High School] Pioneer, 1928-1931*.

Spoelstra, Warren. "Ford Industrial Empire Boosts Sports Notables." *St. Petersburg Times*, July 12, 1943.

Steiner, Jesse Frederick. *Americans at Play*. Recent Social Trends in the United States. New York: McGraw-Hill, 1933.

Stockwell, William Hume [pseud.]. *Rudderless: A University Chronicle*. Norwood, Mass.: Norwood Press, 1930.

"This I Remember." Series of articles in University of Michigan football programs, numbers 26-38, 1965-1979.

Thompson, John. "Yesterdays in Grand Rapids." *Harper's*, May 1969.

Tunis, John R. "Gas and the Games." *Saturday Evening Post*, January 25, 1930.

University of Michigan. *General Catalogue for 1931-1932*.

————. Interfraternity Council. *University of Michigan Fraternities*. Ann Arbor: Interfraternity Council, 1932.

————. *The President's Report for 1931-1932*. Ann Arbor: University of Michigan, 1932.

————. *The President's Report for 1933-1934*. Ann Arbor: University of Michigan, 1934.

Wallenberg, Raoul. *Letters and Dispatches, 1924-1944*. New York: Arcade Publishing, 1995.

Waller, Willard. *The Sociology of Teaching*. New York: Russell and Russell, 1961; first published 1932.

Wells, William S. "Ten Men Who Knocked Gerald Ford on His Ass." *Esquire*, October 1975.

Whitney, Albert W. *Man and the Motor Car*. Lansing: Michigan State Safety Council, 1936.

Whittingham, Richard. *What a Game They Played*. New York: Simon and Schuster, 1984.

Wickenden, Dan. *The Wayfarers*. New York: William Morris and Co., 1945.

Wismer, Harry. *The Public Calls It Sport*. Englewood Cliffs, N.J.: Prentice-Hall, 1965.

Wood, Barry. *What Price Football?* Boston: Houghton Mifflin, 1932.

Books and Articles: Secondary Works

Allen, Roger. *The Story of St. Mark's*. Grand Rapids: Centennial Celebration Committee, 1936.

Armour, David A. "75 Years of Serving Mackinac." *Michigan History*, May/June 2004, pp. 45-51.

Barrett, Paul. *The Automobile and Urban Transit: The Formation of Public Policy in Chicago, 1900-1930*. Philadelphia: Temple University Press, 1983.

Beasley, Norman, and George W. Stark. *Made in Detroit*. New York: Putnam, 1957.

Belasco, Warren. *Americans on the Road, 1910-1945*. Baltimore: Johns Hopkins University Press, 1997.

Bernstein, Mark F. *Football: The Ivy League Origins of an American Obsession*. Philadelphia: University of Pennsylvania Press, 2001.

Bigsby, Christopher. *Arthur Miller, 1915-1962*. London: Weidenfeld and Nicolson, 2008.

Blanke, David. *Hell on Wheels: The Promise and Peril of America's Car Culture, 1900-1940*. Lawrence: University Press of Kansas, 2007.

Booraem, Hendrik, V. *Young Jerry Ford: Athlete and Citizen*. Grand Rapids: Eerdmans, 2013.

Breitman, Richard, et al. *U.S. Intelligence and the Nazis*. Cambridge: Cambridge University Press, 2005.

Canham, Don. *From the Inside*. Ann Arbor: Olympia Sports Press, 1996.

Cannon, James. *Time and Chance: Gerald Ford's Appointment with History*. New York: HarperCollins, 1992.

Carron, Christian G. *Grand Rapids Furniture: The Story of America's Furniture City*. Grand Rapids: Public Museum of Grand Rapids, 1998.

Cassuto, David N. *Cold Running River*. Ann Arbor: University of Michigan Press, 1974.

Charles, Jeffrey A. *Service Clubs in American Society: Rotary, Kiwanis, and Lions*. Urbana: University of Illinois Press, 1993.

Chudacoff, Howard P. *Mobile Americans: Residential and Social Mobility in Omaha, 1880-1920*. New York: Oxford University Press, 1972.

Conklin, E. Dana. *Aims and Methods in School Athletics*. New York: Wingate Memorial Foundation, 1932.

Culver, Mary. "Harry Bennett: Hatchet Man, Architect, Artist, and Animal Lover." *Impressions*, March 2000, pp. 1-5.

Davenport, Horace W. *Not Just Any Medical School: The Science, Practice, and Teaching of Medicine at the University of Michigan, 1850-1941*. Ann Arbor: University of Michigan Press, 1999.

Davis, James S. "Mackinac Scout Service Camp." *Mackinac History* 2 (1975), leaflet 4.

Dinse, Sharon. *Mr. C.M.U.: A Biography of Dan Rose*. Mt. Pleasant: Central Michigan University Press, 1985.

Donnelly, Walter A., et al. *The University of Michigan: An Encyclopedic Survey*. Ann Arbor: University of Michigan Press, 1958.

Dude, Kelly. "Crisis in '34." *Atlanta Constitution*, January 30, 1976.

Eagan, Eileen. *Class, Culture, and the Classroom: The Student Peace Movement of the 1930s*. Philadelphia: Temple University Press, 1982.

Eckert, Kathryn Bishop. *Buildings of Michigan*. Buildings of the United States. New York: Oxford University Press, 1993.

Elliott, Gerald, et al. *Grand Rapids: Renaissance on the Grand*. Tulsa: Continental Heritage Press, 1982.

Engelmann, Larry. *Intemperance: The Lost War against Liquor*. New York: Free Press, 1979.

Gitlow, Liette. *The Big Vote*. Baltimore: Johns Hopkins University Press, 2009.

Gordon, Calvin W. *The Social System of the High School*. Glencoe, Ill.: Free Press, 1957.

Graff, Henry. *Conflicting Paths: Growing Up in America*. Cambridge: Harvard University Press, 1995.

Greenberg, Murray. *Passing Game: Benny Friedman and the Transformation of Football*. New York: Public Affairs, 2008.

Harms, Richard H. "Paid in Scrip." *Michigan History*, January/February 1991, pp. 37-43.

Harris, Reed. *King Football*. New York: Vanguard Press, 1932.

Hawes, Joseph M. *Children between the Wars: American Childhood, 1920-1940*. New York: Twayne Publishers, 1997.

Inabinett, Mark. *Grantland Rice and His Heroes: The Sportswriter as Mythmaker in the 1920s*. Knoxville: University of Tennessee Press, 1994.

Katzman, David M. "Ann Arbor: Depression City." *Michigan History* 50 (December 1966): 306-17.

Kennedy, David M. *Freedom from Fear: The American People in Depression and War, 1929-1945*. Oxford History of the United States, vol. 9. New York: Oxford University Press, 1999.

Kett, Joseph F. *Rites of Passage: Adolescence in America, 1790 to the Present*. New York: Basic Books, 1977.

Keyes, Ralph. *Is There Life after High School?* New York: Warner Books, 1977.

Kirk, Russell. *Confessions of a Bohemian Tory*. New York: Fleet Publishing Corp., 1963.

Krug, Edward A. *The Shaping of the American High School, 1880-1920*. Madison: University of Wisconsin Press, 1964.

Laackman, Blair H. *Gerald R. Ford's Scouting Years*. Grand Rapids: Kindel-Ford Chapter, National Eagle Scout Association, 1982.

Lentz, Charles M. "Grocery Shopping in the 1930s." *Michigan History* 73 (March/April 1989): 14-15.

Leroy, Dave. *Gerald Ford — Untold Story*. Arlington, Va.: R. W. Beatty, 1974.

Levenstein, Harvey A. *Revolution at the Table: The Transformation of the American Diet*. New York: Oxford University Press, 1988.

Logan, Thomas H. *Almost Lost: Building and Preserving Heritage Hill, Grand Rapids, MI*. Traverse City, Mich.: Arbutus Press, 2004.

Lydens, Z. Z., ed. *The Story of Grand Rapids*. Grand Rapids: Kregel, 1966.

Lyons, Eugene. *Herbert Hoover: A Biography.* Garden City, N.Y.: Doubleday, 1964.

Macleod, David I. *Building Character in the American Boy: The Boy Scouts, YMCA, and Their Forerunners, 1870-1920.* Madison: University of Wisconsin Press, 1983.

Martin, Charles H. *Benching Jim Crow: The Rise and Fall of the Color Line in Southern College Sports, 1890-1980.* Urbana: University of Illinois Press, 2010.

Mayhew, John F. *Par Excellence: Highlights of Sixty-Five Years at Barton Hills Country Club.* Ann Arbor, 1983.

McComb, Mary. *Great Depression and the Middle Class: Experts, Collegiate Youth, and Business Ideology, 1929-1941.* Studies in American Popular History and Culture. New York: Routledge, 2006.

McCutcheon, Marc. *The Writer's Guide to Everyday Life from Prohibition through World War II.* Cincinnati: Writer's Guide Digest Books, 1995.

McElvaine, Robert S. *The Great Depression: America, 1929-1941.* New York: Times Books, 1993.

McGregor, Robert. "A Tale of Two Centers." *Ann Arbor Observer,* October 2007.

Meijer, Hank. *Thrifty Years: The Life of Hendrik Meijer.* Grand Rapids: Eerdmans, 1984.

Miller, Arthur. "University of Michigan." *Holiday* 14, no. 4 (December 1953).

Modell, John. "Dating Becomes the Way of American Youth." In *Essays on the Family and Historical Change,* edited by David Levine et al., pp. 91-126. Arlington: Texas A & M University Press, 1983.

———. *Into One's Own: From Youth to Adulthood in the United States, 1920-1975.* Berkeley: University of California Press, 1989.

Murray, William D. *The History of the Boy Scouts of America.* New York: Boy Scouts of America, 1937.

Nelson, Lyle E. "1934 Michigan." *College Football Historical Society Newsletter,* November 1994.

Norwood, Stephen. "Ford's Brass Knuckles: Harry Bennett, the Cult of Muscularity, and Anti-labor Terror in 1920-1945." *Labor History* 37 (1996): 365-91.

Nye, David. *Electrifying America: Social Meanings of a New Technology, 1880-1940.* Cambridge: MIT Press, 1990.

Oriard, Michael. *Dreaming of Heroes: American Sports Fiction, 1868-1980.* Chicago: Nelson-Hall, 1982.

Ortquist, Richard T. *Depression Politics in Michigan, 1929-1933*. New York: Garland, 1932.

Oxford English Dictionary, The. 20 vols. 2nd ed. Oxford: Clarendon, 1989.

Palmer, Phyllis. *Domesticity and Dirt: Housewives and Domestic Servants in the United States, 1920-1945*. Philadelphia: Temple University Press, 1989.

Peckham, Howard H. *The Making of the University of Michigan, 1817-1967*. Ann Arbor: University of Michigan Press, 1967.

Perry, Will. *The Wolverines: The Story of Michigan Football*. Huntsville, Ala.: Strode Publishers, 1974.

Peterson, Robert W. *Pigskin: The Early Years of Pro Football*. New York: Oxford University Press, 1997.

Potter, Robert A. "A Legacy of Leadership: President Ford and U-M." *Michigan Alumnus*, March/April 1986, 30-39.

Rader, Benjamin G. *American Sports*. Englewood Cliffs, N.J.: Prentice-Hall, 1983.

Ransom, Frank Edward. *The City Built on Wood: A History of the Furniture Industry in Grand Rapids, Michigan, 1850-1950*. Ann Arbor: Privately printed, 1955.

Reid, Luman. *Finally It's Friday*. Columbia: University of Missouri Press, 1981.

Ross, Murray. "Football and Baseball in America." In *Sport and Society*, edited by John T. Talamini and Charles H. Page. Boston: Little, Brown, 1973.

Savage, Howard J., et al. *American College Athletics*. Bulletin no. 23. New York: Carnegie Foundation for the Advancement of Teaching, 1929.

Schapsmeier, Edward L., and Frederick H. Schapsmeier. *Gerald R. Ford's Date with Destiny: A Political Biography*. American University Studies, ser. 9, vol. 74. New York: Peter Lang, 1989.

Schmitt, Peter J. *Back to Nature: The Arcadian Myth in Urban America*. New York: Oxford University Press, 1969.

Shaw, Wilfred B., ed. *The University of Michigan: An Encyclopedic Survey*. 4 vols. Ann Arbor: University of Michigan Press, 1951.

Sheridan, Terence P. "Portrait of the Next President as a Young Man." *New Times*, June 19, 1974, pp. 14-25.

Sherrill, Robert M. "What Grand Rapids Did for Jerry Ford — and Vice Versa." *New York Times Magazine*, October 20, 1974, 31-33, 72-92.

Shufro, Nicholas A. "The Great Depression's Effect on Enrollment Patterns at the University of Michigan from 1929 to 1939." Senior honors thesis, University of Michigan, 1984.

Silbar, Howard. "Stars in His Eyes for Vaudeville: Theaters in Grand Rapids — a Personal Perspective." *Chronicle* 26, no. 3 (1991): 6-7.

Smith, Franklin Campbell. *The Diocese of Western Michigan: A History.* Grand Rapids: Diocesan Historical Commission, 1948.

Smith, Gene. *The Shattered Dream: Herbert Hoover and the Great Depression.* New York: William Morrow, 1970.

Soderstrom, Robert M. *The Big House: Fielding J. Yost and the Building of Michigan Stadium.* Ann Arbor: Huron River Press, 2005.

Sponberg, Adryn Lowell. "The Evolution of Athletic Subsidization in the Intercollegiate Conference of Faculty Representatives (Big Ten)." Ph.D. diss., University of Michigan, 1968.

Spring, Joel. "Mass Culture and School Sports." *History of Education Quarterly* 14 (Winter 1974): 483-97.

Sukandasa, Michael E. "Black Varsity Lettermen: 1882-1979." Senior honors thesis, University of Michigan, 1985.

Supinski, Matt. *River Journal* 2, no. 4. Portland, Ore.: Frank Amato Publications, 1994.

Ter Horst, Jerold F. *Gerald R. Ford and the Future of the Presidency.* New York: Third Press, 1974.

Tobin, James. "The Great Raid." *Michigan Today,* June 10, 2009.

Todish, Tim J. *A Legacy for the Future: Reminiscences of Scouting in West Michigan.* Grand Rapids: Boy Scouts of America, Gerald R. Ford Council, 2009.

Treml, William B. "Football Booster." *Ann Arbor News,* April 29, 1987.

Turner, Edward M. *The Good Old Daze.* Kalamazoo, Mich.: Privately printed, 1979.

Vander Meulen, Arnold J. *Skid Row Life Line.* Grand Rapids: Zondervan, 1956.

Van Reken, Donald L. *Ottawa Beach and Waukazoo.* N.p.: Privately printed, 1987.

Van Reken, Donald L., and Russell P. Vande Water. *Holland Furnace Company.* Holland, Mich.: Privately printed, 1993.

Vestal, Bud. *Jerry Ford, Up Close.* New York: Coward, McCann, and Geoghegan, 1974.

Walsh, Richard J. *Zanesville and 36 Other American Communities: A Study of Markets and of the Telephone as a Market Index.* New York: Literary Digest, 1927.

Wandersee, Winifred D. *Women's Work and Family Values, 1920-1940.* Cambridge: Harvard University Press, 1981.

Warren, Harris G. *Herbert Hoover and the Great Depression.* New York: Norton, 1967; first published 1958.

Watterson, John Sayle. *College Football.* Baltimore: Johns Hopkins University Press, 2000.

Wilkinson, Jay. *Bud Wilkinson: An Intimate Portrait of an American Legend.* Champaign, Ill.: Sagamore Publishing, 1994.

Winter-Berger, Robert N. *The Washington Pay-Off.* New York: Dell, 1972.

Woodfill, W. Stewart. *Grand Hotel: The Story of an Institution.* New York: Newcomen Society in North America, 1969.

Works Progress Administration, Writers' Project. *Michigan: A Guide to the Wolverine State.* American Guide Series. New York: Oxford University Press, 1946.

Wylie, Lawrence. *Village in the Vaucluse.* 2nd ed. Cambridge: Harvard University Press, 1975; first published 1957.

Interviews

Ford, Gerald R. Interviews with James Cannon, 1990 (transcripts). GRFL.

Ford, Richard. Interview with author, 2012.

Ford, Richard and Steven. Public interview, October 15, 2010 (transcript). GRFL.

Grady, Jim. Interview with author, 2012.

Grand Rapids Oral History Collection. GRFL.

Grand Rapids Women's History Collection. GRPL.

Hanson, Lin. Interview with author, 2012.

Heibel, Jean. Interview with author, 1997.

Howell, Joseph. Interview with author, 1997.

Keen, Cliff. Interview with David Pollock, 1983 (transcript). GRFL.

Kent County Council for Historic Preservation. Oral history tapes. GRPL.

Olson, Gordon. Report of interview with Gerald R. Ford.

Oosterbaan, Bennie. Interview with David Pollock, 1983 (transcript). GRFL.

Penny, Don. Interview with Richard Norton Smith, 2009 (transcript), GRFL.

South High School, Class of 1931. Notes on interviews by various students with the author, 1998-2003. Author's possession.

Todish, Tim J. Interviews with author, 2012.
Ward, Willis. Interview with David Pollock, 1983 (transcript). GRFL.

Web Sites

Ann Arbor District Library blog. www.aadl.org/node/9306. (DKE house, 1922-1968)
Blog.heritagesportsart.com/2010/08/university-of-michigan-football -uniform.html.
DKE blog. "Brother Gerald R. Ford, Jr., Omicron '35 Remembered."
Dooley, Greg. "Remembering Willis Ward." www.mgoblue.com/sports/m -footbl/spec-rel/101912aaa.html.
Dooley, Greg. "When the Little Brown Jug Vanished (1931-33)." www .mgoblue.com/sports/m-footbl/spec-rel/092611aab.html.
en.wikipedia.org/wiki/1933_College_Football_All-America_Team.
"The Lost Hotels of Minneapolis." www.lileks.com/mpls/hotels/index .html.
michigantoday.umich.edu
Smith, Douglas. Presidential Myth: The Real Story of Gerald Ford, Willis Ward, and the 1934 Michigan/Georgia Tech Game. www.washtenaw-watchdogs.com, January 2014.

Pictorial

Photograph collection, GRFL.
Robinson Collection, GRPL.

Index

Page numbers in bold refer to illustrations